Reconceptualising Lifelong Learning

Concepts of lifelong learning are crucial to the formation of policy and practice in the UK, Europe and globally. However, although taken as given, such concepts and definitions are highly contestable and tied to formations of gender, class and 'race'. Key issues of social inclusion, exclusion, access and participation are inextricably connected to these concepts. This book exposes the politics around which meanings of lifelong learning are constructed, challenged, resisted and reproduced.

Reconceptualising Lifelong Learning argues that the current field of lifelong learning is premised on certain hidden values and assumptions, and exposes the mechanisms by which exclusionary discourses and practices are reproduced and maintained. The book challenges hegemonic understandings of 'knowledge' that shape 'the field' of lifelong learning. Its structure reflects some of those challenges through the use of narrative and through the multipositionings of learners, its readers and the authors of this book. Organised into four sections the book looks at:

- Reclaiming – which draws on feminist and post-structural conceptual frameworks to create a critical analysis of the current 'field' of lifelong learning;
- Retelling – which tells the tales of different multi-positions in lifelong learning;
- Revisioning – which presents a revisioning of learning, providing the critical tools to reconceptualise the field of lifelong learning;
- Reconceptualising – which considers the future of new approaches to, and practices in, lifelong learning.

The book draws on feminist, post-structuralist insights to critique the field of lifelong learning. However, it moves beyond critique to also create spaces for reflexivity, resistances, subversions and possibilities for change, creating a new terrain of possibilities. The authors have engaged with lifelong learning as a site of struggle and invite readers to engage in this struggle, and find their positions and their voices, creating their own spaces of resistances, subversions and new possibilities.

Penny Jane Burke is a Senior Lecturer in Education at the Institute of Education, University of London, UK.

Sue Jackson is a Senior Lecturer in Lifelong Learning and Citizenship at Birbeck College, University of London, UK.

Reconceptualising Lifelong Learning

Feminist interventions

Penny Jane Burke and
Sue Jackson

 Routledge
Taylor & Francis Group

LONDON AND NEW YORK

First published 2007
by Routledge
2 Park Square, Milton Park, Abingdon, Oxon OX14 4RN

Simultaneously published in the USA and Canada
by Routledge
270 Madison Ave, New York, NY 10016

Routledge is an imprint of the Taylor & Francis Group, an informa business

© 2007 Penny Jane Burke and Sue Jackson

Typeset in Times New Roman
by Keystroke, High Street, Tettenhall, Wolverhampton
Printed and bound in Great Britain
by Antony Rowe Ltd, Chippenham, Wiltshire

British Library Cataloguing in Publication Data
A catalogue record for this book is available from the British Library

Library of Congress Cataloging in Publication Data
A catalog record has been requested for this book

ISBN10: 0–415–37614–9 (hbk)
ISBN10: 0–415–37615–7 (pbk)
ISBN10: 0–203–94745–2 (ebk)

ISBN13: 978–0–415–37614–3 (hbk)
ISBN13: 978–0–415–37615–0 (pbk)
ISBN13: 978–0–203–94745–6 (ebk)

Contents

SECTION IV
Reconceptualising practice   **155**

Acknowledgements

This book was developed from the inspiring discussions we shared with the Gender and Lifelong Learning Group. We thank the women who were part of that group and whose voices have inevitably found their way into the book; and the Gender and Education Association, whose financial support enabled the meetings to take place.

Our grateful thanks go to Routledge for making this book possible, and in particular to Philip Mudd, Lucy Wainwright and Amy Crowle, who have supported us throughout. Very many thanks too to Suzanne deVeuve and to Jan Paulus-Maly, who reacted not just positively but with warmth and generosity in allowing us to use their 'tree of life' images; and to Nelson Young Jr. for his equal warmth and generosity in allowing us to use his 'Amazing Grace' image. Our very grateful thanks, too, to Liz Jackson for producing her 'tree of knowledge' illustration for us and to Matthew Ahmet for allowing us to use his photograph.

Enormous thanks to our families, who have put up with us working late into the night and at weekends, yet have stayed enthusiastic in their support for the book and our work. Our families have also been sources of inspiration to us in helping us to develop our critical thinking about lifelong learning.

Finally, our thanks go to each other. Our working relationship has proved to be a source of the rich exchange and development of ideas. We have supported and sustained each other throughout this project, which has enabled us to continue our own journeys as lifelong learners.

Introduction

When a woman sits down to write, all eyes are on her. The woman who is turning others into the object of her gaze is herself already an object of the gaze. Woman, the original Other, is always being looked at and looked over. A women sees herself being seen. Clutching her pencil, she wonders how 'the discipline' will view the writing she wants to do. Will it be seen as too derivative of male work? Or too feminine? Too safe? Or too risky? Too serious? Or not serious enough?

(Behar and Gordon 1995: 2)

In this book we argue that the current field of lifelong learning is premised on certain hidden values and assumptions, and we expose the mechanisms by which exclusionary discourses and practices are re/constructed, challenged and recuperated. The book aims to open up ways of conceptualising learning that take into account multiple and shifting formations of and for learners and learning across different social contexts. In doing so, we aim to broaden what counts as learning and who counts as a learner and to offer different understandings of life-long learning that are able to include currently marginalised and misrecognised values, epistemologies and principles. Reconceptualisations of lifelong leaning need to challenge hegemonic understandings of 'knowledge' especially 'academic knowledge'. The organisation of this book will reflect some of those challenges through the use of narrative and through the multipositionings of learners, of our readers and of ourselves, as the authors of this book.

The book begins with our attempt to reclaim lifelong learning for multiple learners, as well as for ourselves. Here we deconstruct conceptual frameworks, constructions of knowledge, and learning itself, arguing for the revival of radical adult learning that moves through and beyond boundaries of formal and informal learning. This is a concern we take forward into Section II, where we tell the multiple stories of policy-makers, lifelong learning managers, teachers and learners. Our concern in this section, however, moves beyond the stories and the issues they raise to consider and challenge academic literacy. Section III returns to some of the issues raised in Section II, exploring them again through the key themes of identities and subjectivities, emotions and resistances. Finally we turn again to the title of the book and in Section IV question the possibilities of reconceptualising life-long learning. Throughout the book we critique neo-liberal constructions of lifelong learning embedded in a hierarchical individualism. In this section we re-visit those critiques, but also argue that for reconceptualisations to have the value they need to be grounded in practice. Taking four areas of practice – pedagogies, curricula, assessment and quality assurance – we offer our own alternative visions for the future of lifelong learning.

Throughout the book we engage with lifelong learning as a site for struggle. In its final section we confront our own struggles, raise questions and suggest some answers, although we also invite our readers to search for answers and raise questions of their own. Whilst our own voices have been explicit throughout the book, we have aimed also to give space for our readers' voices, looking for the silences and gaps in the book, as well as within lifelong learning policies and practices. We hope the book is a conversation that can be continued with us and without us: a conversation between those to whom lifelong learning matters.

We have written this book because lifelong learning matters to us. The idea was conceived when we were both immersed in and excited by the issues we encountered at a seminar on gender and lifelong learning, and for which we separately and individually engaged in some auto/biographical writing. At that stage, we did not know each other very well. We have both felt (and sometimes continue to feel) marginalised as academics. We have struggled with issues of gender, social class, culture, ethnicity and age. This includes for both of us entering the academy as non-traditional learners, trying to develop our learner identities and subsequent careers whilst bringing up children and struggling with part-time paid work, homecare and mothering. At times we both find academic life isolating, individualised and certainly non-feminist. We were (and are) excited by the idea of working closely with each other: jointly authoring a book which came from close collaboration, friendship and storytelling.

In this book we will tell many stories – some of which will appear more 'story-like' than others. In the current climate, lifelong learning has been inexorably tied to policy in ways which mean that it is captured quantitatively. Throughout this book we challenge definitions of 'evidence-based' research which rely on quantitative data as though it somehow speaks 'the truth'. Whilst quantitative data can be useful it does not – cannot – tell a complete 'story'; a story needs a narrative. The narrative always of course belongs to the researcher, the storyteller, although it is differently experienced by its audiences. Although narrative may draw on numerous and varied accounts, both qualitative and quantitative, the analysis in the end belongs to the one who analyses, deconstructs, reconstructs again, the 'stories' that are told through the data.

Like all written work, our chapters are a performance (Butler 1997), with the players taking their part on the stage for the (analytic) consumption of the readers of this book. Indeed, we believe that lifelong learning cannot just be described and/or analysed: it has to be performed by both teachers and learners. But performance is risky. Despite being grounded in research, in choosing sometimes seemingly 'non-academic' ways to tell our stories we leave ourselves vulnerable to the risk of being invisibilised, or annihilated, in public places. Like Behar and Gordon (1995) we wonder how our work will be viewed in 'the field'. Whilst we may see ourselves as travellers across and between boundaries, we fully understand the conceptual meanings attached to the boundaries between (perceived) academic and non-academic work.

In arguing that interpretation is both political and contested and that the researcher is a learner in the research process, we believe that lifelong learning research should develop skills of personal reflection and reflexive practices. This is not the case just for the researcher, of course. The researched, too, should have opportunities to learn through the research process, never just an object but a learning subject. Lifelong learning research should not be 'on', but 'for' or 'with'. Methods and methodologies for researching lifelong learning involve learning from each other, questioning and deconstructing 'expert knowledge'. We believe that lifelong learning research should always lead to the development of new know-ledges, with the potential to lead to transformative action. It might, for example, replace or challenge existing knowledges and it is likely to have a commitment to social justice. However, here we face a problem. We argue in this book that 'lifelong learning', as it is currently conceptualised and presented through discourse and policy, is often used more as an agent of social control than as an agent for change and transformative action. We will ask in this book whether 'lifelong learning' can be reclaimed, or whether it has become too embedded in the establishment to ever offer alternative visions.

We too, of course, are enmeshed in the academy. As professionals, even though we may be critical of current frameworks of lifelong learning and constructions of what constitutes 'academic knowledge', we are situated within them. This makes it difficult to challenge, because challenges are connected to our personal security and levels of vulnerability, and this is always gendered, classed, racialised and sexualised. In Section II we take what we believe to be a high risk strategy, which may or may not damage our perceived academic authority, through telling the imagined stories of various 'players' in the lifelong learning arena. The processes were interesting for us: in earlier drafts, for example, we included academic references to justify the stories, and our telling of them. We almost fell into the trap of believing that the only stories worth telling were the ones which claimed 'truth' and 'objective research' rather than ones which recognise different truths and subjectivities, drawing on our own lifelong learning experiences and know-ledges. Yet if we reject 'expert knowledge', what replaces it? Are we just re-placing one set of experts with another (ourselves)?

And yet we also found Section II to be one of the most interesting pieces of work with which we have engaged, enabling us to re-tell the very many stories we have been told, the experiences we have encountered, the readings we have undertaken and the academic work and research that we have developed. Because *all* academic work and research tells a story. Or let us change the emphasis – all academic work and research tells *a* story: one which is likely to be written differently depending on who is doing the telling, to what audience, and in which context. Our stories will of course also be consumed differently. In working with issues such as these we have found post-structuralist approaches helpful in their recognition of multiple stories to be told, as well as feminist methodological approaches with their emphasis on different voices and their challenges to subjective/ objective dichotomies.

Feminist work has clearly demonstrated epistemological as well as method-ological frameworks for research (see e.g. Maynard and Purvis 1994; or more recently Ramazanoglu and Holland 2002; Hughes 2002; Letherby 2003; Richie and Lewis 2003). Epistemologies are about ways in which we think about and understand not just what we do but how we conceptualise the world. We argue in this book for similar conceptual frameworks for lifelong learning research, which we believe shares much with feminist research. Whilst we do not argue that life-long learning research has distinctive methods attached to it, nor that it should inevitably be developed from qualitative methods, we do in this introductory section want to consider all of its elements: the 'life', the 'long' and the 'learning': we will return to this in our concluding chapter.

In our focus on 'life' we consider the (sometimes interweaving, sometimes com-peting or opposing, always interconnected) positions of both the researched and the researcher. Like learners and teachers, researchers as well as the researched are people in material and ideological positions, and so are always located in their research. The relationship between the researcher, the researched and the social context always needs to be made explicit. Although we will shortly turn to 'long' we also wish to draw attention to 'lifewide' learning. The researched, as well as the researcher, are positioned both as subject and object. They are always part of a plurality of complex social relations, living far beyond that tiny piece of them which is present in any particular research 'moment'.

In considering 'long' our focus turns to the biographical. This is not necessarily to argue for methods such as life-history approaches, as useful as they can be. Quantitative data can also tell stories of and about lives, cultures and societies. The key issue here is that a holistic approach should be taken, capturing longi-tudinal surveys and momentary snapshots, individual and collective fragments, moments and stories, with a focus on narratives. Learning in the present reaches both back into the past and out into future possibilities. Our potential lives as learners depend on our past and present lives, and on the lives of those around us, as well as on our material, structural and cultural realities.

Finally we turn to the 'learning', which we believe should be placed at the centre of the research. Learning, of course, always goes beyond the research moment and/or the relationship between the researched/researcher. Research serves little purpose without dissemination, although it has been suggested (Hughes 2006) that a more appropriate focus is on sharing. Dissemination can infer a top-down approach ('I will tell you what I have learned from this project') whilst sharing involves its audience in challenges, debates, and emotional as well as other responses. In this book we aim to involve ourselves and our readers in collective debate about the issues we raise, although that debate is unlikely to happen on a public stage. Nevertheless, we are individually and collectively responsible for voicing challenges and encouraging change, although those challenges can be small moments that collectively have the potential to make a difference.

We cannot leave our opening discussion without saying something about ethics in general, and our ethical positioning in particular. Judith Butler (2005) locates social and political critique at the core of ethical practice, and in writing this book this has remained a central concern for us. We have sometimes struggled with such critiques, wanting to both problematise, and yet hold onto, lifelong learning. We have been concerned that critiques can be – and sometimes are – taken up by policy-makers without context and within different political agenda. We have tried to include in our critiques both a dismantling of hegemonic discourse, policy and practice, and an offering of alternative visions and strategies. In addition, the ethics that Butler envisions is one in which the ethically responsible self knows and respects the limits of her knowing, and through this critically interrogates the social world. It has been our aim in this book to interrogate the social world of lifelong learning through the limits of our knowing, whilst espousing the continual creation and recreation of different knowledges. Part of the development of different knowledges has also involved the inclusion of multiple voices in this book – the voices of the other writers on whose own knowledges we have drawn; and the voices of the countless others we have engaged with on our own journeyings and lifelong learnings. We hope that this book will add something to those different knowledges of meanings, constructions and (re-)conceptualisations of lifelong learning.

Section I

Reclaiming lifelong learning

I am enough of an artist to draw freely upon my imagination. Imagination is more important than knowledge. Knowledge is limited. Imagination encircles the world.

(Albert Einstein, 'On Science')

The illiterate of the 21st century will not be those who cannot read and write, but those who cannot learn, unlearn, and relearn.

(Alvin Toffler, 'Re-thinking the Future')

This section will begin with a critical analysis of the current 'field' of lifelong learning, whilst arguing that there are multiple and conflicting fields. We will argue that lifelong learning extends beyond formal post-compulsory education and training to diverse sites of informal and formal learning. This section challenges the narrow ways of conceptualising learning in the current field of lifelong learning and argues that there are a range of different formations of and for learners/learning across different social contexts. In addition we will reveal the ways in which the current skills-based agenda is classed and racialised as well as gendered, examining the politics around the emphasis on instrumental, technical and mechanical sets of skills, outcomes and competencies. We will shift the current focus in mainstream literature to deeper level concerns, setting out to expose exclusionary practices in pedagogy, methodology and practice, as well as constructions of 'learning', 'skills' and 'knowledge' apparent in academic conventions. We will introduce the notion of educational journeys, which we go on to develop in the next section.

Chapter 1

Reclaiming conceptual frameworks

Introduction

The chapter will critically review 'the field' of lifelong learning as it is currently presented in both policy documents and academic literature. We will argue that in the main 'the field' is described as though it is neutral, ahistorical and uncontestable, with little account given of a wide range of different histories and competing 'fields', including those of adult and continuing education, community based learning, and the personal and political learning that takes place in, for example, trades unions, women's groups, or groups for other marginalised people, such as gay and lesbian groups, Black and minority ethnic groups and so forth. 'The field' as it is currently described assumes a particular history, tells a particular story, without acknowledging, or maybe even recognising, that there are multiple possibilities and analyses. We argue that 'the field' is un(der)theorised, and draw on feminist and post-structural analyses to examine the different and competing conceptual frameworks that are currently available, and to consider the ways that these constrain or open up opportunities for lifelong learning. We identify some of the key discourses in current writings on lifelong learning and consider the ways that these might contribute to exclusionary or inclusive practices within post-compulsory education and informal learning.

'Lifelong learning' has become part of a discourse of education, training and learning opportunities, used by the politics of the left and the right, and by governments worldwide. And yet its meanings are shifting and fluid and far from clear, although the term is used politically in ways which suggest hegemonic understandings. What we do not intend in this chapter is to put forward a newly presented but definitive view of the field. Instead, we invite the reader to participate in the processes of reclaiming conceptual frameworks of the multiple fields of lifelong learning. 'Lifelong learning' in political and educational discourse is presented without acknowledging that the stories that are told are particular and partial, that there are other stories to be told, and other tellers of tales. So are you sitting comfortably? Then we'll begin.

From education to learning: telling (some of the) stories

During the last few decades, there have been strong shifts in educational discourse: teachers no longer have a responsibility to educate or teach; rather learners have a responsibility to learn. Teachers no longer set objectives for their lessons and courses; instead they describe the outcomes that learners will be expected to achieve. Whilst we support a move from 'education' to 'learning' there are some important implications for how lifelong learning is conceptualised in contemporary educational policy. The focus has moved from teacher to learner, and from formal education to include both nonformal and informal learning. So learning is not confined to educational institutions: it happens everywhere, and learners must grasp opportunities to continually 'develop' (or train, or re-skill), including in the workplace. Lifelong learning is a continuum of all the learning we do, if not from cradle-to-grave then at least from pre-school to retirement (and sometimes beyond). There has been a strong and often persuasive movement towards highly individualised learners who take responsibility for choices made and opportunities grasped. Today it has become our individual responsibility to ensure that we are able to take our places in a competitive and global knowledge economy. In such a society there is a requirement for continual (re-)training and updating of skills, with a growing emphasis on individual rather than collective learning experiences.

'Lifelong learning' as a concept appears to be comparatively new. On coming into power in 1997, the new Labour government appointed Britain's first Minister for Lifelong Learning. Green (consultative) and White (policy) Papers followed in successive years. In his Foreword to the Green Paper *The Learning Age: A Renaissance for a New Britain* (DfEE 1998), David Blunkett – then Secretary of State for Education and Employment – stated that the fostering of an enquiring mind and a love of learning are essential for future success, both of individual and of State. In a much quoted statement, David Blunkett asserted that as well as securing economic stability and growth:

> Learning has a wider contribution. It helps make ours a civilized society, develops the spiritual side of our lives and promotes active citizenship. Learning enables people to play a full part in their community. It strengthens the family, the neighbourhood and consequently the nation. It helps fulfil our potential and opens doors to a love of music, art and literature. That is why we value learning for its own sake as well as for the equality of opportunity that it brings.
>
> (DfEE 1998)

The wider benefits that learning might bring include a sense of belonging and identity, social cohesion and inclusion, personal growth and development, and improved health and a sense of well-being. However, although David Blunkett's

Foreword to the Green Paper might suggest wider benefits to lifelong learning, in the same Green Paper the Prime Minister demonstrates a prime motive for promoting learning: 'Education is the best economic policy that we have' (DfEE 1998).

The Learning Age emphasises the links between education and employment and the benefit of gaining skills to 'increase earning power' (Sand 1998: 26). The two key proposals of the document are Individual Learning Accounts (ILAs) and a University for Industry (UfI). ILAs are identified to encourage individual investment in learning, allowing people to 'take control of their learning'. The University for Industry, it is argued, will

> put the UK ahead of the rest of the world in using new technology to improve learning and skills. . . . It will act as the hub of a brand new learning network, using modern communication technologies to link businesses and individuals to cost effective, accessible and flexible education and training.
>
> (DfEE 1998: 18)

Current government policy in the United Kingdom relies heavily on a view of learning that is about gaining qualifications, especially vocational qualifications. If 'Education is the best economic policy that we have' then policy on learning will inevitably focus on employment. Yet the employment market is gendered and racialised, with far from equal opportunities or conditions of pay or employment and real tensions in a supposed public/private divide. There is a clear policy interest in producing an efficient and productive workforce – but this workforce is one where opportunities are still created or denied according to class, gender, ethnicity, disability and age.

If public policy is driven by largely economic concerns then competitiveness becomes a primary focus (Field 2000: 3). Yet Field has also pointed out that 'For the past two decades, the wider policy agenda in the European Union has sought to balance the demands of competiveness with the maintenance of social cohesion' (Field 2005: 135).

The European Commission declared 1996 European Year of Lifelong Learning, and from the late 1990s onwards lifelong learning became part of the new educational landscapes of Europe. In a Memorandum, drawn up in Lisbon in 2000, a 10-year Mission was set for Europe to become the most competitive and dynamic knowledge-based economy in the world, capable of sustainable growth with more and better jobs and greater social cohesion (European Council, Lisbon, March 2000).

However, European adult learning participation rates are lower than those of Europe's major global competitors, including in higher, adult and vocational learning. The Commission identified technological and digital developments, intercultural relations, ageing populations and global markets as key areas for strategies. The thrust to increase and, to a lesser or greater degree, to *widen* participation in higher education in most European societies is associated with a number of themes within the larger banner of lifelong learning. They include 'the economic imperatives created by global competition, technological change and the challenge of the knowledge economy, individual responsibility and self-improvement, employability, flexibility of institutions and individuals, social inclusion and citizenship' (Osborne 2003: 6).

There have been worldwide concerns expressed by both international bodies and national governments that there are strong economic reasons for *increasing* access and for *widening* the constituency that higher education serves by including those groups who have traditionally been excluded. These strands of thought are evident in key statements of many international organisations such as the Council of Europe (1998), UNESCO (1998a; 1998b), the International Labour Office (ILO) (2000) and many others (Osborne 2003).

It has been argued that although people need basic education, they also need individual motivation and expanded opportunities to meet personal choice. Furthermore, it has been recognised that formal learning has dominated policy thinking and that nonformal and informal learning have been largely ignored. Six key messages were identified by the European Commission:

- New basic skills for all
- More investment in human resources
- Innovation in learning and teaching
- Valuing learning
- Rethinking guidance and counselling
- Bringing learning closer to home.

However, as we go on to show, it is the first of these that carries the heaviest emphasis in policy initiatives and funding, and formal learning continues to dominate over nonformal and informal learning.

The Bologna process has helped to place a strong emphasis on the creation of transferability of credits gained through formal lifelong learning across different courses, institutions, countries and regions. A new European Qualifications Framework (EQF) is currently being developed with a consultation document produced by the Commission of European Communities on 8 July 2005. The paper outlines the main purposes and functions of an EQF, including the creation of a 'meta-framework increasing transparency and supporting mutual trust' (Commission of European Communities 2005: 4). It is proposed that the EQF would consist of three key elements:

1   common reference points that refer to learning outcomes within a structure of eight levels;
2   a range of tools and instruments to address the needs of individual citizens; and
3   a set of common principles and procedures to provide guidelines between stakeholders at different levels (ibid.).

Three different types of learning outcomes are identified, which are knowledge, skills and wider competencies. It is envisaged that an EQF is offered on a voluntary basis only and carries no legal obligations.

There are certain assumptions underpinning the emphasis on transferability that deserve close attention. First, there is an assumption that developing a framework will create an inclusive structure whereby the learning of diverse groups across different localities and regions can be fairly and equally recognised. This is seen to allow for greater coherence and continuity of formal learning provision so that learners are able to gain credits for different learning that they do and transfer these to new contexts, creating flexibility and the opportunity to pick up learning according to the specific needs of the individual. This is also seen to enhance choice, so that learners are able to make their own choices about what, when and where to study, and can build up credits accordingly.

However, what does not seem to be recognised in these discussions is the way that such a credit transfer framework might significantly restrict the choices of learners. The framework will always have limitations in terms of recognition of learning. Even with the use of AP[E]L, accreditation of previous experiential learning, the range of experiences that can be formally recognised will be restricted by the way that the framework conceptualises what counts as learning. Yet, what counts as learning is highly contested and is tied in with competing constructions of who is a learner, what learning means and where learning can take place. These conceptions are always classed, gendered and racialised. In the current hegemonic discourses of lifelong learning, what counts as learning is bound up with particular middle-classed values and perspectives around the decontextualised individual learner: notions of citizenship that are tied in with lifelong learning; neo-liberal constructions of the flexible learner/worker; and learning that happens in the public rather than private sphere of social life. The emphasis on credit transfer also places emphasis on the outcome of learning rather than on the process of learning, assuming sets of learning outcomes that can be measured through 'objective' assessment methods. The experience of learning is devalued while the end product is the focus of attention, contributing to a credentialist and instrumentalist view of learning. A primary focus on 'competencies' within a heavily credentialised system results in particular constructions of what is valued in learning and who is valued as a (lifelong) learner. The stories of what constitutes lifelong learning are still being (re-)created.

Yet if lifelong learning appears to be a comparatively new concept, lifelong education is not. Key assumptions that underpin contemporary discourses of lifelong learning are identifiable in early twentieth-century expressions of lifelong education. For example, in 1919, the Adult Education Committee of the British Ministry of Reconstruction concluded:

> [A]dult education must not be regarded as a luxury for a few exceptional persons here and there, nor as a thing which concerns only a short span of early manhood [sic], but that adult education is a permanent national necessity, an

inseparable aspect of citizenship, and therefore should be both universal and lifelong.

(1919: 55, in Field 2000: 4)

There are some important connections to be made between the earlier discourses of lifelong education and contemporary discourses of lifelong learning. One is that lifelong education or learning must be available to all adults from different backgrounds and experiences as a matter of importance to nation, interlinked with notions of citizenship, and should be a process of participation throughout an adult's lifetime. Another example comes from one of the first published works that was specifically on lifelong education, which argued that:

Much adult education will never know itself as such, and will be recognized only by leaders and teachers of real insight. It will go on in clubs, churches, cinemas, theatres, concert rooms, trade unions, political societies, and in the homes of the people where there are books, newspapers, music, wireless sets, workshops, gardens and groups of friends.

(Yeaxlee 1929: 155)

A concern to broaden definitions of what counts as lifelong education is then not new, and there is continuity with current ways of understanding what is now termed internationally as 'lifelong learning'.

However, there are some important implications to note in the shift from 'education' to 'learning' for how lifelong learning is conceptualised in contemporary educational policy. In a movement from 'lifelong education' to 'lifelong learning' the emphasis has shifted from formal education to include both nonformal and informal learning, and from teacher to learner. This is a shift that we welcome. Now it is not just 'leaders and teachers of real insight' who recognise and enable learning opportunities to develop, but nor is there an emphasis on the more communal learning described by Yeaxlee, something to which we will return in our final section. There has been another shift towards highly individualised learners who take responsibility for choices made and opportunities grasped. Learners are conceptualised outside of social structures, without identities or subject positionings, and are seen instead as highly individualised beings within a neo-liberal model based in deficit. Today it has become our individual responsibility to work through our 'lack' and ensure that we are able to take our places in a competitive and global knowledge economy. In such a society there is a requirement for continual (re-)training and updating of skills, with a growing emphasis on individual rather than collective learning experiences.

'Lifelong learning' has become part of a discourse of education, training and learning opportunities. The vagueness of the notion has left it open to competing political debates and policies. It can mean all learning from cradle-to-grave; post-compulsory education; formal, nonformal and informal learning; training for and in work; basic skills; and a host of other definitions. It has been used by the politics of the left and the right; and by governments worldwide. The different and competing conceptual frameworks might mean that the term has become meaningless. And yet we do believe it is a concept, and a reality, with which we should engage. At its best, lifelong learning can be inspirational; at its worst, it can produce and reproduce structural and material inequalities. Although the rhetoric emphasises the importance of all learning, in policy and in practice particular types of learning and particular types of learners are prioritised. Arguments abound about whether lifelong learning can lead to the development of a learning society, although what this means differs substantially.

A learning society?

The notion of a learning society is a comparatively new one in terms of policy, signalling the importance of informal as well as formal learning, and extends far beyond the UK. Green (2002) argues that the discourse of the learning society has taken a dominant position globally for three main reasons: the first is related to the ageing of populations common to all developed countries, the second is to do with a cultural shift towards 'lifestyle diversity', and the third is global economic restructuring. However, we argue that it is the final reason that takes precedence in the learning society. Although the rhetoric may appear to value all types of learning, discourses which consider 'the learning society' are guilty of prioritising particular types of learning and particular types of learners. Whilst the rationale for the development of a learning society could rest on a socially cohesive society with active citizens, learning for active citizenship appears to be more about learning to take our places as neo-liberal subjects than about radicalisation as empowered members of local, national and global communities. By neo-liberalism, we refer to a system which discursively states that governments should not inhibit free trade and free enterprise. The rights of individual freedoms are said to supersede state intervention, although we will argue throughout this book that apparent non-intervention is an ideological position which in fact stems from policy decisions and interventions. The development of a 'learning society' means in practice that we are all continually having to re-invent ourselves, to ensure an educated and well-trained workforce that will help the development of a competitive and global economy.

One of the sites for such re-invention is the workplace, with employers (especially but not exclusively large employers in both the public and private sectors) expected to develop learning organisations. According to Senge, a learning organisation is one 'where people continually expand their capacity to create the results they truly desire, where new and expansive patterns of thinking are nurtured, where collective aspiration is set free, and where people are continually learning together' (Senge 1990: 4, in Keep and Rainbird 2002: 65).

However, such a model is weak in its conceptualisation of power relations in the workplace, failing to recognise structural inequalities of gender, class, 'race' and disability, and organisational learning is hindered by cultural and structural characteristics. As Keep and Rainbird (2002) demonstrate, workplace learning can result in continuing discrimination, perpetuating structural inequalities. Age, gender, ethnicity, educational background, disability, hours of work and employment status all have huge influences on the ability of employees to access learning opportunities. The ways in which 'skill' is defined or training designed and delivered is not neutral and, as Anita Devos (2002) argues, training can become part of a struggle for knowledge and power. It is, in the main, those in higher or managerial positions who are able to obtain continuing professional development courses, whilst lower-skilled workers are only able to access basic skills learning. Particularly disadvantaged are manual workers (mainly working-class men) and people working part-time and/or in small workplaces (mainly women).

In learning societies, then, gender, social class and other structural differences and inequalities become embedded and reinforced. Working-class people, for example, do not have the same opportunities or possibilities as middle-class people to self-regulate and self-govern. In the hierarchies of learning that have seen severe funding cuts in further, adult and continuing education, the needs of communities are subsumed under the needs of local economies and employers.

Hughes and Tight go further:

> [T]he function of the learning society myth is to provide a convenient and palatable rationale and packaging for the current and future policies of different power groups within society. . . . Nothing approaching a learning society currently exists, and there is no real practical prospect of one coming into existence in the foreseeable future. Yet this myth has power. [It] is a product of, and also embodies, earlier myths which link education, productivity and change.
>
> (Hughes and Tight 1998: 188)

Foucault (1974) shows the power of such myths, including the determination of what counts as knowledge and 'truth'. For Foucault, central to considering discourse is the idea of power/knowledge, which he describes as inextricably linked: 'Power produces knowledge. Power and knowledge directly imply one another. There is no power relation without the correlative constitution of a field of knowledge, nor any knowledge that does not presuppose and constitute at the same time power relations' (Foucault 1980: 93).

It is the constitution of knowledge claims as 'truth' that is linked to systems of power: those who have the power – institutionally as well as individually – to determine and legitimise 'truth' also have the power to determine dominant discourses. This exercising of power happens so thoroughly, so powerfully, and so ideologically, that the political nature of discourses becomes hidden. Indeed, discourses are themselves acts of power.

Foucault has shown how institutions such as hospitals, prisons and asylums have the power to determine our identities as well as the means of normalisation and control, creating binary divisions such as healthy/ill, legal/delinquent and sane/insane. There is, says Foucault, a 'strange reality' in psychiatric hospitals 'that we call "confinement"' (1988: 96). And in this confinement, discourses of knowledge and truths become institutionalised. Foucault's work can be usefully extended to examine the dominant discourses of institutions of learning, which are full of such binary oppositions as knowledge/not knowledge, sense/non-sense and rational/irrational (Jackson 2004). What counts as sensible, rational knowledge takes on legitimacy through a supposed hegemonic truth, yet remains contestable, partial and disempowering for all but dominant groups. In hierarchies of learning and teaching, the academy becomes the dominant producer of knowledge, although the academy also has its own hierarchies of power and control.

Widening participation

Despite a rhetoric of widening participation which suggests a more inclusive system of higher education (HE), an expanded mass higher education system has generated new inequalities, deepening social stratification (Burke 2002; Reay *et al.* 2005). Although access to HE is increasing, with greater numbers of women undergraduates, patterns of social class remain unchanged and subject divisions are largely ignored or unchallenged. Furthermore, it has been argued that higher education cultures continue to privilege masculinist epistemologies and legitimise the values and assumptions of middle-class and white racialised dispositions. Whilst minority ethnic groups are in the main well represented, groups are clustered around particular higher education institutions and around disciplines, and access and participation varies in relation to age and gender (Connor *et al.* 2004).

Values of individual enterprise, risk-taking and competitiveness are (re)privileged in and through the hegemonic discourses of lifelong learning and this has significant implications for the educational participation of social groups who have historically been under-represented in higher education. The discourse upholds the notion of a meritocratic society in which enterprising individuals grab the (presumed) equally available opportunities to improve their futures by progressing through lifelong learning and into work. It operates to render invisible the ways that it (re)positions subjects hierarchically as classed, raced and gendered, thereby reproducing social inequalities and social exclusions. Notions of meritocracy rest on notions of 'ability' and 'potential' that are seen as natural attributes, fixed, generalisable and measurable (Gillborn and Youdell 2000). We argue that these notions conceal structural, cultural, discursive and material misrecognitions and inequalities, ignoring the ways that 'intelligence', 'ability' and 'potential' are socially constructed in the interests of particular hegemonic groups and communities.

Lifelong learning is often perceived as concentrating on adults returning to study, and yet the 'choices' available to adult learners have become increasingly constrained through recent policy developments. The rhetoric of much New Labour policy of lifelong learning is positive and suggestive of a strong commitment to widening educational participation. Yet the rhetoric is entangled in complex and contradictory policies, which might exacerbate rather than challenge social injustice (Thompson 2000; Burke 2002; Reay *et al.* 2005; Youdell 2006). The operations of institutionalised inequalities are subtle and concealed in complex organisational relations, practices and micro-politics (Morley 1997). As Thompson warns:

> Current trends in adult education policy, theory and practice also require interrogation and caution. Stirred by the progressive tone of some New Labour language, there is a danger that rhetorical assertions about the importance of widening participation, combating social exclusion and recognising social capital, for example, take too little account of the material, gendered, racialised and ideological context in which all these initiatives are located.
>
> (Thompson 2000: 8)

The White Paper on lifelong learning, *Learning to Succeed: A New Framework for Post-16 Education* (DfEE 1999), explicitly connects adult learning to the government's welfare to work programmes (DfEE 1999: 62). Unemployed people are specifically targeted, and are encouraged to upgrade their skills in three main ways:

- Through access to further education without having to pay fees, and undertaking study of their own choice. Those who are claiming Jobseekers Allowance (JSA) may not study, however, for more than 16 guided hours a week and they may remain subject to the availability for work conditions of JSA. This is also the route available for those on New Deal for Lone Parents, New Deal for Partners of the Unemployed, and the New Deal for People with Disabilities.
- People on New Deal for 18–24 year olds and those over 25 have access to further education and training on a full-time basis on the advice of Personal Advisors where this is thought the best way of overcoming barriers to re-entering the labour market. This is paid for under contract from the Employment Service from New Deal funds.
- Through TEC funded work-based learning for adults, which provides basic and occupational skills training for unemployed people over the age of 25.

(DfEE 1999: 62)

The relationship between funding, choice and participation does not go unrecognised by learners. For example, Kate and Shelley – self-defined working-class students on a Return to Study course – demonstrate a clear understanding of constraints around choices about what to study and the government's policy framework:

Shelley: It's like if you want to do computers or basic reading, you can do that
for nothing, but if you want to do something like counselling you've got to
pay. Already its streaming us, isn't it, into what we can be.

Kate: And really, basically, the government's programming us.

(quoted in Burke 2002: 25)

Shelley and Kate recognise that there are particular areas of educational participation endorsed and supported by government policy, and these areas are at
the lower levels of formal learning. Their discussion reveals their perspective
that opportunities are being severely constrained by the same policy that claims
to be about creating inclusion and equality. The emphasis of lifelong learning policy
for working-class adults is on basic skills, computer literacy and work-based
skills.

On the other hand, the government has set the target for widening participation
in higher education to 50 per cent of 18 to 30 year olds participating in higher
education by 2010. Although the language is about widening participation, critics
of the government target have argued that the policy will only work to increase
participation amongst the same groups who have historically always benefited from
higher educational access. Indeed, experts in the field have warned that policy
strategies are likely to increase the gap between middle-class access to and working-
class exclusion from higher education (Archer *et al.* 2003).

Let us consider the ways that the policy discourse, problematically in our
view, shifts attention away from wider social structures, divisions and inequalities.
Instead the policy gaze intensely targets those individuals who are constructed
as the main problem because, although they might have the 'ability' to benefit from
higher education, they lack aspiration. Indeed, 'raising aspirations' has been seen
as a key strategy for widening participation and Aimhigher has been set up by
New Labour to tackle this 'problem'. The following extract from the home page
of Aimhigher South East sets out the main purpose of Aimhigher and its target
groups:

> While the initiative will work with young people from all walks of life, it
> will concentrate on those who are underachieving, lacking in confidence or
> undecided, yet have the potential to enter higher education. Research shows
> that many such young people come from disadavantaged social and economic
> backgrounds, ethnic minority communities and the disabled.

The main work of Aimhigher staff is seen as 'raising the aspirations' of those
individuals who stand out as having special talent and potential despite their social
positioning. The discourse locates problems of deficit in individuals, families
and communities who are pathologised through the discourse of 'social exclusion'.
It is believed that Aimhigher professionals have the 'right' knowledge and skills
to objectively identify individuals with the potential to participate in higher

education, 'overcoming' the barriers of their disadvantaged cultural backgrounds. Raising aspirations is constructed as a straightforward process that occurs outside of social relations and the micro-politics of educational organisations and institutions (Morley 1999).

Raising aspirations comes out of the New Labour policy discourse of social exclusion, which has been critiqued by sociologists (e.g. Gerwirtz 2001; Archer *et al.* 2003) to expose the ways in which it leaves complex operations of power unexamined. Shifting the attention to 'exclusion' and away from inequality, injustice and misrecognition is a mechanism to re-privilege what is presented as a core British society which has universally shared values and perspectives. The assumptions are that the values of the core society are fundamentally good and are detached from politics and unequal social relations and misrecognitions. Those constructed as 'excluded', on the other hand, are also constructed as having flawed values and perspectives and lacking cultural capital, but want, or should learn to want, to be 'included' in this perceived superior society through higher education (Stuart 2000). The effect of this discourse is that specific cultural values and perspectives (i.e. middle-class, heterosexual, white and male-centred) are legitimised without problematising the implications of these values and perspectives for issues of social justice. Those groups who are constructed as 'excluded' are refashioned as deficient and disadvantaged and are reconstituted as marginalised selves through the discourse. The struggle over who is fashioned as an 'ideal' learner, which is tied to struggles over cultural values and epistemologies, is strategically left hidden (Skeggs 2004).

The discourse of 'raising aspirations' conceals the ways that subjectivities and values are re/fashioned through the discursive sites and practices of schools, colleges and universities. The emphasis on individual aspirations overlooks the interconnections between a subject's aspirations and their classed, racialised, (hetero)sexualised and gendered social positionings and identifications. It ignores the institutional and cultural contexts in which certain subjects are constructed, and construct themselves, as not having potential and ability (Gillborn and Youdell 2000). Furthermore, it fails to acknowledge that those classified as 'non-participants' might decide not to participate in higher education for a range of valid reasons (Archer and Leathwood 2003) and might prefer to participate in learning outside of formal institutional spaces.

Non-participation in higher education has been increasingly linked to boys' educational underachievement. The increasing concern that boys, particularly those from working-class groups, are at risk of educational exclusion has been documented and linked to a perception of a wider 'crisis' of masculinity (Epstein *et al.* 1998; Skelton 2001). This literature has argued that we need to understand what is going on in relation to complex formations of class, ethnicity, gender, race and sexuality and to avoid homogenising 'boys' and 'men' by ignoring differences between them. In order to make sense of differences in educational aspirations between boys and girls (and boys and boys), a close examination of gendered educational experiences is required. This needs to take notice of the ways these are connected to national and cultural identifications and complex sets of influences that shape learning orientations and aspirations. Currently the debate on boys/men and education draws heavily on statistical data, which misses out on the complex social processes of learning and often leads to simplistic explanations of gender differences that rest on notions of essentialism – that boys and girls are naturally different. Such assumptions about the natural differences between boys/men and girls/women have been particularly criticised as leading to the redirection of scarce resources in favour of boys and men.

The concerns about boys and schooling have been extended to men in post-compulsory education (McGivney 1999; Marks 2003), with recent quantitative data suggesting that widening participation to men from non-traditional back-grounds poses a serious policy challenge (HEFCE 2005). This is connected to the over-exaggerated but popular image that 'women are taking over', despite the evidence that shows continued institutional gender inequalities, with universities continuing to be male-centred institutions (Quinn 2003). For example, research on women students from working-class and ethnic minority backgrounds has highlighted the significant obstacles that they often have to overcome in terms of issues of funding, debt, access, familial support and fitting into a context that still privileges masculine ways of learning and knowing (Bowl 2003; Quinn 2003). Furthermore, feminist research reveals that the organisation, structure, curriculum and pedagogy within higher education has not changed to accommodate the needs and interests of women students from different cultural backgrounds (Morley 1999; Morley 2003; Quinn 2003). As a result of the ongoing construction of boys as victims of the educational system, and the dominant reasoning that if women are doing well then men are losing out, concerns around widening participation have shifted firmly from girls to boys (Epstein *et al.* 1998). This perspective takes an anti-feminist stance that perceives girls' and women's success as always at a cost to boys and men.

The picture is complex however, and attention does need to be drawn to men's gendered experiences of accessing higher education, particularly with regard to the ways that marginalised masculinities effect men from working-class and minority ethnic backgrounds. A recent UK study suggests that being female increases the chances of higher education participation by 18 per cent (HEFCE 2005), although it does not engage with other sets of differences such as social class and ethnicity. Earlier work identifies men from socio-economic groups IV and V as most unlikely to participate in higher education (Dearing 1997), and more recent figures from the Quality Assurance Agency show that 74 per cent of access students are women (QAA 2003). Similarly, qualitative data have revealed that male 'non-participants' often strongly disidentify with university students, seeing 'participation as incompatible with notions of working-class masculinity' and as 'entailing numerous costs and risks to masculine identities' (Archer and Leathwood 2003). These data show that certain groups of men are having difficulties in accessing higher education and it is important to understand how men's gendered identifications interact with other social locations and differences.

Research on widening educational participation has shown that access to learning must be understood in relation to deeply embedded relations of inequality and misrecognition that operate at multiple levels. One important point made in the literature is that the assumption that higher education participation is the preferred and superior route for young people will only deepen existing exclusions and inclusions. We argue that policy must help to work towards a situation where all young people genuinely exercise the choice of whether or not to participate in university level study, and where higher education institutions are inclusive of a range of ontological and epistemological perspectives and frameworks. Yet, policy must also help to create a situation where other kinds of learning are equally valued in society, including vocational and practical learning. Gary Hawkes, Chairman of Edge, an organisation campaigning for practical learning, argues that:

> Young people are being given phoney choices. They are told there is a vocational route in school when in reality there is not. They are told that vocational education matters, when in reality vocational learning is perceived only suitable for the less able.
> Gaining university entrance is the only goal, a process that alienates a significant minority of young people. A world where half are qualified and motivated and employable and half are unskilled and de-motivated is a recipe for social and economic disaster.
>
> (Hawkes 2005: 3)

Furthermore, there is a single route into higher education that continues to be upheld and privileged as the preferred and 'best' route: the Advanced ('A') level (Williams 1997). It is difficult for students entering higher education through alternative entry routes, such as Access to Higher Education courses and General National Vocational Qualification (GNVQ), for example, to be considered for those universities constructed as 'elite'. The hierarchies between higher education institutions however matter in terms of the status of the student and how she is perceived by potential employers. Such favouring of the traditional 'A' level student also helps to exclude mature students from certain universities with status, as mature students are more likely to enter HE through Access to Higher education programmes. This is in the context of credential inflation and an increasingly competitive employment market.

Conclusions

In this opening chapter, then, we have started to tell some of the stories of lifelong learning: stories that will continue to be developed throughout the book. Here we have told stories of shifting currents between education and learning; of credit transferability and of widening participation; of learning for the love of learning, of learning for work, and of learning to develop basic skills; of learning societies, and of discourses of learning; of competition and flexibility, and choices and con-straints; and stories of learners and 'non'-learners and of inclusion and exclusion. In the next chapters we will continue our theme of storytelling to consider constructions of knowledge and of learning.

Chapter 2

Reclaiming knowledge

Introduction

This chapter argues that in order to reconceptualise lifelong learning, we need also to deconstruct formations of knowledge that are currently privileged within academic and policy discourses. Drawing on feminist post-structural theoretical frameworks, we will expose the hegemonic, masculinist truth-knowledge claims that permeate the current field. We argue that there is a dichotomous and hierarchical separating out of 'knowledge', with higher education seen as 'more academic' than further education and other forms of learning. This is not straightforward, however, as there are more subtle power relations and hierarchies between higher educational institutions, with institutions differentially positioned in relation to 'knowledge' and 'skill'. Furthermore, legitimated knowledge is persistently constructed as neutral, objective, apolitical and value-free, while we argue that all knowledge is always tied to power, and is classed, gendered, racialised and sexualised. The lack of recognition that knowledge is socially constructed and contextualised exacerbates cultural, discursive and material inequalities, which remain embedded in lifelong learning policies and practices.

De/constructing and re/constructing knowledge about lifelong learning

This section will consider how lifelong learning is being constructed in the field and what we can know about it through the available discourses at play locally, nationally and internationally. What kinds of research about lifelong learning are being conducted and legitimated in the field? Who is contributing to the discourses of lifelong learning – and who is not? In what ways does this limit what we can mean when we talk about lifelong learning? We will explore these key questions in this section.

Meanings of lifelong learning are constructed in competing ways through the different epistemological frameworks available to researchers. This is connected to wider discourses about what counts as knowledge and what counts as 'good research'. Foucault's (1972) notion of discourse is particularly useful in shedding light on the processes by which meanings of lifelong learning get constructed through policy, practice and research. 'Discourse' captures the ways that knowledge and power are always intertwined, profoundly shaping national, local and institutional practices and policies, structures and disciplinary technologies. Discourses are produced within shifting cultural contexts and continually refashioned through changing power relations. Discourses constrain and create the kinds of spaces we live in, the ways we give meaning to our experiences, the positions we take and, importantly for the construction of knowledge, the kinds of questions we raise in research (Foucault 1972, 1973). Discourses of lifelong learning institutionalise and regulate gendered and normalised understandings about what learning is and who counts as a learner. However, discourses of lifelong learning are contested so that there are multiple and competing meanings of lifelong learning across time and space.

Competing discourses shape the kinds of questions that are asked about lifelong learning and so it is important to have an understanding of the different contexts in which discourses are re/produced locally, nationally and internationally, struggling for hegemony. At the national and international levels, multiple meanings of lifelong learning are constituted by the often contradictory discourses at play in lifelong learning policy including globalisation, economic stability and competition, changing and new technologies, ageing populations, needs of industry, market-forces, citizenship and social justice. Researchers concerned with deconstructing the meanings and motivations behind the increasingly broad international focus on lifelong learning have identified the competing discourses running through policy as devices of persuasion: 'Globalization, the rise of new information technologies, or the ageing society are just some of the keywords also used by national as well as international bodies to justify the need for lifelong learning' (Dehmel 2006: 49).

Nicoll and Edwards (2004) go further than Dehmel, analysing policy to expose the particular rhetorical devices that construct the problems and possibilities of lifelong learning in an attempt not only to persuade but to mobilize individuals and groups into a certain way of understanding change. Drawing on the UK Green Paper *The Learning Age*, they are interested in deconstructing the effects of the 'new age' being produced through the text. Their work is concerned to understand the ways that rhetorical strategies fabricate and mobilize the new age. They ask:

> What rhetorical strategies are involved in representing it [the learning age]? With what effects? If we can go some way to answering such questions, then we may begin to understand how policy works as persuasion and become more discerning as to the way in which problems and possibilities are framed and fabricated. We may also be able to reconfigure our responses to policy.
>
> (Nicoll and Edwards 2004: 43)

Nicoll and Edwards argue then that deconstructive research not only contributes to understanding the effects of lifelong learning policy but also creates the spaces for resistance through reconfigurations. Similarly, Patrica Cross who investigates what we can know about learners and how we can know it, argues that research is only the first step to raising new lines of inquiry and understanding (Barkley *et al*. 2005).

These authors raise some important questions about research and knowledge production. First of all, what kind of knowledge is constructed through research and for what purposes? The researchers above recognise the potential of research to not only shape understanding but also to create possibilities for change and resistance. However, what we would like to point out in relation to Foucault's concept of discourse is the way that research is always constrained by the discourses at play within any particular space and time. It is not possible for the researcher to move outside of the discursive field in which they are located and the hypotheses or questions they formulate will always be shaped by the discourses available to them at any given time. This is not to argue, though, that researchers are without agency, and the kinds of methodological frameworks they decide to draw on profoundly shape the kind of epistemological perspectives they contribute to.

However, lifelong learning research is dominated by certain assumptions that constrain the kind of research possible and most likely to be seen as valuable and valid in relation to wider social norms and practices. For example, large-scale research that claims objectivity, validity and reliability continues to be universally privileged. This phenomenon is linked to enlightenment assumptions that privilege methods modelled on the natural sciences. This construction of social research assumes that by using scientific methods the researcher is able to uncover pre-existing truths, ensuring value-freedom and neutrality, to contribute to forms of valid and reliable knowing and knowledge about the social world. Lifelong learning is constructed as an objective reality that can be scientifically measured and known. However, feminist post-structuralist methodologies deconstruct the claims to objectivity and neutrality made by scientific social researchers arguing that all knowledge is situated, politicised, gendered, partial, contextualisied and discursively constituted. Binaries between objectivity/subjectivity, large-scale/ small-scale, breadth/depth, rationality/emotion, quantitative/qualitative have been seen by feminists as enduring regimes of truth that re/privilege masculinised, white racialised and Westernised ways of knowing.

Lifelong learning as a field of study has been affected by such regimes of truth, often undermining the voices of those whose understanding is perceived as 'too subjective', experiential and localised (coded as feminised ways of understanding). These struggles are crucial to understanding the meanings of lifelong learning and the power relations that make some knowledges central and others marginalised and ignored. For example, although there is a growing body of practitioner-based research in the field, which is researched in local sites and often by teacher-researchers, such research is likely not to be seen as 'robust' enough to influence decisions at institutional and national levels (Burke and Kirton 2006). This is not to underestimate the important contribution of such research, which often makes a difference to classroom-based practices and should, we argue, be disseminated widely to deepen our understanding of lifelong learning practices, processes and experiences.

Most educationalists, including policy-makers, managers and teachers, would hope that policy is informed by high quality research and knowledge. However, there are several issues that affect the chances of a piece of research being used by policy-makers to help to develop policy of lifelong learning. First are the assumptions about 'rigorous research' and these are tied in with the privileging of certain scientific forms of knowledge. Knowledge that has been produced through large-scale research methods for example is often preferred; breadth rather than depth and statistical rather than experiential knowledge is seen as 'more scientific'. This is because notions of objectivity are premised on the assumption that there is an observable social reality that exists and can be measured by the researcher using scientific methods. It is thus difficult to argue for national policy on the basis of in-depth qualitative inquiry, which focuses on the discursive construction of experience and meaning. The processes by which some discourses become hegemonic are always tied in with privileged epistemological frameworks and social positions. Research that fits in with positivist frameworks is more likely to be used as evidence for policy-making and individuals in high status social positions are more likely to significantly contribute to the production of meanings. Critical researchers who might challenge positivist assumptions are less likely to have an influence on policy-making, partly because the knowledge produced through this kind of research is often localised, contextualised and tentative, resisting the tendency in much large-scale research to make universal claims that might simply be applied to educational policy and practice. Critical researchers are more likely to raise further questions and to take a position of uncertainty. Policy-makers need the supposed certainties of large-scale research that claims scientific rigour to persuade their audiences that their strategic decisions are based on hard core evidence.

This means that those at the centre of knowledge about learning, the learners themselves, are the least likely to contribute to mainstream knowledge production and policy formulation. Even those in the most senior positions are unlikely, due to hegemonic epistemological frameworks, to draw on their knowledge of lifelong learning from the perspective of experience. Moreover, many learners do not occupy the kinds of social positioning and status that would enable them, as individuals or communities, to have a significant influence on knowledge or policy of lifelong learning. We are not suggesting that there is a single monolithic meaning of lifelong learning nor are we arguing that learners have no affect on the production of meaning and knowledge. However, we do argue that there are particular ways of thinking about lifelong learning that have gained hegemony and these have a profound effect on the policy and practice of lifelong learning and yet these are largely uninformed by the complex, contradictory and multifaceted experiences of learning. This is largely due to the processes and politics of knowledge validation and the ways that these operate around shifting and complex inequalities.

Lifelong learning and the knowledge economy/society

This section will build on the above discussion of the ways that knowledge gets constructed in hegemonic discourses of lifelong learning. Lifelong learning has been identified as a key strategy to address the needs of changing economies and societies. Knowledge, skills and ideas are seen as central to national stability and competitiveness in the context of globalisation and new information and communication technologies. This section will consider the kinds of knowledge that are privileged within the discourses of the knowledge society and the implications for lifelong learning and learners. Whose knowledge is marginalised within these discourses? What kind of learning gets constructed? What kind of knowledge is desired? The section will present critiques of these constructions of the knowledge economy/society.

The dawn of the twenty-first century has been seen internationally as posing numerous challenges and risks for individuals, communities, societies and governments, including the changing nature of work, technological change, globalisation, environmental uncertainties, terrorism and war, and the general uncertainties of the times. Indeed, part of the attraction of scientific methods is that they are seen to produce reliable, objective and valid data that help to manage the risks connected to a range of threats and uncertainties. The right kind of knowledge, it is assumed, will enable us (those in powerful and/or privileged positions particularly in the over-developed world) to control our environments and minimise risk. Creating a 'knowledge economy' will, it is assumed, reduce the threats for certain individuals and communities facing what is seen as an increasingly volatile world. Lifelong learning is seen as a key strategy in relation to this.

The creation of a knowledge society is also related to the rapidly changing nature of work and the increasingly competitive global markets that challenge national economic stability. John Field says:

> Particularly in western societies that are shifting from manufacturing towards services and must adopt high productivity and high added-value work processes if they are to survive in an increasingly competitive environment, these factors are also combined with a new emphasis on the role of knowledge itself as both a driver of change and a basic prerequisite of competitive success.
>
> (Field 2005: 114)

Lifelong learning has been identified as a key strategy to build the knowledge capital of different, and competing societies and to then face the challenges and risks confronting late modernity, particularly with regard to the key themes of innovation, change and flexibility. The twenty-first century has been discursively constructed as an age of uncertainty and of ever increasing levels of risk which need to be carefully monitored, managed and regulated. Increasing knowledge capital therefore is a key policy strategy, locally, nationally, regionally and globally, in managing and regulating risk and instability. Lifelong learning could be seen as a disciplinary mechanism to control and regulate global citizens and communities within the context of this constant threat of risk. In lifelong policy across different nations and regions, the notion of a 'knowledge society' has become widely adopted, leading to increased levels of attention to 'lifelong learning'.

As we have said above, a central concern of lifelong learning policy is to accumulate technological and scientific knowledge in order to better manage the risks that face societies and communities. This prevailing concern constructs 'the lifelong learner' in particular ways and ignores the ontological questions underpinning the concern to develop particular kinds of bodies of knowledge (e.g. technical, technological and scientific) and 'knowers' (e.g. scientists and business-men). Class, gender, ethnicity, sexuality and race are largely seen as separate from the pursuit of knowledge, and questions about identity and difference are often excluded from debates about who should participate in the different kinds of life-long learning available and why. Yet, the ontological position of those producing knowledge that is publicly recognised, legitimated and validated is crucial to under-standing the characteristics of that body of knowledge in terms of its underpinning values, assumptions and the contexts in which it is produced.

There are certain interconnected ontological issues between 'learning', 'learner' and 'knowledge' that deserve closer attention. The kind of knowledge that is privileged within the 'knowledge society' is (believed to be) scientific, rational, objective, specialised, technological and apolitical, traits that are closely tied up with masculinised, middle-classed and white racialised ways of being. On the other hand, within an increasingly service sector centred economy, certain feminised traits are required, including for example being friendly, providing 'customer care', being flexible, having generic sets of skills and being diligent at work. These traits are often constructed as sets of skills (rather than knowledge) that can be acquired through training, rather than education. The current discourse of 'learning', which has shifted the focus away from 'education' allows slippages between 'knowledge' and 'skills', as if they were equally valued and recognised within society. Yet, the differences between specialised knowledge and generic skill is highly gen-dered and classed, and makes material differences in terms of access to income, social capital and status or social positioning. We would argue therefore that the construction of the 'knowledge society' as an ungendered, apolitical and universally shared goal is highly problematic and raises particular issues about who has access to (the different kinds of) learning and knowledge and who is (a particular kind of) learner and knower. Certainly, the emphasis of much government policy is to raise the literacy levels of the poor and to provide excluded groups with access to learning up to Level 2. On the other hand, for those who are seen to have high levels of 'ability' and 'potential' and are between the ages of 18–30, government policy aims to provide access to higher education. Classed, gendered and racialised identities are intermeshed then with the different constructions of 'learner' and 'knower', and who has access to education, rather than training, is embedded in wider social relations and inequalities.

Access to meaning-making through lifelong learning

Higher education in particular is seen as central to the production of new knowledge in the context of competing economies and societies responding to the pressures of global change. Access to HE becomes of increasing importance, expressed through policies of widening participation, and the UK government's target of 50 per cent participation of 18 to 30 year olds by 2010. Research conducted within universities is also seen as of major importance in policy on higher education (DfES 2003a) but the implications of increasing hierarchies between 'diverse HEIs' is not being explicitly addressed. Who is seen as worthy of HE access? Who is able to participate in producing new knowledge and in what contexts? What kind of knowledge is privileged through policy mechanisms that regulate the kind of research that is produced? What is the role of the university in relation to the 'knowledge economy/society' and what are the different perspectives within these debates?

Feminist scholars have argued that hegemonic knowledge within academia is oriented towards those qualities associated with masculinity, and operates around traditional binaries that privilege the masculine over the feminine (Alcoff and Potter 1993; Morley 1999; Currie et al. 2002). Knowledge that is legitimised by universities is constructed as objective, rational, and value-free (Morley 1999; Quinn 2003). It is seen as detached from the personal and political, although critical theorists have argued that knowledge is always tied to wider power relations that are classed, gendered and racialised (Lather 1991). The production of knowledge therefore always operates in the interests of certain groups over others. Feminist theorists point out that knowledge is always situated and who the knower is, the ontological politics of meaning-making, are as important as epistemological questions about what counts as knowledge (Haraway 1988; Collins 1990; Harding 1993; Stanley 1993).

Access to meaning-making is policed by the changing structures, discourses, unequal relations and conventions of the academy. Higher education diversity has become a celebratory discourse that constructs differences between HEIs as simply a positive thing. Of course, diversity is something to work towards and recognise positively but we argue that unless considerations of diversity also address issues of difference, (mis)recognition and (in)equality, then exclusions from contributing to knowledge production will continue to operate in subtle, insidious and almost invisible ways. Access to the resources and space needed to produce research, for example, is gendered. This is partly because women tend to occupy lower positions within higher educational institutions and often are on part-time, temporary contracts, although it is a vicious circle of course, because the less research produced the more unlikely promotion, recognition and esteem. The picture for women in university is not as glowing as much of the hegemonic discourse about 'women taking over the university' might suggest (Quinn 2003). For example, only 13 per cent of professors in British universities are women, in the USA the figure is 16 per cent and in Australia it is only 11 per cent. As Currie, Thiele and Harris explain, drawing on their study of American and Australian universities:

> Based on our study and review of the literature, we conclude that universities are dominated by masculine principles and structures that lead to advantages for male staff and disadvantages for female staff. The most valued activities in universities are those that reflect male patterns of socialization: individualist rather than collective, competitive rather than cooperative, basd on power differentials rather than egalitarian, and linked to expert authority rather than collegial support.
>
> (Currie *et al.* 2002: 1)

The micro-politics within and between universities operate in subtle ways to reinforce these gender divisions. The divisions are further strengthened through quality assurance structures that separate out teaching and research, which we explore in detail in Chapter 14. Those who spend more time teaching than conducting research and writing for publication are likely to be concentrated in lower status universities. Access to knowledge production is linked in with the power relations of differently valued HEIs, the relationship between teaching and research, part-time, temporary work and access to powerful networks within academia. All of these different aspects are heavily gendered and racialised. However, the micro-politics of universities help to reveal the 'myriad ways in which women are undermined and excluded from access to resources, influence, career opportunities and academic authority' (Morley 1999: 4).

Micro-politics operate in myriad ways to block access to meaning-making for many students as well as academic staff, particularly those who are constructed as 'widening participation students'. Students are expected to meet the specific conventions of the academy, although these conventions are themselves contested, contextualised and heterogeneous. Particular constructions of 'academic knowledge' regulate what can be claimed and who can claim certain meanings. Knowledge that is seen as 'subjective' or 'personal' is at risk of being discounted and there are certain rules of the game that must be adhered to if a student is going to succeed in higher education. Other bodies of knowledge that the student might bring to their work are often invalidated if the student does not construct that knowledge to fit in with the expectations of the academy. For example, students must frame their understanding not in terms of practical or professional knowledge but in relation to academic knowledge, the literature 'out there' that will then validate the points they want to make.

Teresa Lillis argues that the dominant literacy practice within Western higher education is 'essayist literacy', which operates around particular taken-for-granted practices. Essayist literacy 'privileges the discursive routines of particular social groups whilst dismissing those of people who, culturally and communally, have access to and engage in other practices' (Lillis 2001: 39). There are several important key points that Lillis makes that are of relevance to our argument here about the ways that the politics of meaning-making operate across ontological and epistemological struggles, inequalities and misrecognitions. The dominant practice of essayist literacy, Lillis argues, exposes that students are expected in formal educational institutions to take part in a very particular kind of literacy practice. Those students who are unfamiliar with this practice are often wrongly constructed as intellectually inferior or lacking ability. She also points out that this practice 'involves and invokes particular ways of meaning/wording, and can consequently serve to exclude others' (Lillis 2001: 40).

The essayist literacy practice positions the knower in specifically gendered, racialised and classed ways as the masculine, white and middle-class subject who is objective, decontextualised and rational, and who is reflecting rather than constructing reality. The complex social relations by which knowledge gets produced are perceived as apolitical and/or irrelevant in such practices, and other literacy practices are not recognised as legitimate or valuable. Those who do not produce written texts in the right ways will not have access to the high status forms of learning that are most rewarded in terms of job, status and income. Furthermore, those who do not conform to essayist literacy practices are least likely to have access to the production of knowledge. As a consequence of such practices, certain epistemological positions are reprivileged through the formal sites of lifelong learning.

Policy on lifelong learning nationally also plays a key role in legitimising particular kinds of knowledge and dismissing other bodies of knowledge as less important. As we argued earlier, claims to the importance of some kinds of knowledge – and skills – are often made in the name of the economy. Indeed, as we have already considered, the notion of a 'knowledge economy' illuminates the significance that is placed on knowledge for economic advantage in many contemporary policy documents. The following quote from *The Future of Higher Education* demonstrates well the close links policy makes between knowledge production and economic concerns:

> We have to make better progress in harnessing knowledge to wealth creation. And that depends on giving universities the freedoms and resources to compete on the world stage. To back our world class researchers with financial stability. To help turn ideas into successful businesses. To undo the years of under-investment that will result in our universities slipping back.
>
> (DfES 2003d: 2)

The emphasis in this White Paper is clearly on scientific and technical knowledge, although 'other' kinds of knowledge are also mentioned. Knowledge however is repeatedly valued in relation to its contribution to economic and business prosperity.

> Research lays the long-term foundations for innovation, which is central to improved growth, productivity and quality of life. This applies not only to

scientific and technical knowledge. Research in the social sciences, and in the arts and humanities can also benefit the economy – for example, in tourism, social and economic trends, design, law, and the performing arts – not to speak of enriching our culture more widely.

(DfES 2003d: 23)

Let us consider for example the kind of knowledge that is privileged through the national curriculum in schools and the kind of knowledge that is ignored as less important. The national curriculum privileges subjects that are seen to provide children with the key knowledge and skills required to participate as active citizens and to be included in society – in particular to be in paid work in their adult lives. We are not disputing that the national curriculum subjects are important for learning but the ways that curriculum and pedagogy are approached within this framework might be argued to reinforce wider injustices and exclusions rather than to ensure an equal and just society. This is partly because of the ways that knowledge gets reconstructed through curriculum, pedagogy and assessment, with the teacher and pupils often as passively positioned in relation to meaning-making. The teachers, in the context of multiple levels of expectations, in particular around league tables and raising levels of achievement on exams, have minimal agency within such tightly regulated frameworks (Gillborn and Youdell 2000). Possibilities of creating knowledge with pupils becomes limited when the teacher has little role to play in the design and development of curriculum, pedagogy and assessment. Similarly pupils have limited agency within these disciplinary frameworks, where what the pupil learns is dictated by a set curriculum and by the examinations that need to be successfully undertaken to increase life chances. The ways that class, gender and race operate within these highly constrained contexts to reproduce injustices and exclusions are ignored and there is little opportunity for intervention by teachers and pupils. This then affects the opportunities for marginalised groups to contribute to meaning-making and to bring their perspectives into what they experience and know as significant.

For example, citizenship education was introduced in 2002 as a compulsory national curriculum subject in secondary schools, requiring that pupils aged between 11 and 16 are taught the three key areas of social and moral responsibility, community involvement and political literacy (see http://www.dfes.gov.uk/citizenship). The first of these requires that pupils are taught appropriate behaviour both in and beyond the classroom towards those in authority and towards each other. Appropriate behaviour to those in authority is likely to confirm dominant and hegemonic practices, especially in ways which confirm classed and racialised positionings. Political literacy means that pupils learn the skills, values and knowledges required in a 'democratic society', issues that we engage with both in this chapter and throughout the book. Although it has been shown that citizenship education has the potential to develop pedagogic approaches that can enhance student learning and achievement (Citizenship Education Research Strategy Group 2005) in practice the Review indicated that there is a lack of teacher training to enable them to develop such approaches. In addition, teachers are constrained by a proscriptive curriculum that leaves limited scope for manoeuvre or resistances.

Curriculum therefore is a space that is often regulatory and reproductive. Yet it also provides a space for resistances and challenges and is a key discursive site in the formation of knowledge. Furthermore, the ways that we know about the operations of classed, gendered and racialised identities and inequalities is left at the tacit level and is rarely explicitly addressed within formal curricula except by specialist courses such as Women's Studies. However, such courses are themselves highly marginalised both within educational institutions and wider society. Martino, drawing on interviews with Australian boys aged 15–16 in a Catholic high school, argues that schools should include gender studies in their mainstream curriculum. This he argues will provide a critical space for boys and girls to study the impact of masculinities on social relations and individual experiences. He argues that the deployment of texts, which encourage self-reflexive practices, would enable boys to understand the significant gendered effects of certain formations of masculinity and to thus adjust their behaviours and modes of thinking. Schools, he argues, should develop curricular strategies designed to:

> encourage boys to reflect on and to recognise the injustices in their own lives as a basis for enabling them to develop and value capacities for empathising with other people's experiences of injustice [see also Martino 1996, 1997]. In this way, a critical practice that helps students to interrogate heterosexist and homophobic versions of masculinity can be developed. Within such a peda-gogical context of self-problematisation and adjustment, certain practices and modes of thinking, acting and behaving are linked to the enactment of particular problematic forms of masculinity and this is made explicit for students. That is, the links made between modes of behaviour and the enactment of forms of masculinity selected for analysis and adjustment become the target of a critical practice. Such gender equity initiatives, designed to encourage boys to engage productively with issues related to the politics of masculinity, are presented as complementing attempts to improve and enhance the achievement and social situation of girls in schools.
>
> (Martino 1999: 260)

Martino's argument highlights the importance of critical knowledges that are not currently taught through the formal curriculum but should become an integral part of learning and knowing about ourselves and how this relates to wider social practices, relations and contexts. These knowledges are subjective and situated, linked to the body and to emotion, and are embedded in lived practices and ways of being. We would argue that if governments are to take seriously the links they make in policy texts between lifelong learning and social justice then Martino's approach is crucial. However, this would not just involve pupils at school to interrogate forms of masculinity and how they are connected to social inequalities but also would involve students at university, in further education colleges and other informal sites of learning to consider how gender, class, 'race' and sexualities play out in relation to the creation of meaning and knowledge. This would feed into informal sites of learning, including the workplace and the home, so that lifelong learning encompasses wider social issues beyond utilitarian or economic concerns.

Conclusions

This chapter has considered the project of reconceptualising lifelong learning in relation to competing constructions of knowledge, some that are hegemonic and privileged within discursive educational fields and practices, and others that are marginalised. We have considered the politics around the production of knowledge, and the specific roles of policy and higher education within such processes of meaning-making. We have drawn on feminist critiques of positivism to position ourselves epistemologically as researchers who construct knowledge as always tied to power and as classed, gendered, racialised and sexualised. We argue then that a lack of recognition that knowledge is constructed and contextualised means that social, cultural, discursive and material inequalities remain embedded in lifelong learning policies and practices thus serving to reinforce social injustices through lifelong learning discourses.

We have also considered in this chapter the ways in which lifelong learning is being constructed through research and the ways that the currently hegemonic frameworks limit what we can know about it. We have considered the ways that certain knowledge about lifelong learning is legitimated and how some voices are heard louder than others. This is understood as being connected to democratic processes by which we can all agree on certain sets of value and assumptions about what is right and valid. However, the operations of selectivity and meaning-making are tied up with complex politics about what kinds of knowledge are seen as useful, valuable and valid, and these operations, we have argued are highly classed, gendered and racialised. Through subtle and insidious mechanisms of exclusion, claims are made in the interests of certain individuals, communities and cultures. Knowledge about and through formal lifelong learning therefore privileges the perspectives of those in more powerful positions. Furthermore, knowledge about informal and nonformal learning is marginalised both in the field and in terms of the experiences of different learners.

Building on such deliberations, the final section of this chapter has considered issues of access to knowledge and access to meaning-making. We have drawn on Lillis's work to argue that essayist practices work against the interests of marginalised groups, and we will return to this in the next section of the book. We continue these discussions in the next chapter, where our focus shifts from knowledge to learning, although we see the two as inextricably bound together.

Chapter 3

Reclaiming learning

Introduction

This chapter challenges the validation of learning that only takes place in formal educational institutions to the exclusion of other forms of learning. We examine the implications for equity and inclusion when certain kinds of learning are given higher levels of esteem and status than others, arguing that hierarchies of learning exist between and within institutions as well as outside of them. Although we argue that different forms of learning are equally important, this does not erase the structures in place that reinforce the privileging of learning in higher education and the costs to individuals who do not participate in higher education. Furthermore, we will critique the value that is given to certain kinds of learning within higher education institutions especially as policy seems to be increasing levels of differentiation within HE through its emphasis on vocational learning for 'widening participation' students.

We go on to examine the range of learning that takes place in further and community-based education colleges, highlighting some of the innovative programmes and practices that often take place within these institutions and questioning how much recognition is given to the contribution that they are making to lifelong learning. In this section of our discussion, we pay attention to the groups who are able to access learning in these institutions and the implications for policy and practice. We move on to consider the learning that takes place outside of these formal institutional contexts, including home, community and in the workplace. We end the chapter by arguing that education is always political, and outline ways in which the radical politics of learning have in many ways become overshadowed by the discursive practices and politics of neo-liberalism. In reclaiming the complex and contested journeys of informal learners, we will shed light on the ways in which lifelong learning might be reconceptualised and the value of learning that takes place outside of higher education.

Changing educational landscapes

We begin by considering higher education, not because we prioritise it over other forms of learning, but because it will enable us to begin our critique of dominant educational discourses and structures. Half a century ago higher education was still primarily the domain of young, white and mainly middle-class men. However, during the 1960s, in a time of apparent emancipation and freedom, as social and educational aspirations grew, so did the demands for increased access to higher education (Pratt 1997). By the end of the 1960s eight new polytechnics were created, and with them a growth in vocational courses for working-class men. Women still had very limited access to higher education and there was initially little diversity in the student body. Despite this, the advent of the new polytechnics was seen by many as the dawn of a new era, setting out to revolutionise higher education. With demands for education to step outside its ivory towers and into the lifelong learning agenda came greater hopes for more equal opportunities. Indeed, there were expectations amongst some that the universities would be unlikely to survive. Instead it was the polytechnics that disappeared. The Education Reform Act of 1988 first (in 1989) took the polytechnics out of local authority control and then in 1992 enabled the polytechnics to become universities or, more specifically, 'new' universities, perhaps still seen as 'the comprehensive schools' of higher education (Robinson 1968), with little but a change in name altering the status between 'old' and 'new' universities (Jackson 2004).

It is not surprising that there is a continuing divide between the pre-existing discourses and cultures of the 'old' and 'new' universities. Although the post-1997 Labour government has been keen to speak a language of lifelong learning, if there *are* any new discourses of higher education they are tied to an emphasis on vocationalism rather than to lifelong learning, especially within the 'new' universities. There is no agreed paradigm of learning by higher education institutions, and such agreement might be very difficult to reach, with an ensuing 'clash' between the cultures of learning developed within 'old' and 'new' universities (Duke 1992). Ainley (1994) suggests that in universities today – and especially in the 'new' universities – there is an emphasis on work and industry, with the 'new' universities more likely to put an emphasis on vocationalism, and the 'old' universities on a more 'traditional' or 'liberal' education.

Ainley (1994) argues that at both 'old' and 'new' universities, work has become modularised and fragmented, with an emphasis on building credits and on assessments. Assessment continues to be based on a very limited range of criteria, so benefiting particular groups of students. Although there is a growth in entry for women, working-class, minority ethnic students and mature students, the greater the prestige of the higher education institution, the lower the percentage of these groups, with the exception of women. There is, however, still a clear gender difference between subjects. Gender differences for engineering and physics, for example, are apparent across age bands. A report on widening participation in higher education has suggested that this means that efforts to persuade females to enter these subject areas have had little effect (UUK/SCOP 2005). However, this report takes no account of the sexism embedded within institutions and within the workplace, instead placing the blame firmly with women for not taking up supposed opportunities offered.

Jocey Quinn argues that mass entry of women is the most dramatic change universities have seen. For some women, higher education becomes a protected space, where entering through the gates means leaving behind their gendered positionings in the home and entering a space set aside entirely for the 'studying self'. If power exists in being exercised, she states, 'then women are truly powerful: they are exercising their power to think' (2003: 148). Although feminists have continued to describe the university as a male space, Quinn argues that we can no longer think of the UK university in such a way, although we do still need to explore the academy as a place of women imbued with masculinist notions.

However, majority numbers do not necessarily equate with power. As Jocey Quinn acknowledges, women are still positioned as gendered, as Black, as working class, as mothers. Yet she concludes that women are truly powerful in the exercising of power, including the power to think and deconstruct, emerging as ambiguous but powerful subjects. However, there seems to us little evidence that women have changed the face of HE so that it can no longer be configured as a man's world. As Jocey Quinn herself states, 'the curriculum has not been reconfigured: women are still marginal territory and feminism has not shifted the paradigms of what is valid knowledge' (2003: 148).

Whilst 'old' universities have increased their student numbers, there has been a lower rate of increase for non-traditional entrants and minority ethnic groups, who are more likely to seek places at 'new' universities. With the formation of the polytechnics into universities, there are now much wider opportunities for such groups of students to gain university admission. However, this does not necessarily suggest that such students have been able to find more innovative teaching, nor does it equate with growth in equalities of opportunities.

A study on *Young Participation in Higher Education* (2005) demonstrates the extent and scale of the inequality of access to higher education by young people from affluent and poorer areas throughout the country. The study of participation rates in every region of England reveals that the most advantaged 20 per cent of young people are up to six times more likely to enter higher education than the most disadvantaged 20 per cent (HEFCE 2005: 97). Although a greater proportion of males compared to females from higher socio-economic groups are accepted at universities, the reverse is true with regard to lower socio-economic groups. Additionally, young people from disadvantaged backgrounds, and minority ethnic students, are clustered in 'new' universities, where they are most likely to make successful applications (UUK/SCOP 2005) whilst those from more advantaged groups are more successful at obtaining places at 'old' or more elite institutions. Inequalities are more marked for young men living in the most disadvantaged areas, and are compounded by the fact that young men are less likely to complete their HE courses and gain a qualification than young women (HEFCE 2005: 28).

One important change within higher education institutions has been the increase in older learners. Whilst for most higher education institutions, 'mature' students (over the age of 21) are seen as the exception rather than the rule (whether or not this is so in fact) two UK higher education institutions for whom virtually all their students are 'mature', with a good proportion of those students over the age of 50, are the Open University and Birkbeck, University of London. It may be no coincidence that both of these institutions specialise in learning opportunities for students studying part-time, a mode of study especially appreciated by older learners. What these two institutions also have in common is the wide variety of venues in which learning takes place: for the Open University nationally and for Birkbeck – through its Faculty of Continuing Education – across the Greater London area. This is particularly appreciated by older learners, especially for some groups of older learners, including women. Additionally, classes are offered at times which suit learners, giving increased flexibility. Other institutions might well want to consider ways in which they can support older learners through a greater consideration of the needs of part-time students, such as appropriate times and venues, including outreach work and types of learning opportunities offered to older learners.

However, not all decisions are in the hands of the universities. There is little evidence that the government is prepared to shift from its focus on 'skills' based accredited courses for full-time 18–30 year olds to show that genuine social inclusion should also apply to older learners, including those studying part-time. Although, as we have shown above, many older learners engage in learning for their own personal growth and development, there is currently an insistence that all courses need to be accredited in order to obtain funding. This is in particular an urgent issue for university continuing education departments, who traditionally offer a large range of shorter and previously non-accredited courses, which are very attractive to older students (see Carlton and Soulsby 1999; Jackson 2004). Pressures from funding councils to move to accredited courses may well prove to the detriment of older learners (see Jamieson and Adshead 2001; Jackson 2005a).

The link between definitions of 'completion', assessment and funding is a key institutional issue. The Higher Education Funding Councils need to have a clear understanding that the mission and methods of university adult and continuing education are ill served by an insistence on a conventional approach to issues in these areas. The result of current approaches means that lifelong learning is being defined in narrow and inappropriate ways, whether viewed in economic or social terms.

Today there is confusion as to the purpose and aims of higher education, and its intended participants. This has increasingly been the case as universities have opened their doors – albeit not always very widely – to growing numbers of students. Within the last decade, student numbers in higher education have increased in developed countries by an average of 40 per cent, whilst in the UK they have reached a massive growth of 81 per cent (Scheutze and Slowey 2000: 3). Nevertheless, as we showed in Chapter 1, this has not necessarily led to more equity.

Currently, one of the few ways for universities to be able to obtain additional funds to increase student numbers is through a widening participation scheme via a 'postcode' system, primarily aimed at attracting young people from apparently disadvantaged areas into full-time university opportunities. Widening participation remains one of the four core strategic aims of the Higher Education Council for England, and an influential component of policy development in all areas. Yet expansion has done nothing to improve levels of access for more disadvantaged socio-economic groups. Neither has it altered an academy which is imbued with gendered and classed ways of knowing (Jackson 2004).

However, and despite the confusion, the HE sector broadly retains its identity. The further education (FE) sector on the other hand has been transformed (Jackson and Clarke 2003), although it still lacks a clearly recognised and shared core purpose (Foster 2005). In the early 1990s the Training and Enterprise Councils (TECs) were established, with the aim of promoting closer links between education and industry, channelling public funds into delivering the skills required by local firms. At the same time, the Further and Higher Education Act (1992) removed non-HE post-16 learning from local authority control to the Further Education Funding Councils (FEFC). However, the Labour administration elected in 1997 proposed the abolition of both TECs and of the FEFC in order to establish a new Learning and Skills Council (LSC), responsible for funding all post-16 education and training outside universities, including school sixth forms. The Learning and Skills Act 2000 established the LSC as the single largest non-departmental public body in England, responsible for funding school sixth forms, FE and tertiary colleges, work-based learning, and voluntary sector organisations (including the WEA, see below) (Jackson and Clarke 2003). Such financial control means that particular types of learning can be cut at a stroke, and the focus on vocational training was self-evident from the outset:

> The LSC exists to make England better skilled and more competitive. We have a single goal: to improve the skills of England's young people and adults to make sure we have a workforce that is of world-class standards. We are responsible for planning and funding high-quality vocational education and training for everyone. Our vision is that by 2010, young people and adults in England have the knowledge and skills matching the best in the world and are part of a fiercely competitive workforce.
>
> (www.lsc.gov.uk)

Soon after its inception, the Learning and Skills Council was interpreting its brief as post-14 rather than post-16 year olds and, in 2005, it launched its 'agenda for change', a programme of reform for further education with regard to the skills agenda for 14–19 year olds.

In his Foreword to *Agenda for Change*, Bill Rammell, Minister of State for Higher Education and Lifelong Learning, is very clear about the focus of further education:

Further Education is the engine room for skills and social justice in this country. It equips businesses with the skills they need to compete and opens up opportunities for people of all ages and from all groups in the community to build the platform of skills and qualifications to get and keep jobs, to develop in their jobs to skilled, well-paid employment and to progress to higher education. Thus far an unsung hero, FE is well placed to keep Britain working.

(LSC 2005: i)

The Foster Review of Further Education (2005) shared much of this vision and focus on skills and employment, asking where, amongst the three broad categories of FE activity (which it identified as building vocational skills, promoting social inclusion and advancement, and achieving academic progress), the emphasis should be placed. It concludes:

Although the diversity of the FE offer is often celebrated, it became clear during the review that many stakeholders believe the unique core focus of FE should be in skill building for the economy. This is the tradition from which much of FE developed, but it is a tradition that has been diluted in recent years. We therefore propose that skills, an economic mission, is the route for FE.

(Foster 2005: 22)

It recognises that this will have implications for 'non core' activities, including learning for leisure and personal development purposes, and states that such learning must remain a valuable and important part of overall lifelong learning: 'However, recognising its value does not mean that all colleges should provide it, or that the Government must pay for it in full' (Foster 2005: 23).

This will leave a real gap in the possibilities open to current and potential learners. The sector as a whole has around three and a quarter of a million learners, comprising both school-age and adult learners. There are more females than males, with 78 per cent of learners from white ethnic groups. Colleges have more learners (both 16–19 and adult) who are relatively disadvantaged compared to the population as a whole and to learner populations in other educational establishment types (Foster 2005). Yet if these learners want wider opportunities they may have to look outside and beyond further education colleges, although choices are dwindling, especially for younger learners. For older learners, other possibilities for learning may be found outside of universities and colleges.

It is clear that sites of formal learning are imbued with hierarchical discursive practices. Within universities this includes the value judgements that exist and are perpetuated with regard to pre- and post-1992 universities, as well as through gendered and classed disciplinary bases. There are also seemingly immovable hierarchies between universities and colleges, including the definitions of and values attached to 'knowledge' and 'skills' which we considered in the previous chapter.

Within educational structures and institutions, as within other social fields, there are both negotiations and struggles for resources. The concept of 'capitals' can be used as a metaphor for the assets accumulated by individuals and groups (see e.g. Bourdieu and Passerson 1977). Status can be determined by the accumulation of capital, although not all capital is equally regarded. Identities of social class, gender and 'race' (including 'whiteness') structure, and are structured by, the capitals on which individuals and groups can draw. It is clear that the opportunities for career development offered by different sites of learning will impact differently for different groups both with regard to the human capital (including access to differently valued educational qualifications) and to the economic capital that individuals can expect to accumulate in their lifetime. Learners will also differently accumulate cultural capital, which Ball and colleagues have described as integral to understandings of classed positionings (Ball et al. 2000). The cultural symbols recognised and used by learners, teachers and institutions will be markedly different within differing educational contexts, some of which will have hegemonic value, and some of which will not.

An important aspect of all learning experiences is the social networks that people develop, enabling them to accumulate social capital, the connections amongst individuals and the social networks and norms of reciprocity and trust that arise from these connections. According to Putman, social capital can help to mitigate socio-economic disadvantage (Putman 2000: 319–25), although as John Field shows, social capital can be used to exclude as well as include: 'Communications may not be shared with outsider groups, and new ideas and skills may be ignored because they come from outside the network' (Field 2000: 129).

We have shown how exclusionary social networks operate within the hierarchies of formal educational institutions. However, we turn now to networks of learning outside of conventional post-compulsory education.

Alternative landscapes of learning

In considering alternative possibilities for learning, we start with gender as a central focus, whilst indicating that we are never just women or men, but women and men who are not only gendered but classed and 'raced'; have differing levels of dis/abilities; different cultural and family backgrounds; are geographically diverse; and so forth (Jackson 2005a). Whilst much research and policy today is focused on failing boys and men (Francis and Skelton 2001), there have been very many less educational opportunities for girls and women both in formal and workplace learning. For older women this is more likely to be true. Naomi Sargent (1997) has shown that the less likely people are to have continued education whilst young, the less likely they are to participate when they are older. As Tom Schuller (2002) states, 'in education, the more you have had the more you are likely to get', or, to put it another way, the chances are that if at first you don't succeed, you don't succeed. For many women aged 50 and over, but especially for working-class women, continuing at school or in further education beyond the age of 15 was not considered an option (Jackson 2003). Both working-class women and men will, throughout their lives, have had low access to education, especially higher education. But women are less likely than men to have received workplace learning or apprenticeships, or to hold higher educational qualifications; and more likely than men to be poor, to have no occupational pension, to live alone and to live longer (Jackson 2004).

In addition, any engagement that women have had with more formal education is likely to have marginalized their experiences or made them invisible (Jackson 2004). This is especially true for women who have worked at home bringing up children and who find, once their children have grown and left home, that academic subjects seem to bear little relationship to their lives. However, there is also an assumption that the roles of housewives and mothers are the ones that women of 50+ will have played: women who are living other lifestyles, including for example non-mothers, or lesbians, may find themselves even more marginalized. However, for mothers, 49 per cent of 'non-learners' who mentioned childcare as a barrier to learning said some form of childcare support would encourage them to learn (Snape et al. 2003).

The picture is additionally complicated by demography (Tuckett and McCauley 2005), including a rural/urban divide. Women in particular are dependent upon public transport, but this differently affects women living in towns and in the countryside. In rural areas, a severe lack of public transport may prevent women from attending educational centres, and the older women are, and the lower their economic group, the more likely they are to be dependent on public transport. If they have a physical disability, public transport options can become non-existent. Ninety per cent of 'non-learners' mentioning transport as a problem said transport improvement or assistance would encourage them to learn (Snape et al. 2003). However, there are learning opportunities in villages, including the Women's Institute, that we will raise below. In urban areas, public transport might be more frequent and available, but there is a (perceived) risk of personal danger that prevents women from travelling after dark, which in winter means from mid-afternoon (Jackson and Clarke 2003).

Almost entirely located in urban areas, there are huge gender issues for older learners from Black and minority ethnic communities, as well as a lack of awareness of religious and cultural differences for both women and men. Stella Dadzie (1993) shows that many elders from Black and minority ethnic communities came to Britain from necessity rather than choice, in search of work or education, or from political or economic desperation. As far as education is concerned, for many the search is fruitless, and there is little recognition of the past learning experiences, skills and resourcefulness of people of diverse cultural, social and ethnic backgrounds. As participants in a survey for the Collaborative Widening Participation Project shows, racism and ageism are a double barrier: 'The universities have not understood the needs of our community . . . they are not targeting anyone in these communities. . . . It's your age: they are not interested in people like me' (*Student and Community Voice: 4* 2002). How then can educational institutions demonstrate their understanding of, and interest in, 'people like me' (see also Bowl 2003 and Jackson 2005a)?

Naomi Sargent shows that the three main reasons given for participating in learning are work-related; education and progression; and personal development (Sargent *et al.* 1997). For those with an interest in lifelong learning as personal development, much can be learned from sectors other than formal educational institutions (see Chapter 12 for further discussion).

The University of the Third Age (U3A), for example, recognises that lifelong learners are teachers as well as students, and that many older learners have the skills to organise, teach and learn in autonomous learning groups in local communities. Currently in the UK there are well over 100,000 people learning in almost 500 local groups (http://www.u3a.org.uk). Members of the groups are responsible for choosing and setting the curriculum, times and modes of study, subject content, teacher and optimum number of learners. The Workers Educational Association (WEA) too is a major adult education organisation, with over 100,000 students nationally. Like the U3A, the WEA is controlled by its members, who are actively involved in the planning and promotion of courses. It is the UK's oldest provider of adult education courses in the voluntary sector (Roberts 2003). One of the aims of the WEA is to 'provide high quality learning opportunities for adults from all walks of life, but especially those who may have missed out on learning in early life, or who are socially and economically disadvantaged' (http://www.wea.org.uk). This certainly applies to many older learners. Like the U3A, the range of local and community-based centres in rural and in urban areas used by the WEA is of particular benefit to older women learners.

Another key provider of active learning opportunities for older women is the National Federation of Women's Institutes. The NFWI offers a wide range of choices and learning opportunities for its quarter of a million members, the majority of whom are over 50 (see Carlton and Soulsby 1999). Within their local branches, women are able to develop their own learning opportunities to meet their needs and interests, primarily through invited speakers. The Federation also has its own college, Denman, which runs residential courses for WI members throughout the year. Its prospectus lists almost 500 courses, many of which are accredited. The vast majority of the programme consists of arts, crafts and other leisure courses, but also includes a group of courses headed 'personal development', and around 40 courses headed 'social studies, history and public affairs'. Adult eduction is currently a key campaigning issue for the NFWI. It is concerned that, as a result of changes in Government funding priorities, many adults are finding that local colleges and community education centres have cut courses and increased fees, making adult education inaccessible to many people. This is true, too, for the NFWI which is finding it increasingly difficult to offer non-accredited courses for older women learners. It is concerned that adults, particularly women, are losing access to education and is encouraging its members to take action. The NFWI is right to be concerned, and it is apparent that its members value a 'safe space' for older women learners, and find the learning opportunities particularly helpful in times of transition, including changes in family life, transitions from work to retirement, and the transition to widowhood, enabling them to gain confidence and develop new interests (Jackson 2006). As one member of staff commented: 'Denman . . . is still primarily a safe learning experience and an almost entirely women-only environment. The feedback that I have had from students is that really it makes a difference in a women-only environment and a safe learning experience' (in Jackson 2006: 80).

Women indicated many ways in which learning in and through the NFWI enhances their experiences and personal development. Benefits include:

- to have a voice, locally and nationally;
- a sense of belonging;
- companionship, loyalty and mutual support;
- to develop new interests;
- be part of the community/involvement in community work;
- involvement in village life;
- get to meet people/make new friends;
- awareness of the world around me'.

(Jackson 2005b: 4)

We shall return to a discussion of the U3A, the WEA and the NFWI in Chapter 12. From all three organisations, it is apparent that learning can bring a sense of belonging and of community, and one educational arena with a history of 'social purpose' is that of community education, which can include both education within community settings, and education for communities, focused on transformative action and change (Jackson 2006). Especially important for community education is nonformal learning rather than the more formal and accredited learning which attracts government funding (Benn *et al.* 1998; Colley *et al.* 2003; Field 2005). However, despite the wide(r) benefits of community education both to individual learners and to the wider community, it is not proving possible to convince policy-makers and funders that it is worthy of investment (McGivney 1999), and community educators, learners and policy-makers can have very different understandings of what constitutes successful learning (McGivney 2002).

As Marjorie Mayo and Jane Thompson (1995) demonstrate, in an ever-changing and postmodern world, adult education finds itself (continually) restructured towards market forces and vocationally based needs. Community education appears to be being nudged, or pushed, away from transformative learning. Finger and Asun argue that 'the instrumental rationality which dominates the market and the organisation of labour has now also become adult education's dominant frame of reference' (2001: 132).

With its beginnings emanating in community education, before moving into higher education and then back out again, we turn to Women's Studies to show ways in which pedagogic practice can be adapted and developed. Feminist pedagogic practices of Women's Studies argue for a need to:

- strive for egalitarian relationships in the classroom;
- try to make all students feel valued as individuals;

- use the experience of students as a learning resource;
- question the role and authority of the teacher;
- consider questions of difference; and
- consider personal experience.

(Jackson 2004)

Practitioners of Women's Studies have long argued that traditional constructions of what counts as 'academic' are insufficient to enable marginalised voices to be heard, when to be 'academic' generally excludes the experiential, the personal and the emotional. Work that is intellectual and academic can, though, also be 'creative', especially when there is an opportunity for learners to put their 'own ideas and thoughts' into the work. Students have stated that work in Women's Studies offers more scope for individuality, style and creativity (Jackson 2004: 74). For example, the creativity of Women's Studies for some students is to do with discovering ways to express their 'own individual point of view . . . having the chance . . . to express my own individual voice' (Jackson 2004: 75). For many women, such creativity has been discovered through journal writing, an area where learners are particularly able to explore a range of issues, and to link their theoretical discoveries with their personal experiences and lifelong learning. As one Women's Studies student stated, she found journal writing creative and reflective:

> allowing her to 'toss' ideas around, including ideas about 'myself and who I am and my inner and outer self'. She had found this process very challeng- ing, and described ways in which she had changed since starting her degree. She felt that previously she had never had to 'question things . . . we weren't allowed to argue about politics or religion'. The range of people she was meeting, as well as the ideas she was encountering, was making her reappraise herself, and the journal gave her the opportunity to try out new ideas. The course opened lots of issues for Winnie regarding patriarchal structures, causing her to question her original feelings as well as issues in her life. Journal writing can be a constructive and powerful way for women to consider their lifelong learning experiences, and not to see them separately to or differently from their 'academic' learning experiences.
>
> (Jackson 2004: 64)

Indeed, the use of auto/biography has been central in feminist work, placing individual experiences into wider contexts. Journal writing can be an ideal way to explore such experiences, and we will explore some of this writing in Section II.

This is not to argue for the current moves towards 'personalised learning' (see e.g. the DfES 2004c), which appears to be more about menu choices than about the development of personalised learning styles or personal relevance. Current approaches that emphasise personalised learning have too great a focus on individuals rather than on the collaborative or communal approaches advocated in Women's Studies. Learners have come to value the pedagogic approaches of

Women's Studies as much because of the chance to develop learning through deepening processes of participation in communities of practice which recognises that learning is social and develops from our experiences of participating in daily life (Lave and Wenger 1991) as for the different ways to be academic (Jackson 2004). Women's studies has been described as 'transformational' for its learners as well as for its teachers, although its ability to transform the academy itself has not been realised (Jackson 2004).

Both outside and inside of formal education institutions there is, then, much good practice in enabling learners to facilitate and negotiate their own active learning. In the next sections we shall explore ways in which teachers and education institutions can draw on this work to develop active and effective learning.

Adapting and changing pedagogic approaches

In much university teaching, there remains an assumption that lecturers are the possessors of knowledge which is to be imparted to students, and that this happens in neutral, impartial and objective ways (Jackson 2004). However, learning is about making meaning, and learners can experience the same teaching in very different ways. Students (as well as teachers) are part of complex social, cultural, political, ideological and personal circumstances, and current experiences of learning will depend in part on previous ones, as well as on age, gender, social class, culture, ethnicity, varying abilities and more. All learners have valuable experiences and transferable skills which they bring with them into the classroom that can be developed into learning and teaching points. It is important that learners recognise this of themselves, and that both teachers and other students recognise this of the learners in the classroom. Students can learn as much or more from listening to each other in the classroom as they can from teachers or from their engagement with academic texts.

Whilst some learners in the academy have engaged with 'academic' learning in the past, others will be non-traditional applicants. This is likely to be especially true for women, for working-class people, and for those from minority ethnic groups. One way to facilitate successful learning in higher education is to enable learners to recognise themselves *as* academic. To do this, teachers need to consider a range of ways to encourage active and participatory learning, and to make subjects relevant to the lives of their students, exploring ways to encourage and enable the use of personal experience in theoretical and analytical approaches (see Jackson 1999). Additionally, texts used, examples drawn, and seminar and other discussions should recognise and include the lives and experiences of older people. Teachers need to find ways to make the subject content appear more relevant to the lives of their learners and, where necessary, to adapt and change the curricula to include and value the diverse experiences of their students.

Education is a political act, and teaching can never be divorced from critical analysis of how society works. According to Freire, teachers must challenge learners to think critically through social, political and historical realities within which they are a presence in the world (Freire 2004). It is the task of progressive education to inspire students' critical curiosity. Today there is an especially great need for these curiosities, as neo-liberal discourse and ideology can be immobilising.

Freire believes that

> education makes sense because women and men learn that through learning they can make and remake themselves, because women and men are able to take responsibility for themselves as beings capable of knowing – of knowing that they know and knowing that they don't.
>
> (Freire 2004: 15)

It is the responsibility of teachers, says Freire, to challenge oppressed groups to overcome certain portions of their knowing as they begin to show their 'incompetence' to explain facts, although teachers should not arrogantly impose their knowing upon oppressed groups 'as the only *true knowing*' (Freire 2004: 64, original italics).

Freire tells the story of a young man struggling to understand his material and subject positioning:

> If yesterday he blamed himself for it, now he became able to realise that he was not responsible for finding himself in that condition. . . . His struggle was more important in constituting his new knowledge than the messianic, authoritarian militant's discourse.
>
> (Freire 2004: 65)

However, although the young man of the story obtained 'new knowledge', all knowledge is not equally privileged and what is 'known' and who are the 'knowers' is highly politicised. As we have shown in Chapter 2, some knowledges count, whilst others do not, legitimising and de-legitimising beliefs. Education is always a certain theory of knowledge put into practice, and it is therefore always political (Freire 2004: 71). Different realities, different ways of knowing and experiencing the world, need to be acknowledged and understood. There are questions to be asked regarding the power and authority of teachers, and knowledge and truth claims. How do beliefs become legitimised as knowledge, who can be a 'knower' and what things are 'known' (see Harding 1987). There are epistemological questions to be answered about the nature of knowledge, its foundations, limits and validity. The 'new knowledge' that has been acquired by the young man in question may well bring insight and political awareness, but of itself will not bring about the power to implement change or transformation, although challenges to ways of knowing can lead to collective action.

Freire believes 'there are questions all of us must ask insistently that make us see the impossibility of *studying for study's sake*'. Instead, we should ask 'In favour of what do I study? In favour of whom? Against what do I study? Against whom do I study'? (Freire 2004: 60, original italics). These are important questions. Although, as Rossatto (2005: 145) shows, educators can construct nonfragmented knowledge by relating daily life experiences to academic content, ruling groups are able to exercise control over both what is taught and how it is taught, maintaining hegemonic control. Neo-liberal discourse and ideology can be immobilising, promoting adaptation and a fatalism which means that we compromise with reality rather than transforming it. An absence of, or the opposite to, solidarity comes from neo-liberal discourses (Rossatto 2005). Neo-liberalism emphasises accountability, audits and managerial control, with funding regimes working to the detriment of adult, continuing and liberal education. We are increasingly seeing the decline, even death, of adult 'liberal education' programmes, and the question of choosing whether or not to study for studying's sake will soon, to coin a phrase, be academic.

Additionally, there are challenges to adult education posed by new technological restructuring. Freire describes neo-liberalism as the transference of knowledge for industrial productivity (Freire 2004: 77). 'A critical reading of the world implies the exercise of curiosity and the ability to challenge in order to know how to defend oneself from the traps ideologies . . . will place along the way' (Freire 2004: 92). Education has come to be about technical knowledge, training learners in skills which enable them to adapt to economic globalisation, but leaving little space for utopian dreams.

> The more education becomes empty of dreams to fight for, the more the emptiness left by those *dreams* becomes filled with technique, until the moment comes when education becomes reduced to that. Then education becomes pure training, it becomes pure transfer of content, it is almost like the training of animals, it is a mere exercise in adaptation to the world.
>
> (Freire 2004: 84, original italics)

When education and knowledge are described purely in terms of technology and training, then 'in a postmodernity touched at every moment by technological advances' 'new pedagogical proposals become necessary, indispensable, and urgent' (Freire 2004: 107).

By stripping education of its political nature and reducing it to dexterity training, the object subsumes the subject and the 'liberated voice' disappears. Neo-liberal ideology and politics produce educational practices that contradict fundamental requirements of technological advances. Critical subjects should respond to change, but more than that they need a knowing that is part of a broader universe of knowing.

In his consideration of schooling, Basil Bernstein (1996) said that 'we can ask about the acoustic of the school. Whose voice is heard? Who is speaking? Who is hailed by this voice? For whom is it familiar?' (Bernstein 1996: 7). The same questions can be asked about the acoustics of adult education institutions, including universities. In order to attract older learners, institutions could start by looking at their publicity and prospectus. What images are being projected? What are images and text saying about the ethos and the culture of the institution? All learners need to recognise something of their current and potential selves in their choice of institutions, including older learners. Universities could also develop more flexible entry requirements and highlight possibilities for non-traditional learners in their publicity. The accreditation of prior experiential learning, for example, would contribute to the positive recognition of the experiences and achievements that learners have already acquired.

All learners should be entitled to education as a right. This might be especially true for those who have been disadvantaged in terms of educational stakes. There are clear equity issues in considering lifelong learning opportunities, yet there are also economic and social benefits to wider society in investing in older learners. People who engage in lifelong learning are more likely to be active citizens, to engage in volunteering, to enjoy better relationships within their families and social networks, and to enjoy better physical and mental well-being (see e.g. Hammond 2002; Schuller *et al.* 2004). The wider benefits of learning are clear and well documented by the Centre for Research on the Wider Benefits of Learning (http://www.learningbenefits.net). Participation in learning sustains active, independent lives and empowers citizens.

In his work on *Pedagogy, Symbolic Control and Identity*, Basil Bernstein called for three rights for children in schools: the right of individual enhancement, the right to be included socially, intellectually, culturally and personally, and the right to participate in discourse, practice and procedures. These are all rights that should also belong to all participants in lifelong learning (Jackson 2002). As we showed in Chapter 1, David Blunkett indicated in his introduction to *The Learning Age* (1998), the first right, that of individual enhancement, should be applicable for all learners, at whatever age. There is much that education institutions can do to facilitate the inclusion demanded in the second right, inclusion. However, it is the third right – the right to participate in discourse, practice and procedures – that will embed the voices of learners in the academy. If participation is to mean more than to just take part, but to be actively involved in setting meaningful agenda, then other adult education institutions could well turn to some of the successes of the University of the Third Age and the Workers Educational Association, for ways forward.

Nevertheless, these three rights will still not be sufficient to ensure that (lifelong) learning is accessible for all. '[E]ducation', says Bernstein (1996: 5), 'is a public institution, central to the production and reproduction of distributive injustices'. There is currently little evidence that policy-makers are enabling universities or further education colleges to become more socially inclusive for all learners. Whilst funding, for example, depends on 'completion'; whilst part-time students miss out on access to grants and bursaries; and whilst the government's widening participation agenda continues to focus on vocational learning, some learners become *less* likely to participate.

Conclusions

Too often in the UK and beyond, the lifelong learning agenda is one that has been focused on skills-based vocational learning. However, even the White paper, *21st Century Skills* (2003), recognises the need to safeguard a varied range of learning opportunities for personal fulfilment, community development and active citizenship. There is also ample evidence to show that lifelong learning and continuing education can mobilise individuals into civic and political participation, but only if a radical, democratic tradition of adult education survives. Lifelong learning can develop social capital, social cohesion, and voluntary and community involvement, engaging people in common concerns and leading to social inclusion and neighbourhood renewal. In addition, non-accredited courses are often the start of people's learning journeys, developing personal and social confidence and progression. We have argued here against a primary focus on 'skills' based accredited courses for full-time 18–30 year olds, as important as they are, and have suggested ways in which learners, teachers and institutions can adapt and change pedagogic approaches to facilitate social inclusion and democratic renewal, reclaiming something of the social purpose of adult education and lifelong learning.

In the next section, we shall continue to explore policies and practices of lifelong learning through the (imagined) voices of learners, teachers, managers and policymakers.

Section II

Retelling

> Consult your own understanding, your own sense of the probable, your own observation of what is passing around you.
>
> (Jane Austen, *Northanger Abbey*)

In Section I we outlined something of our approaches to reconceptualising lifelong learning, arguing that lifelong learning extends beyond formal post-compulsory education and training to diverse sites of informal and formal learning. We set out to challenge some of the ways in which conceptualisations of lifelong learning are limited through exclusionary practices.

One such practice is the use of an academic language that excludes the voices of many learners and teachers. As part of our challenge to exclusionary practices, this section will be written in the mode of storytelling and will tell the tales of different multipositions in lifelong learning. In Chapter 2, we drew on the work of Teresa Lillis, who argued that 'essayist literacy', the dominant literacy practice within Western higher education, privileges the discursive routines of dominant social groups. These practices constrain access to meaning-making, regulating what writers are able to say, and who they can be (Lillis 2001: 39). As we showed in Chapter 2, essayist literacy positions the knower in specifically gendered, racialised and classed ways as the masculine, white and middle-class subject who is objective, decontextualised and neutral and who is reflecting rather than constructing reality and truth through rational and scientific methods. Other literacy practices are neither legitimated nor valued, something that we aim to challenge in this section of the book through the stories that we will tell. We additionally aim to challenge the hierarchical and linear practices of academic writing. We therefore invite you the reader to engage with the stories in ways of your own choosing. The chapters may, for example, be read in any order, as may the different institutional contexts of Chapter 4, the various sections of the minutes in Chapter 5, the stories of the teachers you will meet in Chapter 6, or the journals of the learners in Chapter 7. In doing so, we hope that you will de/re/construct the stories for yourself.

This section will be written in narrative style, developing the voices of (imagined) characters and reflecting on the multiple, contradictory and shifting experiences of learning. The narratives will explore the different ways that learners are positioned and position themselves in relation to a range of social, cultural, material, political, structural and discursive contexts. These might include, for example, policy, hegemonic practices, gender and class relations, age and other social inequalities. The stories will include those of learners both in formal and informal educational settings. We will also include stories about 'non-learners' and other subject positions within lifelong learning such as policy-makers, educational managers and academics. We want to tell the stories of 'the learner' whilst capturing how the position of learner is multiple and contested. Moreover, stories of learners do not and cannot exist separately from the stories of other players and stakeholders, including policy-makers, managers and teachers – all of whom may also be learners. Additionally, learners can and do influence policy; teachers are also managers; and managers and policy-makers are differently situated institutionally as well as through their gendered, classed and racialised positionings.

The chapters will be written in narrative style to tell the (imagined) stories of some of the key participants of lifelong learning. We have chosen a narrative style to challenge the conventions of academic writing and to illustrate the fluidity of these different positionings within lifelong learning and the contested nature of their trajectories and perspectives. Throughout this section, all names, characters, groups and organisations are fictitious.* However, personal stories – even imagined ones – make political points. Throughout Section II, we will illuminate through narrative the power relations in play in different contexts and in relation to competing identity positions within lifelong learning. We will ask the reader to read between the lines of the stories, looking for the gaps, the silences, the fissures and the contradictions, and to use the stories as a lens through which to explore changing political contexts.

As we continue into Section III we will move away from narrative to analysis, revisioning the stories by highlighting some key issues and concepts.

---

* Any reference to people either living or dead is purely coincidental.

Chapter 4

Retelling the stories of policy-makers

Introduction

In this chapter we consider some of the stories of policy-makers, to examine the processes and micro-politics of policy formulation. We will explore the different positionings of policy-makers in relation to authority, decision-making and influence to reveal the complex relations and contexts in which policy formulation happens and is contested. The voices retelling the stories will include those in senior positions as well as those in less powerful posts within national government agencies, such as the Department for Education and Skills (DfES). It will also include voices from those working within local education authorities, and those making policy decisions within institutional contexts, for example senior managers within further education colleges and higher education institutions.

This chapter will present the stories of such individuals through the emails that they send within policy-making networks. Emailing has become a dominant literacy practice within educational institutions and is a primary form of communication between colleagues. It is also used as a form of pedagogical support. New policies are often constructed and reconstructed through the processes of email communications and we would argue that email as a form of literacy practice has its own sets of particular cultural practices, discourses and etiquette. It is often seen as an informal mode of communication and the language of the email can often be much less formal than the language of 'hard copy' documentation. Yet, there are different practices with email writing and these are tied to institutional and social relations of power, positioning and identity. Emails might be seen by the subjects constructing them as personal communications and yet they are highly accessible – they can be forwarded, used as evidence and represent legalistic levels of agreement. The use of emails across different social networks can be democratic and inclusive but they can also be used in exclusive ways, outside of formal meetings and supporting different subjects' access to social capitals. Emails can be synchronous or asynchronous and they can be sent across oceans, in different time zones and to the colleague in the office next door. Emailing as a social practice is central in these ways to the formation of policy across time and space; it is contextualised and yet can be formulated in virtual spaces. In this chapter, the email messages are imaginary, however they are based on the everyday concerns and issues currently faced by UK policy-makers across these different educational contexts. The 'characters' in the narratives are fictitious, as are the messages, but draw on a range of sources such as literature in the field, policy documents and our own experiences as participants in the policy-making framework.

The Further Education College context

To: kbattley@cityregionalcollege.ac.uk
From: mmehmet@cityregionalcollege.ac.uk
Subject: student support

Dear Kimberley
In light of the meeting yesterday to discuss the college's changing structure around student support, as the college representative for student support staff, I would like to make some points regarding agenda item 3a (the role of support staff in retaining students). If you remember, you talked about appointing one key member of staff who acts as a co-ordinator for the student support staff to oversee their work in the classroom as teaching assistants. It occurred to me that it would be a good idea to get the support staff together to discuss their ideas about how this would work in relation to the issue of retention. This way we could get them involved with identifying key aspects of the job in relation to the work that they do, from their perspectives. If possible, it would be good to get such a meeting together before the next senior management meeting next month. I would appreciate your views on this and, if you think it's a good idea, I wonder if you would chair such a meeting?

With best wishes
Mustafa Mehmet
Student Support Worker representative

To: mmehmet@cityregionalcollege.ac.uk
From: kbattley@cityregionalcollege.ac.uk
CC: crobertson@cityregionalcollege.ac.uk
Subject: Re: student support

Dear Mustafa
Thank you for this. I think it would be a good idea and would like to suggest the following way forward. It would be best if you arrange and co-ordinate such a meeting in the next week or so with the student support staff to identify some key issues. If these issues could then be reported to me no later than 8 March, I will feed them back at the next senior

management meeting. Could you please liaise with Cathie
Robertson and Cathie would you please take the minutes of
the student support workers' meeting?

Kimberley
Kimberley Battley
Head of School of Lifelong Learning
City Regional College

To: kbattley@cityregionalcollege.ac.uk
From: mmehmet@cityregionalcollege.ac.uk
CC: crobertson@cityregionalcollege.ac.uk
Subject: Re: student support

Dear Kimberley
Great, I will get a meeting together next week and let
Cathie know of the date.
I appreciate your support.

Mustafa

To: dmackintosh@cityregionalcollege.ac.uk;
tpaisley@cityregionalcollege.ac.uk;
asamar@cityregionalcollege.ac.uk;
tanida@cityregionalcollege.ac.uk
From: mmehmet@cityregionalcollege.ac.uk
Subject: student support

Dear Diane, Tracey, Anisa and Tony
At a recent senior management meeting, it was decided that
student support workers should be contributing a key role
in student retention. They are proposing to set up a new
structure for support workers with a member of staff (it
might be someone new recruited for this post) to manage the
work that we do, rather than our work to be managed by our
programme area manager, as it is now. I suggested that we
all meet together so that we can contribute to these changes
by making our perspectives clear to senior management. I
have put this by Kimberley Battley who has said we should go
ahead and meet and then feedback our points to her (through
Cathie Robertson). Could we please meet sometime over lunch
next week? Could you meet next Tuesday?

Thanks
Mustafa

To: dmackintosh@cityregionalcollege.ac.uk
From: tanida@cityregionalcollege.ac.uk
Subject: student support

Hi Diane
What do you think of this? I think it's awful — you and I
have worked hard to pull the team together and yet again
our efforts are ignored. It would be fatal if someone from
outside the team manages us — they won't have clue what we
do, what we're about. If this happens, I'm looking for
another job. What do you think?

Tony

To: tanida@cityregionalcollege.ac.uk
From: dmackintosh@cityregionalcollege.ac.uk
Subject: Re: student support

Hi Tony
I agree with you. It's not right and it's not going to help
us at all. I think Mustafa's doing a good thing to ask for
this meeting. If the four of us get together and think of a
plan and an argument, I think we can make our position
clear. Let's talk about it over lunch — you want to meet in
the staff room at 12:15?

Best wishes
Diane

To: dmackintosh@cityregionalcollege.ac.uk
From: tanida@cityregionalcollege.ac.uk
Subject: Re: student support

See you at 12:15 — you're always more optimistic than me — I
could use some cheering up!

Tony

To: crobertson@cityregionalcollege.ac.uk
From: mmehmet@cityregionalcollege.ac.uk
Subject: meeting of student support staff

Dear Cathie
The student support staff has decided to meet next Tuesday
(26 February) at 12:15-1:15 in room 204, Building C. We are
all bringing our own sandwiches and I'll be providing some
coffee and tea. I hope you will be able to attend this
meeting to take minutes (as requested by Kimberley Battley).

With best wishes
Mustafa

To: mmehmet@cityregionalcollege.ac.uk
From: tpaisley@cityregionalcollege.ac.uk
CC: dmackintosh@cityregionalcollege.ac.uk;
asamar@cityregionalcollege.ac.uk;
tanida@cityregionalcollege.ac.uk

Dear Mustafa
I'm not able to go to the meeting but I did want to have the
chance to say something about this.

I feel very strongly that it should be one of us who gets to
oversee the student support workers. I wouldn't want someone
from outside. I think we work really well together as a team
and that each of us have strengths to bring. We have a
different kind of understanding to the teachers about
supporting students on their courses and I think our
understanding is important. I don't think someone else could
just come in and take over after all the hard work we've put
into building a team and working together. I know that we've
had our ups and downs but that's all part of it. In terms of
retention, a lot of the work we do is what keeps the students
in. We help explain things more clearly — we usually relate
to the students better than the teachers do. I think there's
an important relationship that we have with the students
that sometimes is the reason they stay.

I am sorry I can't be at the meeting but I really feel
strongly about this and wanted to say something. I don't
know how others feel about this but that's how I feel.

Thanks
Tanya

To: tpaisley@cityregionalcollege.ac.uk
From: asamar@cityregionalcollege.ac.uk
CC: dmackintosh@cityregionalcollege.ac.uk;
tanida@cityregionalcollege.ac.uk;
mmehmet@cityregionalcollege.ac.uk

Dear Tanya
I agree with you. We do something different from the main
staff and we should have credit for this. Anyone who manages
our work should come from inside our team. Let's talk about
this more at the meeting

Best wishes
Anisa

To: kbattley@cityregionalcollege.ac.uk
From: mmehmet@cityregionalcollege.ac.uk
CC: crobertson@cityregionalcollege.ac.uk
Subject: Re: student support

Dear Kimberley
The student support team have now met and Cathie Robertson
has taken minutes of the meeting. In the meantime, I wanted
to highlight what we thought were the key issues:

*** Appointment of student support co-ordinator**
We feel it would be best if someone was appointed internally
from our team, as we have a good understanding of our work
within the college and the students' needs. It would take an
outsider some time to gain insight into the key issues that
we face and we feel also that having an internal appointment
from within the existing team would build on the trust that
already exists within our team. It would also bolster morale
and show the value of the work that we contribute to the
college.

*** Work of student support workers**
We would like the opportunity to clarify our role as student
support workers, as the work we do is not really transparent
at the moment. We carry out a wide range of duties from
taking registers, to behaviour control with the year 10/11
students, to helping students in the classroom with their
work, to supporting mature students with their key skills
development. There is some confusion amongst academic staff
about how to best use our skills in the classroom and we feel
that this is the opportunity to make all this more clear. We
would like to propose that we draw up a working document for
further discussion at the senior management meeting.

*** Retention**
Support workers already significantly contribute to the
retention of students in the day-to-day support that they
provide. We are able to provide a sometimes 'more
accessible' support system than tutors and are able to
develop good relationships with students. This puts us in a
very good position to help students who might be considering
dropping out of their courses and help keep them on track.
With the changing structures, we are concerned that our
knowledge about this area of our work might become lost. We
would like to be part of the conversations about changing
policies of this area of our work.

*** Issues for careful consideration**
There are many complicated issues that need careful
consideration by senior management around the issue of

retention. For example, one member of our team was recently harassed and threatened by a 17-year-old student. When he reported the incident to his line manager, he was told to leave the college site. However, he waited around for at least two hours before finally leaving with his older brother. The next day my colleague was rather shocked to find that there was a meeting going on, with the student concerned, his father and his line manager. He was not included in the meeting, and the student was allowed back in to the college despite the excessive nature of his threats to my colleague.

Another colleague was left to teach a class on her own, without any guidance, and this has happened on more than one occasion. Clearly this not only affects the kind of staff development training and support that we as student support workers should be getting, as well as our work profile, but also raises issues about the quality of education for the students and their decision to stay on course.

There are a number of other issues that were discussed at our meeting and Cathie should be getting the minutes to you soon. We would really appreciate you keeping us posted about how this all develops.

With many thanks
Mustafa

The National Government context

To: d.greene@dfes.gov.uk
From: r.marks@dfes.gov.uk
Subject: first draft of WP paragraph

Dear David
Please find below a draft of my paragraph on widening educational participation and ICT. I have tried to take into account the points that were made at yesterday's meeting.

Best wishes
Rachael
Rachael Marks
Executive Assistant, Widening Participation

Widening educational participation is a national priority and it is every citizen's responsibility and right to have access to lifelong learning. The changing nature of information and communication technologies mean that we require a national workforce that is able to update their skills continually in order to compete in increasingly

competitive global markets. We need each and every citizen
to reach their potential and to have the ability to use
information and communication technologies in relation to
the requirements of their employers. However, access
to lifelong learning is not only about economic
competiveness, it is also about social justice. As
information and communication technologies become more
important in our lives, not only as employees but also as
responsible parents and active citizens, it is important
that all citizens have the basic and key skills needed in
ICT.

To: a.m.davis@dfes.gov.uk
From: d.greene@dfes.gov.uk
Subject: WP paragraph

Anthony,
I have received a first draft from Rachael Marks of the
paragraph on WP and ICT. I have made some minor changes
(please see below).

Regards
David

Widening educational participation is a national priority
~~and~~. We have already set out our proposals to widen
participation in higher education in The Future of Higher
Education. Widening participation to other forms of
education and training are also important throughout
a citizens' life. We are living in a time of rapid
change in work and industry as a result of the ongoing
development of new technologies. Consequently, it is
every citizen's responsibility and right to have key
~~access to lifelong learning~~ skills in ICT and to update
their skills in relation to the needs of their employer.
The changing nature of information and communication
technologies means that we require the knowledge to take
a leading role in the development of new technologies
~~a national workforce that is able to update their skills~~
~~continually in order to compete~~ in the context of
increasingly competitive global markets. ~~We need each and~~
~~every citizen to reach their potential and to have the~~
~~ability to use information and communication technologies~~
~~in relation to the requirements of their employers.~~
However, access to lifelong learning is not only about
economic competitiveness, it is also about social justice.
As information and communication technologies become
more important in our lives, not only as employees but

also as responsible parents and active citizens, it is important that all citizens have the basic and key skills needed in ICT. It is our plan to set up basic skills in ICT centres in every local education authority in the country so that all citizens will be able to learn these basic skills.

I need to work on this section and I'll also include a section in the HE context, which links in with LEAs.

To: d.greene@dfes.gov.uk; r.marks@dfes.gov.uk
From: a.m.davis@dfes.gov.uk
Subject: WP paragraph

Dear David and Rachael
Thank you for your work on this. This looks good and will now be integrated into the main consultation document for widening educational participation across educational sectors, with some minor modifications as necessary. David, please send in your text on the HE context no later than Friday morning.

With best wishes
Anthony

To: a.m.davis@dfes.gov.uk
From: d.greene@dfes.gov.uk
Subject: Re: WP paragraph

Dear Anthony
Please find my paragraph on the HE context drafted below.

David

Widening educational participation in higher education has been identified as key to the nation's economic position and stability in the context of globalisation and increased levels of competition. We must liberate all human potential in the United Kingdom in order to maintain and secure our leading position in research, scholarship and teaching. This is becoming increasingly important in an exciting time of rapid change, new developments and major breakthroughs in the fields of science and information and communication technologies. The United Kingdom has the talent to continue to take the lead in these fields. We need to ensure that we utilise higher education as the best economic policy we have by avoiding the wastage of the most talented citizens in our society. In Britain we cherish both equality of opportunity and equality of worth and our policy will ensure a higher education system in which all citizens are socially mobile according to their potential and talent, rather than their privilege or class. We are a wealthy nation in relation to talent and knowledge and every British citizen who is given the opportunity to fulfil their talent adds to our national wealth. This is a matter of economic strategy as well as social justice.

To: d.greene@dfes.gov.uk
From: a.m.davis@dfes.gov.uk
Subject: Re: Re: WP paragraph

Dear David
Many thanks for your superb work on this. This will now go forward for inclusion in the green paper, subject of course to the usual modifications by our team.

Best wishes
Anthony

The HE context

To: allstaff@centraluni.ac.uk
From: G.Davies@centraluni.ac.uk
Subject: Time Sheets
Attachment: TimeSheetform.doc

Dear colleagues
Please note that it is now university policy for every member of staff to fill out a time sheet on Friday of each week to record their schedules for the following week. Time sheets are now available from your School's administration office. You will need to record where you will be over each week of term including office hours, meetings, working from home, teaching and tutorials and course administration.

It is extremely important that we have these records at the end of each week from every member of staff before our audit next term. Thank you in advance for your co-operation with this.

Best wishes
Gerry Davies
Quality Assurance Officer

Time sheet

Name

School

Date

	Morning	Afternoon	Evening
Monday			
Tuesday			
Wednesday			
Thursday			
Friday			
Saturday			

To: G.Collier@centraluni.ac.uk
From: N.Hankes@centraluni.aca.uk
Subject: article

Dear Gerri
Hi! Hope you're well. I'm really looking forward to Friday
when we'll be meeting up to work on our article. There is a
School meeting that day though — do you think, given the new
policy on time sheets, that we will be able to say we are
working from home on the book proposal? Should we attend the
meeting and reschedule our day? I would really prefer to get
on with our book proposal, especially while our ideas are
fresh — what do you think?

Nancy xx

To: N.Hankes@centraluni.ac.uk
From: G.Collier@centraluni.ac.uk
Subject: Re: book proposal

Dear Nancy
I think we should stick to our plans and get on with our book
article. I feel this is very important especially as I was
first author on our first joint article — we need to get on
with this so we can submit it in time, so that you can be
lead author on this one and get recognition for it in the
RAE. I think this is more important than the school meeting
— and I don't think we should feel harassed by these new
managerialist policies — especially if it starts to
undermine the little space and time we can find to write.
Looking forward to seeing you Friday.

Love
Gerri xx

To: ProgrammeDirectorsSSH@centraluni.ac.uk
From: c.topps@centraluni.ac.uk
Subject: annual review 2003/04 — module evaluation summaries

Dear all Module Leaders
Please note that the deadline for all annual reviews is
5 January 2005. This means that I will need all summaries
of module evaluations submitted no later than 3 December
2004. Please do use the main headings for your summary (see
handbook for module leaders). If you have any questions
about this, or the annual review process in general, please
do let me know.

Best wishes
Cathy
School Manager, School of Social Sciences and Humanities

To: c.topps@centraluni.ac.uk
From: k.thittrall@centraluni.ac.uk
Subject: Re: annual review 2003/04 — module evaluation
summaries

Dear Cathy
Greetings from Barcelona!
Please find a summary of the evaluations of my module
'Introduction to the Social Sciences'. Please note that we
have discussed the evaluations in detail at the course
committee meeting last month where some key issues raised by
students have been addressed. The concern that students were
finding the module 'too theoretical' we have discussed as a
course team in some detail. We have decided that next
academic year we will be offering 'theory workshops' to help
the students become familiar with different perspectives
within the social sciences and provide them with some of the
tools they'll need to read and write critically. This is the
main area that has emerged as needing attention by the
course team. As you'll see, the evaluations suggest that the
students are very satisfied with the module and the teaching.

With best wishes
Karen Thittral

To: k.thittrall@centraluni.ac.uk
From: c.topps@centraluni.ac.uk
Subject: Re: annual review 2003/04 — module evaluation
summaries

Hi Karen
Thanks for this. I hope you're having a good time in
Barcelona — don't work too hard and have a drink on me.

See you soon
Cathy

To: allstaff@centraluni.ac.uk
From: K.Brownly@centraluni.ac.uk
Subject: RAE review
Attachment: RaeReview.doc

To all staff
Please note that the university will be undergoing an
internal review in preparation for the 2008 RAE. All
academic staff must complete the attached form. Please see
the attached guidance notes for the review and for the form.
Your head of school will be getting in touch with you to
arrange a meeting over the next month to go through the form
and then to write up a short report, which will be submitted
to the internal RAE review panel for close scrutiny.

It is absolutely essential that every member of staff
completes the review process by the end of August.
Thank you for your co-operation.

Keith Brownly
Dean of Research

To: L.Derrie@centraluni.ac.uk
From: M.Periosos@centraluni.ac.uk
Subject: advice please

Dear Lisa
Could I talk to you sometime soon? I would really like your
advice about the RAE stuff before I meet with the Head. So
far, I only have one published article, but I have just
submitted one recently and I'm working on another. Do you
think this is going to affect my chances of getting a
permanent post? Please let me know what you think, I feel so
anxious about it.
Thanks!

Marianna

To: M.Periosos@centraluni.ac.uk
From: L.Derrie@centraluni.ac.uk
Subject: Re: advice please

Dear Marianna
First of all, don't be worried. You are doing very well to
have had your first article accepted in a very prestigious
journal — you have another submitted and are working on
another right now. This shows your potential and there is
still plenty of time for you to have your fourth article in
time for the RAE.

I would be happy to meet up for a coffee to talk it all over.
I could meet later today — after 3 if you're around? If not,
how about Thursday at 4?

All my best
Lisa

Conclusions

This chapter has considered some of the different voices involved in the production
of educational policy, drawing on email as a dominant form of literacy practice.
These accounts have been fictional but have highlighted some key issues about
the processes of policy-making in relation to the different sectors of lifelong
learning. We have seen, in the further education context, the attempt of a small
community of support workers to define their role in the context of organisational

change and institutional policy around retention. In relation to the national government context, we have seen how meanings within policy get made and remade by different authors, until perhaps the final version is unrecognisable to those who first produced the original text. In the higher education context, we have seen moves towards a greater level of managerialism leading to policies that are imposed on staff and students to a large degree. We will in the next section, be analysing these fictional accounts to consider their implications, the silences and the opportunities for resistance, change and subversion.

Chapter 5

Retelling the stories of educational managers

Introduction

In Chapter 4 we began to (re-)tell some of the stories of policy-makers. Here we explore the stories of educational managers in relation to policies and practices of lifelong learning and their role in reinforcing or challenging these. For example, their positioning within competing discourses such as 'quality' and 'widening participation' might pose contradictions for how they see themselves as facilitators of or participants in lifelong learning. The stories that we tell will include managers working within further and higher education, as well as those managing projects such as AimHigher, working with refugees and asylum seekers and community projects.

In this chapter we present some of the stories of educational managers through the (imagined) minutes of a meeting of the Lifelong Learning Managers Network. We have chosen this format as minutes of meetings are ways of telling (partial) stories of events, determining action plans and managing sometimes competing agenda through hierarchical positioning. Minutes formalise those stories, which then form an established part of the history of the event that has taken place. They are often produced hierarchically, tied to institutional power relations, in that the Chair of the meeting (normally someone with authority) is likely to have the power to agree the final version that is circulated. The final version of the minutes formally determines the record that is kept of what was said, and is often publicly available for consumption. The record of the minutes also determines action plans, including what does not get actioned, as well as what does, by whom, and in what ways, so playing a key role not just in the stories that have been told, but in the future stories that will be developed and ultimately recorded. The production of the minutes is likely to be gendered and based in institutional practices. The draft minutes that we show here, for example, are discursive and make reference to people by their given (first) names. The final circulated and recorded version may look somewhat different.

Whilst the Network and its participants are our invention, the issues are not. They are developed from our own attendance at similar meetings; from informal discussions with colleagues; from interviews with educational managers; and from a range of reports and other sources.

Agenda

Lifelong Learning Managers Network

1   Introductions and welcome

2   Apologies for absence

3   Purpose of the meeting

4   Funding
    4.1   Higher Education
    4.2   Further Education
    4.3   Age-related funding
    4.4   Funding for lifelong learning

5   Recruitment
    5.1   Under-represented groups
    5.2   Outreach
    5.3   Flexible learning
    5.4   Expansion

6   Retention and progression
    6.1   Foundation degrees
    6.2   AimHigher
    6.3   Learner support

7   Modes of delivery
    7.1   Work-based learning
    7.2   Flexible delivery and ICT

8   Part-time workforce
    8.1   Institutional issues
    8.2   Managing part-time workers

9   Quality Assurance
    9.1   Institutional requirements
    9.2   Benefits of quality assurance
    9.3   Disability Discrimination Act

10   Any other business

11   Date of next meeting

DRAFT (to be confirmed by the Chair prior to circulation)

Minutes of the 1st meeting of the Lifelong Learning Managers Network

Present

Andy Johnson	(Higher education) (Chair)
Hafsa Akil	(Centre for supporting refugees and asylum seekers)
Narindar Batra	(Adult education centre)
Edith Colebridge	(Centre for older learners)
Linda Edwards	(Learning in libraries and museums)
Stephen Frost	(Further education)
Judith Gold	(Learning now)
Jalaal Ismail	(Learning through volunteering)
Sally Martin	(14–19 learning and teaching network)
John Peters	(The corporate university)
William Sheldon	(Learning in the community trust)
Sarah Thomas	(Centre for continuing education)
Jessica Wilson	(Learning at work)

1 Welcome and introductions

1.1 WELCOME

The Chair welcomed everyone to the first meeting of this newly formed Network. He thanked people for adding items to his suggested agenda, and asked if someone would be willing to take Minutes of the meeting, and Hafsa agreed.

2 There were no apologies for absence.

3 Purpose of meetings

Andy opened the meeting by reminding those present of the purpose of the Network meetings, which was to share common issues and concerns, and to explore opportunities for collaboration. Recent reports by the Adult Learning Inspectorate and the Office for Standards in Education had reminded us all that the contribution of educational managers to improve learner outcomes and provider effectiveness has grown in importance in the last few years. In the current climate, students and learners have become 'customers'. It is key that lifelong learning managers re-evaluate the ways in which we best serve these customers. There is increasing competition to attract more customers. This competition is fuelled by the impact of technology and increased competition in the form of distance learning. Andy believes that key issues for this group to consider include managing information and resources, budgets, quality, inspections and accountability. Whilst not all of those present agreed with this assessment of key issues, Andy stated that there would be opportunities for further discussion during the morning. Andy introduced the agenda for the morning, and thanked colleagues for letting him have suggested topics.

4 Funding

4.1 HIGHER EDUCATION

Andy stated that one of the primary aims of educational managers should be to ensure high-quality cost-effective learning experiences for all our students, and suggested we need to look increasingly towards partnerships to secure funding. We should be finding ways to move towards collaboration, franchising and partnership arrangements to ensure the delivery of high quality, accessible and cost-effective programmes.

He told the meeting that the Dearing Committee's enquiry into higher education had recommended that responsibility for funding all categories of publicly funded higher education in England should be taken on by the Higher Education Funding Council for England. As a result the Government had agreed that the funding of all first degree, postgraduate, Higher National Diploma and Certificate, Diploma of Higher Education and Certificate of Education courses be transferred from the Further Education Funding Council to the HEFCE from the academic year 1999–2000. Since then, new approaches have been developed for the funding and development of higher education in further education colleges. These included developing sets of funding options for direct funding, franchising and consortia. Although his main concern was with higher education, Andy thought that there were excellent examples here that could be followed by other members of the Network.

4.2 FURTHER EDUCATION

Stephen added that many further education colleges are involved with higher education provision. They had been asked to make strategy statements with regard to funding. Stephen reminded colleagues that funding cannot be separated from recruitment and from strategic planning, especially as under-recruitment can result in the reduction of funds. Whilst larger colleges with around 100 full-time equivalent higher education students could apply for funding in their own right, this was not the case for colleges with a smaller amount of HE provision. However, funding had been set aside so that those colleges with fewer than 100 HE FTEs could submit consortia applications, although around 40 per cent of these colleges had experienced significant holdback of funds due to under-recruitment. He agreed with Andy about the benefit of developing partnerships.

4.3 AGE-RELATED FUNDING

Narinder said that she thought the current focus on funding that seemed to favour 'skills' based accredited courses for full-time 18-30 year olds did little for social inclusion, and argued that the social purpose of adult education needs to be reclaimed. Hafsa agreed and argued that learning opportunities for personal fulfilment, community development and civic participation should be fully funded. Non-accredited courses are often the start of people's learning journeys, developing personal and social confidence and progression.

Edith supported this view. In around 30 years time nearly half the population of Britain will be over 50, with growing numbers of elderly people for whom learning could take on increasing importance. However, few of these learners or potential learners are interested in assessment. Older learners often want to learn for leisure reasons whilst funding is generally directed towards vocational learning. Edith felt that a special case should be made for funding older learners.

4.4 FUNDING FOR LIFELONG LEARNING

Linda said that lifelong learning managers in libraries and museums shared these concerns. Whilst some museums managed to attract largely middle-class learners who could afford to pay for learning opportunities, much more needed to be done to support funding for non-traditional learners. Sarah asked that the Network take a clear position with regards to social inclusion and exclusion. In managing fees, for example, lifelong learning managers should support the retention of part-time students from under-represented socio-economic and other disadvantaged groups.

William added that funding was an issue for voluntary and community organisations, who do excellent work in connecting with and encouraging access to learning for the most disadvantaged communities. His funding, for example, comes from several sources. These include the Learning and Skills Council, but he has also received funding as part of the community regeneration programme, and he is currently funding two key community lifelong learning officers from lottery funding. Their work in particular involves trying to find ways to make learning meaningful and relevant to 'non-learners'. Currently they are working with two identified groups in the community. They are trying to encourage unemployed and underemployed fathers into schools, with the aim of introducing them to learning opportunities for themselves as well as to encourage them to take a greater interest in their children's learning. They are also working with disaffected young men with little or no expectations of future opportunities. He sees the role of these workers as crucial to the development of the community learning programme, but they are only funded for two years, after which the project will come to an abrupt end unless additional funding can be found.

4.5 OTHER FUNDING ISSUES

Sarah stated that the group should be making formal representation on the current position in the UK, where public funding was only available for students who complete assessment.

Action: Sarah offered to produce a short paper for the next meeting outlining the key issues regarding funding.

5 Recruitment

5.1 RECRUITMENT AND UNDER-REPRESENTED GROUPS

Sally stated that young people in manual social classes remain under-represented in education generally, and specifically in higher education, where participation remains significantly below that for non-manual social classes. Despite overall rises in participation, increased numbers have come almost entirely from learners from non-manual social classes, especially with regard to higher education. Whilst in the last ten years or so participation in higher education for young people from non-manual social classes had increased from 35 per cent to 50 per cent, there is still less than 20 per cent participation from those from manual social classes. There is still a large gap in entry to higher education by social class, with students from middle-class backgrounds three times more likely to go to university than those from poorer backgrounds. She suggested that recruitment would be most effective if targeted at young people from manual social classes.

5.1.2 Age Edith felt it a mistake to target any recruitment campaigns at younger people as older learners become doubly disadvantaged. Many older learners left school at 15 or earlier, many of whom continue to have no recognised qualifications. Older learners should be encouraged to re-enter education to make up for lost opportunities.

5.1.2 Black and minority ethnic groups Edith told the Network that a report by the National Institute for Adult and Continuing Education (NIACE) had confirmed that in delivering adult learning there is a tendency to aim recruitment at those who have traditionally presented themselves as willing to participate in what we have to offer. If we wish to encourage more adults to participate in learning we need to find ways to overcome the barriers to learning experienced by different groups. In particular, the proportion of older people from Black and minority ethnic communities will continue to rise significantly over the next 20 years, and this is an important group on which to focus recruitment. Talking with potential learners to identify needs could help with recruitment.

5.1.3 Refugees and asylum seekers Hafsa expressed concern about support for refugees and asylum seekers, and thought that any campaign for recruitment needed to consider these groups of people. She was also concerned that where there is an attempt to recruit refugees and asylum seekers, this was often phrased in terms of 'lack' and the need to develop new skills to rectify that lack. Whilst it is important that language skills are developed, there is often little or nothing that recognises or values the skills and abilities that refugees and asylum seekers bring to a new country, nor is there much understanding or acknowledgement of the differences between refugees and asylum seekers, nor between different groups of refugees and different groups of asylum seekers. Whilst Andy recognised that these were groups who could be considered disadvantaged, he reminded the meeting that the percentage of students from minority ethnic groups accepted into higher education institutions had increased, something for which he believed universities could feel justifiably proud.

5.2 RECRUITMENT AND OUTREACH WORK

5.2.1 Working with communities William agreed that important points had been made, and asked that when colleagues consider recruitment they give good attention to their local communities. Many centres of learning fail to recognise, let alone understand, the needs of community members, and rarely specifically target people living in the local community. Where they do, recruitment for specific learning opportunities is often inappropriate. For example, recognition should be given to the past learning experiences, skills and resourcefulness of people of diverse cultural, social and ethnic backgrounds, as well as to the needs of parents and older learners. William suggested that forward planning prior to any plans for recruitment should include a clearer understanding of the groups that constitute local communities. He asked that all managers include a member of their local community on the recruitment planning group.

> **Action: All managers agreed to identify a member of their local community to take part in the recruitment planning group.**

5.2.2 Reaching 'non-learners' Linda said that she was concerned that recruitment too often focused on people who were already likely to engage in some form of learning, and said that her main concern was in trying to reach people who do not currently see themselves as learners, often because they had had negative learning experiences whilst younger. These were the most challenging groups to recruit, but outreach work moving towards recruiting 'new' learners could also be the most satisfying. Outreach is also important to Judith, who said she empathised with some of the early learning experiences of apparent 'non-learners'. She also stated that in some areas of her work recruitment was not always a primary issue. In prisons, for example, some of the learners were doing courses compulsorily, although the courses – primarily basic skills – were not always the most appropriate learning experiences. Whilst recognising its importance, Judith was also concerned that the probationary services took basic skills as their main focus for community learning. Judith suggested that recruitment partnerships could be very effective in outreach work with non-traditional learners and hoped the Network could explore this further.

5.3 RECRUITMENT VIA FLEXIBLE LEARNING

Stephen said this was good advice, and something which he already routinely does. However, he wanted to remind the Network of changing global economic climates coupled with changing expectations of the purposes of learning and education. He believed that more and more learners wanted to engage in diverse learning paths, including part-time study, distance learning, engagement with new technologies, and in particular with vocational learning. The challenge for managers in terms of recruitment was not just in reaching diverse groups of learners but also in planning for and managing their learning in terms of flexible modes of delivery and multi-site delivery with an increasingly part-time workforce. He thought that there were important structural issues that needed to be decided before commencing recruitment.

5.4 RECRUITMENT AND EXPANSION

Andy warned lifelong learning managers that they needed to pay close attention to expansion, and related funding, before embarking on recruitment campaigns.

Action: Andy to circulate a brief paper outlining policy issues regarding recruitment, expansion and funding, for further discussion at the next meeting.

6 Retention and progression

Andy said that retention and progression are vital for all institutions to ensure funding, growth and development. Lifelong learning managers need to be as concerned with retention and progression as they are with recruitment. Sally thought it would be helpful if, rather than looking at their own groups of learners, the meeting considered ways to retain people in learning processes more generally. She noted that there was wide representation for managing lifelong learning at the meeting, and was particularly interested in the question of transitions. She hoped that the group would be able to explore ways of managing learning for younger people through to older people, and between learning in the community, through voluntary work, and in paid work, as well as learning in more formal educational settings.

6.1 FOUNDATION DEGREES

Stephen thought that foundation degrees were good examples of links between further education colleges, universities and work-based learning, and thought that

14–19 year olds looking for vocational education and training should be encouraged in this direction. There were clear progression routes set out for them, and it was likely that they would remain in education at least until the end of their foundation degrees. The learning support and information and communications technology that was an integral part of many foundation degrees would also help with retention, progression and completion.

6.2 AIMHIGHER

Andy said that he was overseeing the AimHigher work within his own institution, a government initiative to help widen participation in UK higher education, particularly amongst students from non-traditional backgrounds, minority groups and disabled people. AimHigher also offered information and assurance on financial matters to students entering higher education, specifically information about financial support and advice. Andy said that clear advice at the early stages of a learner's enquiries plays an important part in progression into higher education and could help retention. He suggested that managers should be developing new performance indicators and associated benchmarks to assess the success of AimHigher and other widening participation projects with regard to retention and progression.

Sally stated that she thought there was already evidence of success. AimHigher specifically sets out to improve the attainment, aspirations and motivation of young people aged 14–19. She said that she had found the AimHigher campaign helpful for young people considering progression into higher education, particularly through Partnerships for Progression. She explained that this is a joint initiative which aims to bring together universities, colleges and schools with other stakeholders in a region to form comprehensive partnerships for the development and delivery of a regional plan to raise aspirations and achievement of young people, to encourage progression into higher education.

William had some experience of managing an AimHigher project, and agreed that it could help with progression. He had been involved in a community project which involved mentoring young people still at school and involving them in community initiatives, which he believed had been successful. Sarah expressed some concern about AimHigher, though, and suggested that managers should also consider ways to address some of the structural barriers to learning. However, Andy said that AimHigher was specifically targeted at young people from disadvantaged backgrounds, with bursaries offered to those aged under the age of 21 and from low-income families.

6.3 LEARNER SUPPORT

Edith reminded the meeting that older learners too had to overcome many barriers to learning, including cost, inaccessibility and unsuitable learning environments. However, once older learners had started to re-engage with learning, they were keen to continue and it was important to retain them. Institutions needed to move away from an over-emphasis on vocational and accredited learning, and to broaden their curriculum range to make it relevant to the learners whom they want to attract.

Hafsa agreed and said that the development and implementation of learning support as an aid to retention and progression should be of concern to all lifelong learning managers. However, she was concerned that learning support too often focused on basic skills when at times what was needed was the development of understandings of cultural differences. Learners from some cultures, for example, believe that it is disrespectful to speak out in class; or that it is wrong to critique the work of academics. Other learners needed support in the development of confidence. Managers should be prepared to put funding into this type of support work, which would not only have human benefits but also financial ones, as they would be more likely to retain learners.

Action: Stephen offered to bring to the next meeting some data on foundation degrees and retention.

7 Modes of delivery

7.1 WORK-BASED LEARNING

John said he believed that corporate universities are an excellent example of flexible modes of delivery. He explained that in the USA corporate universities are the fastest growing sector of HE: in Britain corporate universities have mainly been developing since the mid-1990s and there are now around 20 corporate universities. They were created to deliver learning at appropriate times, to a wide range of audiences, using a variety of methods. Sometimes training is delivered within the organisation, often by a mix of learning professionals and senior staff. At other times it is outsourced. Several corporate universities also have partnerships with traditional universities, offering a range of learning opportunities for their members. Many employees in corporate universities are engaged in accredited learning whilst others make use of learning resource centres or other training opportunities. All corporate universities offer on-line learning: through utilising the latest technologies, companies can economically and effectively deliver distance learning and 'virtual' learning. Members of staff are encouraged to complete personal development plans, and corporate universities see themselves as very meaningful participants in the development of lifelong learning.

Jessica added that work-based learning occurs within many smaller organisations, not just corporate universities. It includes learning *for* work, linked to work placements, and learning *through* work, linked to formally accredited further or higher education programmes, as well as her own main area of concern, learning *at* work. She said that the trades unions were often particularly active, with union learning representatives playing an important role in many organisations. She explained that she manages lifelong learning for smaller organisations that have introduced, or plan to introduce, learning at work.

Sally said that vocational and work-based learning was increasingly important for young people. Over a quarter of a million learners are currently on apprenticeship schemes: these had been particularly successful with regards to business administration, engineering, hairdressing and beauty therapy, land-based provision, retailing, and health and social care.

Jalaal said that learning through volunteering also offers different modes of delivery which are equally meaningful. Volunteering is an excellent way to gain new experiences and develop new skills, or to enhance existing ones. Many volunteer placements enable people to study and develop key skills, whilst some volunteers receive vocational training in specialist areas such as social care, working with the elderly, or working with children.

7.2 FLEXIBLE DELIVERY OPTIONS AND ICT

Stephen reminded the meeting that 80 per cent of students in further education are adults, many of whom prefer to study part-time for a variety of work and personal reasons and it is important that providers always consider part-time learning opportunities. Additionally, older people usually prefer daytime classes, whilst for people in employment, evening classes are often the preferred mode. His college offers a range of delivery options, including day and evening classes, full and part-time delivery, and work-based learning. This included the development of foundation degrees and vocational education, often working closely with employees to agree the skills needed for current and future workforces. Currently over half a million people are participating in work-based learning, with engineering and technology being the most popular areas.

Stephen thought that the biggest growth area in his college was information and communication technology, including e-learning. Recent reports – both nationally and within his own college – have shown that e-learning has positive effects on retention and recruitment, enabling the development of student-centred, independent learning. Learners – including older learners – engage very effectively with new technologies. This is especially true when mixed modes of delivery are offered. His college included e-learning in the classroom and at a distance, as well as more traditional classroom based learning and teaching. However, teachers were sometimes reluctant, or lacking in skills, to effectively deliver in mixed modes, and lifelong learning managers need to take a lead to ensure quality across subject areas and departments and to implement e-learning institutionally. Sally added that e-learning had proved to be motivating for younger learners, who might not otherwise effectively engage with learning. There is also evidence that e-learning can give good support to disabled students.

Sarah said that whilst she could see that it might be beneficial to introduce e-learning in the classroom as well as at a distance, this would prove impossible for her to implement for her continuing education students. Her classes are offered at multiple sites, which is seen as key to outreach work and to the delivery of learning opportunities for students who may not be able to get into the centre. Multi-site delivery was essential for under-represented groups, including women (especially those with school age children or for older women), people with disabilities, people from particular ethnic communities and older people. This was a view shared by Narinder. Whilst most of her delivery is single site, the management of outreach is also an important element of her work. Of the almost one million people enrolled in adult and community learning, the vast majority are women, many of whom find it difficult to get into the centre for classes. Her centre offers classes in local centres which attract older women who are reluctant to attend 'evening classes', and women with children who appreciate local classes that are held in school hours.

Action: Stephen offered to give a demonstration of flexible delivery and ICT at a future meeting.

8. Part-time workforce

8.1 INSTITUTIONAL ISSUES

Andy explained that in higher education almost half the lecturers are employed part-time, with the vast majority of these on hourly paid contracts. Stephen said that in further education, the position is even worse. Around two-thirds of all teaching staff are part-time, and large numbers of casual staff have been employed to replace the redundancy/early retirement of 20,000 permanent staff. However, with many part-time workers able to claim equal rights with full-time workers, managers had a burden of responsibility to the part-time staff, to the institution and of course to the learners.

Sarah asked the group to remember that part-time staff are not representative of the work-force as a whole. Around 70 per cent of part-time and hourly paid staff are women; numbers of older workers are above the national average; whilst numbers of disabled staff are almost double the national average. However, staff from minority ethnic groups working part-time in lifelong learning are less than the national average. She said that lifelong learning managers needed to be aware of these statistics, and to consider issues relating to equality of opportunity with regard to specific groups. Sarah stated that lifelong learning would collapse in the UK without the work undertaken by a part-time workforce, the majority of whom do not receive pro-rata pay and terms of conditions of service. Indeed, many of the teaching staff in lifelong learning, and some of the administrative staff, are employed as casual workers on an hourly paid basis. For teaching staff, almost all are appointed to teaching only posts. A large number of part-time lecturers teach the same number of hours as full-time lecturers yet their level of pay is often below the bottom point of lecturer scales.

8.2 MANAGING PART-TIME WORKERS

Linda said that working with part-time staff poses a range of issues for managers. Of particular concern to her is the balance between making part-time (and especially hourly paid) members of staff feel included and part of her team, and yet being unable to pay them for attending meetings. Additionally, whilst she encouraged them to engage in continuing professional development, this also could not be supported financially.

Andy said that educational managers must give urgent attention to staff development for hourly paid staff in particular. Such staff are not always aware of how to comply with new policies, and this is especially important with regard to disability. This includes clerical and administrative as well as teaching staff. Managers need to be fully aware of ways in which part-time work is governed by institutional policy, audit regulations and employment law. However, despite the possible pitfalls, there are considerable benefits to using part-time staff. Part-time contracts allowed for flexibility in managing the delivery of programmes, and broadened the scope of teaching by including specialist contributions. Equally importantly, using hourly paid staff provides a way of dealing with contingencies such as unexpected absence or unplanned but temporary increases in workload.

Judith was concerned that the discussion had turned from 'support' to 'compliance'. She hoped the Network could explore ways to implement staff development for hourly paid staff which would enable them to develop themselves and their careers and which would support them within their institutions.

> **Action: Judith to produce a paper on staff development and sessional/ part-time contracts.**

9 Quality assurance

9.1 INSTITUTIONAL REQUIREMENTS

Andy said that a key issue facing lifelong learning managers is both the assurance and the improvement of quality. Stephen explained that for post-16 providers funded by the Learning and Skills Council, comprehensive self-assessment reports had to be produced based on the Common Inspection Framework. These had been jointly developed by the Adult Learning Inspectorate and the Office for Standards in Education. In addition, institutions were expected to participate in regular and ongoing review and evaluation. Although some people have found this helpful, this process has added enormously to the workloads and stress experienced by lifelong learning managers, highly exacerbated when an institution is due for a formal inspection, which takes place once every four years. Andy informed the meeting that his institution was due for a Quality Assurance Agency institutional audit, which was bringing increased pressure on managers with regard to preparation of documents etc., including contributing to the institution's self-evaluation document.

9.2 BENEFITS OF QUALITY ASSURANCE

Narinder said that although much of the emphasis on quality assurance appears to be over-burdensome and teaching staff can be resentful, she had tried to demonstrate that some aspects of review and evaluation can be helpful and developmental, and tried to involve staff in more positive experiences of self-assessment and evaluation, including observations of teaching practice. She had worked with staff to introduce peer assessment of teaching as well as the more formal observations of teaching which take place. Sarah agreed, and said that observations of teaching should be undertaken in a climate of supporting learning and learners.

Hafsa emphasised the importance of listening to learners, who were key to issues of quality assurance and development. She had introduced systems where termly meetings were held between students, tutors and managers to monitor developments and seek to improve the learning experiences taking place. John said that he believed that whilst it is important to listen to a variety of voices – learners, tutors and administrative staff – it was crucial that managers took responsibility for managing. He produced annually a clear strategy and action plan which could be effectively monitored and assessed.

9.3 DISABILITY DISCRIMINATION ACT

There was some concern among managers about the requirements of the Disability Discrimination Act and its implementation. This had implications for both human and financial resources. Whilst Andy, Stephen and John had clear institutional support structures and guidelines in place, this was not the case for several of the other managers. In particular, Hafsa and Sarah noted that there were special issues with regard to outreach work; and Jalaal and William noted the challenges when working with community and other groups. It was agreed that this is an important area and should form a separate item at a later meeting.

Action: Andy to invite a speaker on the DDA to the next meeting.

10 Any other business

Narinder expressed concern about the workloads of lifelong learning managers. There was a general discussion about the amount of paperwork and emails generated, as well as the vast numbers of meetings managers are expected to either attend or initiate. In addition, there was concern about the amount of documents with which lifelong learning managers have to familiarise themselves, including institutional policies, new legislation, etc. Narinder said that although she only manages a small section, her 'open door' policy means that the paperwork can become overwhelming. She suggested that it might be helpful if the group use the Network to consider personal and professional development.

Narinder explained that her past experiences of trying to move into a management role in a further education college led her to believe that she was better suited to working with adult and community groups. In her view, FE and HE institutions were unwilling to address the needs of Black staff and learners. However, she told the group that a survey into leadership and management that was conducted by the Learning and Skills Development Agency showed that adult and community learning leaders emerged as having the greatest need for development and support across the widest range of management activities.

She would like to explore the possibility of setting up professional development groups for women managers or managers from minority ethnic groups. Black staff are under-represented amongst lifelong learning managers, and she suggested that professional development, mentoring and job-shadowing would all be positive initiatives. Narinder said it would be useful, for example, to work with colleagues to update knowledge about the education sector and issues facing Black adult learners, from training and employment to funding, learning and partnership/working opportunities.

However, Andy stated that he did not think this was the purpose of the Network.

Jalaal asked that a fuller discussion take place about the purpose of the Network, as he thought that there had not been enough discussion about matters that included the interests of all of those present. William seconded the proposal. He said he has some concerns that although the Network is targeted at lifelong learning managers, their interests may be too diverse to form a meaningful group. He felt that the meeting had been useful and believed it had given them all some insight into their relevant sectors, but he wasn't sure where the Network would go from this point or what the real possibilities were for collaborative working. Andy asked if other colleagues agreed with this view. Whilst Judith understood William's point, she suggested that the Network continue to meet termly for one year, and to then review its usefulness and benefit to its members. It was agreed that this was a useful suggestion, and that the purpose of the Network would form an agenda item at the next meeting. Other future agenda items suggested by members of the group include managing resources, partnerships for progression, knowledge exchanges, foundation degrees, and managing disability. Jalaal asked that the purpose of the Network form the main item: he was concerned that there was a danger that too big an agenda would prevent collaboration between the members rather than enhance it, leading to William's concerns. It was agreed that the two main items for the next meeting would be the purpose of the Network and the development of knowledge exchanges, although Judith hoped that there would also be an opportunity to return to some of the items that had been raised at this first meeting, including support for hourly paid staff, as well as professional development for themselves.

11 Date and place of next meeting

Date and place to be agreed and circulated later.

Conclusions

We have in this chapter shown some of the issues facing managers in a variety of lifelong learning contexts. Some of the managers have issues and concerns that they share, such as managing a part-time workforce; managing through different modes of delivery etc., although how they deal with these differ considerably. These differences arise not just because of the differences in the lifelong learning contexts themselves (e.g. formal or nonformal learning) but also due to the hierarchical positions of institutions and of managers. Some voices are dominant from the outset: Andy, for example, as Chair of the meeting, as a manager in a higher education institution, and as a white man, shows a confidence not just in voicing his opinions, but in believing that he can impose those opinions on others. As Chair he will also determine the version of the minutes that is eventually circulated and, in a legalistic and quality assurance framework, the final version of the minutes will be taken as a 'true' record of the meeting. Minutes of meetings have become a dominant form of storytelling and record keeping in educational institutions. However, what has not been shown in this chapter is what does not get minuted: informal discussions, jokes, sarcasms, subversions, resistances, emotions, body language or silenced voices are impossible to 'read' from the minutes alone, yet these too are parts of the stories of educational managers. We will return to issues of identities, emotions and resistances in the next section.

Chapter 6

Retelling the stories of teachers

Introduction

Chapter 6 moves its focus from educational managers to teachers. The narratives in this chapter will include the stories of teachers both inside and outside of formal educational institutions. Some of the stories will uncover the contradictory experiences of teachers who are concerned with processes of learning and teaching but who have external pressures that place emphasis on product and outcome. Stories will highlight the realities of working within contemporary educational contexts, which involve crossing institutional and cultural boundaries, addressing multiple and contradictory demands, and reinventing identities to respond to differently located contexts.

The stories in this chapter are told through the imagined discussions of an Action Learning Set for those who are teaching in lifelong learning, including practitioners in hourly paid, fractional or full-time teaching posts. Action learning is a process in which a group of people come together more or less regularly to help each other to learn from their experiences, encouraging personal and professional development. It is a continuous process of learning and reflection, supported by colleagues, through which individuals learn with and from each other by working on real problems and reflecting on their own experiences.

Membership of this (imagined) Action Learning Set fluctuates, although there is a steady core. Membership has included practitioners working in further education, adult or continuing education, higher education, youth work, arts practice and the cultural industries, community development, nursing and health services, prison work, adult education, the careers service, staff development in the public and not for profit sectors, and independent trainers. In following some of their stories here, we ask our readers to look for what is not said as well as what is said, and consider resistances, identities and emotions, all of which we will return to in Section III.

In writing this chapter, our thanks go to colleagues with whom we have participated in Action Learning Sets of our own, as well as to our colleagues in the range of institutions in which we have taught; and to the students on our teaching certificates and lifelong learning and education Masters courses, from whom we continually learn.

Teaching in Lifelong Learning Action Learning Set

We ask you to imagine a group of people gathered together on a weekday morning in October, near the start of term. There are 18 members of the Action Learning Set, including the facilitator: although this is a large number for an action learning set, only 11 people are present this morning. They have all poured themselves a cup of tea or coffee, and have had a few minutes to stand chatting in twos and threes. Chairs are set in a circle.

Margaret, the facilitator, asks those present to take a seat. She welcomes everyone to the group and reminds them of their differing roles. As facilitator, she will mainly keep everyone to time to ensure that people have a chance to develop and reflect on any issues they wish to raise. She asks who has an issue that they would like to bring to the group this morning. Aisha, Jim, Sally, Chris and Dave all say they would like to present an incident or issue to the group, and the rest of the participants confirm they are happy with this. Margaret reminds the Set that presenters should be allowed to speak without interruption. Participants should neither offer advice nor appear judgemental. However, they should look at the problem from their own perspective, and may challenge underlying assumptions. Presenters should be helped to move on in their understandings, and to come to see possible ways forward.

Aisha's story

Aisha tells the Set that since they last met in July she has started teaching part-time in a further education college on one of their foundation degrees. She was pleased to get the work as the outreach work that she had been doing with her young women's groups had been cut, and she needed to develop some more teaching hours. The Set will remember, she says, how distressed she was last time they met both at the thought of not having sufficient teaching, and at losing work to which she was strongly committed. The last meeting had helped her to realise that she needed resolution and closure. At least the uncertainty is over – the outreach work is gone, but she can move in different directions. When she took on this new job she was also interested in the new opportunities offered as a lot of her background is in widening participation. She expected that she would be working with learners who were conventionally harder to reach, and that her students would in some ways be similar to those with whom she had worked with in the past. She started the term feeling very positive.

However, although she realises it is early days in a new job, she has become increasingly disappointed and disillusioned. Having felt a valued member of a small team, she now feels like she has become invisible and that the only people her FE colleagues have time for are their HE partners. She is expected to go into college and teach the contracted number of hours, but she is left out of team meetings, plays no part in curriculum development or other planning, and isn't even on the circulation list for staff information. She has no desk, no computer, no phone. If she wants to give any of the students support – and many of them need either pastoral support, study skills support, or both – she has found herself talking to them in corridors in her own time, and without pay.

She feels that all her past experiences and professional qualifications count for nothing. She was even told that if she wants to stay working at the college – especially if she wants to develop her work – she will have to do a teaching certificate. She doesn't object to continuing professional development – she feels that is what she does all the time – but the way she was told made her feel that she is considered unqualified and inexperienced.

She is also disappointed in the foundation degree and in her students. She has tried to engage them in reflective learning, and keeps pointing out to them that they can all learn from the experiences of each other. However, on the whole she finds her students pragmatic at best and instrumental at worst. She is worried that far from widening their possibilities she is doing little or nothing to initiate change.

Aisha stops talking. There is silence for several minutes, broken by June asking Aisha what she sees as the main issue.

Aisha thinks. She isn't sure. 'I suppose', she eventually says, 'it is about my own sense of worth'. She feels that she is no longer sure who she is. What she used to be was a community tutor involved in outreach work and widening participation. She cared passionately about the work and believed that she was empowering the young women with whom she worked to make choices for themselves. The work mattered, and she knows that she made a difference. She tried desperately hard for most of last year to secure additional funding but despite all her efforts this wasn't to be. Now she is paid an hourly rate doing what she has been made to feel is unskilled work. She doesn't seem to make a difference to her students' lives, and the work could as well be done by any other teacher.

Katrina intercedes. 'So what you are saying', she suggests, 'is that you are able to judge the worth of their learning for your students. How do you *know* what difference their learning makes to them?'

'I suppose I *am* assuming that job development isn't as important for my students as personal development', agrees Aisha. Of course eventual employment matters for her students – she knows that – but this isn't why she became a teacher.

Jane asks whether Aisha is really talking about self-worth. She suggests that because Aisha doesn't feel that the work she is doing matters, then she also thinks that *she* doesn't matter. 'Do you think you *are* your work?' she asks.

'I hope not', Aisha retorts, and then says she is surprised at the passion with which she gave her response. She is remembering an incident that happened just this week. She wasn't sure before she came today if she wanted to or was able to speak about it, but thinks she should. Maybe she *does* fall into a trap of believing she is what she does, but if that is so maybe she feels like nothing because she *does* nothing.

The incident happened in the classroom and, later, in the staffroom. She has one student in her class – an older learner – whom she feels is continually challenging and trying to undermine her. She doesn't know why he is taking the foundation degree as he wouldn't join in when she asked students for their reasons for taking the course. He stated in class at the time that he was there to get his qualification, and wanted to get on with it. In trying to get members of the class to draw on personal experience, Aisha introduced a piece of writing by a Black woman writer. The student in question stood up and said that the writing was irrelevant and politically correct, obtaining a laugh from other class members. Aisha was particularly upset by this incident, as she feels there is a sub-text which is also dismissing her as irrelevant and her appointment as politically correct. When she happened to meet another teacher on the foundation course in the staffroom later that day and recounted the incident, she was told she was being over-sensitive and she had to learn to bluff it out. And anyway, her colleague added, there is only limited classroom time and every part of it has to count. After all, we do need to ensure that we retain our students and that they end up with the qualification they want. Maybe, her colleague suggests, she *should* stick to more conventional texts. 'Well', says Aisha, 'maybe I should'.

Aisha stops and is silent.

'Well', says Bill, 'using only so-called conventional texts is one solution to the problem, but maybe there are others'. He suggests that Aisha think about what assumptions are being made by some of those involved, and consider whether those assumptions could be challenged.

Aisha says she knows what assumptions are being made. They think that because she is a woman, and Black, they can say what they like to her. She also thinks they are assuming that because her previous work was in community education, it doesn't carry the same status as work in further or higher education. Her professional qualification in youth and community work also appears to carry little or no value.

Bill asks if other assumptions are also being made about the purpose of education – including foundation degrees – and the role of tutors. 'Yes', says Aisha, 'I think they are'. She is starting to wonder whether foundation degrees were introduced as a way to get working-class young people into work, and to give employers the types of employees that they think they need. Although she said earlier that she recognises that employment matters to her students, she would like to think that she could encourage them to expand their horizons and think about new possibilities. However, in her current role, there seems to be little or no scope for her to do this within the tightly structured syllabus with which she has been presented, and which in turn she is expected to present to the students.

John asks whether this might be the reason that the students don't feel that they can learn from each other or from a range of texts? 'Or from me', adds Aisha.

June suggests that Aisha is feeling very powerless in the college. Sometimes we *are* in situations where we don't seem to have any control, she says, and wonders if there is anything Aisha could do to help her feel more in control. Aisha says she would like to think about this. She needs to consider her role in the classroom and in the college, but she would also like to think about her position as a Black woman in the wider community. She also thinks it would be helpful if she reminds herself that this happens to be a job she is currently doing, rather than a job that defines who and what she is.

Margaret looks to the clock, and reminds Aisha that her time is nearing an end and it will soon be time for the next person to present their incident. She asks if there are any final points Aisha would like to make, whether the session has been helpful for Aisha, and what action Aisha might take as a result. Aisha says that it has been helpful to be able to talk, and not to have her story trivialised. She is glad to have this space where her concerns can be taken seriously. She isn't sure what action she might take, though, and would like to go away and think through some of the issues. After she reflects on these she hopes to make an action plan, and will come back to the Set next time to let them know how she is progressing.

Jim's story

Jim starts off by saying he empathises with Aisha about teacher training. He has a demanding post as a lecturer in a post-1992 university with a heavy teaching load. When he first started at the university he had to take a compulsory certificate in teaching as one of the conditions of satisfactory completion of probation, and he felt it was one more demand on his time. However, whilst he thinks teaching is acquired rather than learned, he found the course useful in many ways. He believes that if teaching is to be respected as a profession, then a commitment to professional standards needs to be demonstrated.

He admires Aisha for bringing some of her issues to the Set, which has made it easier for him to continue. He empathises with her because, as a gay man, he too has been marginalized in the past, although this is not so much the case in his present post. He had previously contacted his union to try and find out how many lesbian, gay, bisexual or transgendered lecturers there are, but the union doesn't monitor for sexual orientation so numbers are unknown.

However, this is not the issue he wants to bring to the Set. It might be connected, but he doesn't think so. This is difficult for Jim to speak about and he needs to take a few moments to collect his thoughts . . .

He feels that his manager is making impossible demands on him. Jim knows that over half of all lecturers feel that they can't cope with the workload, and that many are suffering from stress. However, knowing that lots of other people feel the same doesn't help him. Jim is hoping to apply for promotion soon, and thinks that if he suggests he has too much work he doesn't stand a chance of getting it. His Head of Department will have to support any promotion application but has made it clear to Jim that he is currently not making satisfactory progress. He has given Jim two key tasks to oversee, and doesn't feel Jim is doing either of them as well as he should be.

First Jim has been asked to supervise a move in the department towards e-learning. This wasn't a role that Jim wanted, and he feels that he is weak in this area and doesn't know enough himself to be able to direct the department. He wanted to do some training first, but there was no funding to support him in attending any courses, nor did he really have the time to be able to go even if the money had been found. He feels there might be links between e-learning, widening participation and student-centred learning but hasn't been able to explore these: he is having to react to the demands of the department rather than being pro-active in determining the direction for e-learning.

The second task that has been set though is the one that is really causing Jim stress. The university is due for an institutional audit, and Jim has been briefed to advise and prepare the department. Although the audit is still six months away, Jim is already immersed in documentation and is experiencing the tensions of colleagues concerned about outcomes. There are areas which particularly concern him with regard to the audit, like insufficient student support, but no resources – human or financial – to do anything about it. He feels that if the audit doesn't go well, he will be a convenient scapegoat.

Jim ends by saying that he feels sick at the thought of going to work and has continual headaches. He feels that he is in a cycle from which he can't escape, as he needs his Head of Department to either support an application for promotion or, if Jim decides to move on, to write a good reference for him, neither of which he thinks is likely to happen. He is berated by his Head of Department in private and in meetings, but he really doesn't believe he is as bad at his job as his Head of Department indicates – he gets good student evaluations, for example – but he is working ridiculously long hours, his home life is suffering, and he is not sure how long he can continue like this.

Jim stops speaking and there are a few moments of silence.

Kate asks the first question. She reminds Jim that he started off by talking about a commitment to professional values, and wonders what he means by that.

'Well', says Jim, 'what I mean by professional values is always showing a commitment to my students and giving my best to them. It means being thoroughly prepared for my lectures; and supporting students to develop through their assessed work and the feedback I give them. However, as far as others are concerned, professionalism is about external accountability and a pursuit of excellence which seems to be more about market choices and less about our learners.'

Parminder asks whether this is Jim's concern with regard to e-learning. Jim agrees that it is certainly one of them. The university has the development of e-learning in its strategic plan for learning and teaching, and the department needs to demonstrate that it is complying with this, particularly with the forthcoming institutional audit. The department is trying to keep everyone happy except the students! Whilst the students do want e-learning, Jim doesn't think the way it is currently being introduced will benefit their learning and this causes him much concern. He thinks there are exciting possibilities for e-learning, but he doesn't know how to reconcile the scope for opportunities with limited resources, the demands on his time, and the directions in which he feels he is being forced to go.

Amar picks up the thread. 'Is there a way to do this', he asks? How do we find ways to cope with the external pressures and demands of outside bodies, as well as the internal pressures and demands of our own institutions?

Both seem greedy, says Jim, and incessantly demanding. He doesn't think he should *have* to be finding ways to cope. He remembers when he enjoyed his work; when it was about more than *coping*.

Anne asks whether Jim has also thought about involving his union. She knows this is difficult, but she wonders whether Jim would describe what is happening to him as bullying.

Jim becomes distressed as he considers this. He was bullied for much of his childhood, he says, and was determined not to let this happen to him again as an adult. If he brings charges of bullying, it makes him appear weak and unable to cope, and he will not let himself be back in a position of helplessness. 'I am no longer a child', says Jim. 'I am a professional and am determined to be recognised as such.'

'So what', asks Amar, 'do you think is the professional responsibility of your Head of Department, and what should your own professional response be? What can you reasonably be expected to do to work within the changing contexts of learning and teaching, and what can you reasonably expect of the institution?'

Jim thinks it is useful to think about the issues in terms of professionalism and reasonableness. He thinks he might find it helpful to look back at his job description and at his last appraisal, and to make an appointment with his Head of Department to discuss his current workload. He also thinks it might help if there is a third party present – maybe someone from human resources – and he will explore the options. He thanks the Set for their thoughts and comments.

Sally's story

Sally describes herself to the Set as a portfolio worker. She undertakes hourly paid work for a range of different institutions, working mainly in the area of student support. Her main area of expertise is working with students with dyslexia, but she also works in other areas of study skills support. She has worked for many organisations – sometimes only for short periods of time, and sometimes for several years. Currently she is working at an adult education centre; a centre for continuing education; and for the prison service, where she works with young offenders. She has also just been offered work within the lifelong learning centre of a National Health Service Trust, coming in one afternoon a week to give additional learning support to some of the employees. She is very committed to the concept of lifelong learning, and she believes that many learners are let down through lack of support. She believes that her work enables her to help them to continue learning, in sometimes very difficult circumstances.

Whilst she recognises that there are drawbacks to portfolio work, especially with regard to job security, she has always enjoyed the flexibility it brings. She gave up full-time employment when she first had children, and hourly paid work allowed her to have more control over her hours of work. That was a long time ago: she found herself enjoying the variety of teaching situations and the wide range of learners with whom she has contact, and values this aspect of her work. Having heard Jim's story, she also values not being involved in institutional politics, although she does sometimes feel – as Aisha does – a lack of any feelings of community with regard to her colleagues. However, she knows that both staff and students see her work as important, both in terms of supporting learning and teaching, and as a response to external bodies, who want to see evidence of investment in the quality of student experience.

In addition to her support work with students, Sally has recently been asked to run staff development sessions for tutors to help them find more diverse methods of assessment. For students with dyslexia, for example, traditional essays aren't necessarily the best assignments to set. This is another interesting aspect of her portfolio, which she is enjoying very much. Sally can also see that this work has good potential to develop. She has been talking to some of her colleagues in the centre for continuing education where she does some work, and they have also been concerned with problems of assessment. They have told her that their institutions are reliant on students handing in work for assessment in order to get government funding. However, far from needing study skills support, many of their students are very able, and come to the courses because of their passion for the subject. Although committed learners, they often have little or no interest in undertaking assessment or in gaining a certificate or qualification. However, her colleagues are finding themselves under strong institutional pressure to get the students to submit work for assessment. If central funding is lost, either courses will close or students will have to pay vastly increased fees. Sally is considering offering staff development sessions on creative and innovative methods of assessment, and is excited by this new direction.

So, says Sally, the Set must be wondering what issue she is bringing to the group. She is happy and fulfilled in her work, and to a large extent is able to choose the type of work she wants to do, and the hours she wants to work.

However, her personal situation has now changed. At the age of almost 50, she now finds herself without a partner, and reliant solely on her own wages. Although her various hourly paid commitments do bring in sufficient money on which to live, she has been wondering whether she should be more concerned about job security and about building her pension. She has made lists of the strengths, weakness, opportunities and threats in both full-time and hourly paid work, spoken to family and friends, looked at job advertisements, but she still doesn't know what to do. Should she stay with what she enjoys doing, but with each year always bringing a risk as to whether she will have her contracts renewed, or should she move into full-time permanent work?

Edith says she can see why Sally is so concerned with the present situation: it *is* a dilemma. However, she wonders if Sally could just tell them why she entered teaching as a career.

'Almost accidentally', says Sally. She grew up in a working-class area and, although she went to grammar school, there were little expectations that girls would go to university. If girls stayed on beyond compulsory schooling, most either did a secretarial course or went into nursing or teaching. She chose teaching as the other two options didn't appeal, and went to college to train as a secondary school teacher.

She worked full-time as an English teacher in a secondary school until she left to have her first child. After her children were born, she started to think about returning to some part-time work, and noticed that her local college was looking for part-time tutors to teach adult literacy. So she applied, got the job, and has been working in post-compulsory education ever since. 'No grand plans, then', she tells Edith, 'it just seemed to happen'.

Now that she thinks of it, continues Sally, the move she made into post-compulsory education – although a long time ago – was at a time of transition. It was the right opportunity at the right time, when she was adjusting to a period of change: not dissimilar to her current situation. Maybe, she thinks, she shouldn't rush into things but stay with her current work whilst keeping an eye on job advertisements. She might also talk to people in the institutions where she works, and let them know she is looking for more job security. Maybe for this year she has had enough changes in her life. She will keep her options open, but probably shouldn't apply for any full-time job that doesn't excite her. She thanks Edith for her question, and feels that she has started to make a partial decision.

Chris's story

Chris says that she is also starting to develop work in new directions. She is in a different position to the other people in the Set, she believes, because she is employed by a school, although she has close working relations with her local college and with local employers. She also does some voluntary work with youth groups. Chris knows that everyone else in the Set works with post-compulsory learners, but she thinks the divide between compulsory and post-compulsory isn't always helpful in thinking about lifelong learning.

Chris's job specification allows her to teach both at the school and at the college, and to visit young people who are doing work-related learning. Her brief is to work with young people aged 14–19, developing a curriculum for citizenship to equip young people with the knowledge, skills and attributes needed for adult life. This includes the development of positive attitudes to continuing learning, and preparation for active participation within the community.

Chris tells the Set that her task is broad. She has to motivate her students to become lifelong learners, and to take an active interest in their local and wider environments. However, Chris is struggling to find ways to put this into practice when most of her students are disillusioned with learning and with their local communities and see no real futures for themselves. She knows that the government plans for 50 per cent of all 18–30 year olds to enter higher education, but she is concerned about what will happen to the 50 per cent who don't. She recognises that it would be a real achievement if she could get young people who currently see themselves as non-learners to engage with meaningful learning experiences, but she is afraid that the political agenda for the job is more about turning already disadvantaged young people into compliant workers. She is concerned that she is helping to reproduce structural inequalities and injustices.

John asks Chris why she took the job. She tells him that she was previously teaching history and was a form tutor. When the headteacher started to look for someone to facilitate moves towards a curriculum for citizenship, Chris saw a chance to develop her interests in the ways in which young people could become members of the school and local communities. She took on the task, and the work grew from there. She is now employed by the school full-time to develop citizenship and lifelong learning.

'So the job clearly interested you in the beginning', says John. 'Are there still aspects of the job that really matter to you?' 'My students matter', says Chris. 'Their life opportunities matter.'

John says that teachers come to their work with their own value sets, beliefs and politics. He asks how Chris would describe hers, and how she might measure success for herself. Chris believes this is the wrong question. She isn't interested in imposing her value systems on her students. Rather than measure her own success she wants to be able to measure success for her students, although John asks whether this is something that perhaps the students should do for themselves.

Michelle joins the conversation. She remembers Chris saying that the divide between compulsory and post-compulsory is a false one, and she can certainly see what Chris means. However, there is a big difference. The students aged 14–16 are learning because they have to, whilst those over the age of 16 are presumably still learning because they want to. Does it help to think about this sort of divide, she asks?

Perhaps, says Chris. She had thought about working with the older learners to see if they were interested in acting as mentors to the younger learners, and this might still be worth exploring. Chris starts to wonder whether she has been trying to exercise too much control over her students' choices. In worrying about hidden agenda, maybe she has been trying to set her own. She will talk to them again about what matters to them. She could even consider getting them to work in Action Learning Sets! Perhaps she could help to reflect some of their experiences back to them, so that they can critically discuss their engagement with learning and citizenship. Maybe they would then start to see through and challenge hegemonic practices and think about change in their lives. Although she remains concerned about the political agenda for disadvantaged young people, Chris says that she is at least taking away some positive ideas, and she might even find ways to subvert the agenda. To answer John's question, she says, maybe *that's* how she will measure success!

Dave's story

Dave thanks everyone for letting him join the Set. As they know, he is new to the Set and was interested in joining when he met Margaret recently and she told him about action learning. Dave tells the Set that he is just starting his second year as an academic. Although he did some teaching as a postgraduate student, he finished his Ph.D. a little over a year ago and at the same time was successful in finding a job as a lecturer. He enjoys the work and believes he is doing a good job. He prepares his lectures thoroughly, and is confident in his subject. However, he has some students in one of his groups who are continually disruptive. They come in late, sit near the back of the lecture hall, talk, and generally look as though they would rather not be there. Dave would be pleased to learn from more experienced colleagues what he should do.

Margaret intercedes. She realises that Dave has only just joined the Set but she reminds him as well as the other members that the purpose of the Set is not to supply answers but to ask questions, encouraging participants to seek their own answers or ways of dealing with the issues they raise. She asks Dave if he would like to say a little more before colleagues join in.

Dave isn't sure what else he can say. He lectures in economics and realises that lecturing is a necessary part of his job, although he prefers to work on his research. He hopes that as he moves up the academic ladder he will be able to spend less time on teaching and more on research.

Sally says she would find it helpful if Dave could clarify what the main issue is for him, and Dave repeats that it is that he has disruptive students. Yes, agrees Sally, but are you concerned that this is disrupting the learning for the other students in the lecture, or are you concerned that the students whom you see as troublesome are failing to engage in learning?

Well, says Dave, of course these things concern him, but he can't make them learn. He is there to teach them, and he is not sure why they are failing to pay attention to what he has to say. After all, they are at a respected university to obtain a good degree and if they don't listen and learn they will find themselves disappointed.

Anne asks whether Dave will also feel disappointed. He replies that of course he will – if his students get poor results it will reflect back on him.

Anne asks Dave what he knows about the disruptive students. Dave is surprised at the question and says that he has never spoken with them. As soon as the lecture is over they leave, and quite frankly he is pleased to see them go. Anne asks what he thinks might result if he spoke to them. Dave agrees that he could tell them that he is not happy with their behaviour. 'That's true', says Anne, 'but is there anything else you could discuss?' 'I could ask them why they are at university if they aren't interested in learning', replies Dave.

Amar asks Dave whether he has considered finding out what *does* interest them. Dave isn't sure how this will help in the lecture theatre. He knows that some of his colleagues think it is important to take a student-centred approach, but although this might be possible in some subjects he doesn't think it is in his own especially for the first years. The students have to understand some of the basic theories and concepts before they can get involved in discussion, and he doesn't see how knowing more about his students' interests will make any difference to what they have to learn.

'Will it make a difference to how they learn, or to how you teach', asks Anne? Dave doesn't see how it will, but he senses from the questions that colleagues in the Set think he should do this. So next time he sees his disruptive students he will ask them to stay behind and he will try and find out why they insist on talking through his lectures, and he will give some thought to what he might be able to do to get them to listen.

Anne asks whether Dave has any colleagues he could talk to about this outside of the Set. Dave says that he was assigned a mentor last year, but they had little to discuss as Dave felt he was coping well. He is quite happy to take the advice of the Set and to talk to the students, and will report back next time.

Moving on

Margaret starts to bring the Action Learning Set to a close. Members agree that it was a useful session, and several participants say they found the issues raised relevant to their own work. Margaret reminds them again that anything raised within the Set is confidential, and is not to be discussed outside of these meetings. A date is agreed for next term's meeting, and the Set disbands.

Conclusions

Unlike the written and publicly available records presented in Chapters 4 and 5 (emails and minutes of meetings) this chapter has been presented as a transcript of the dialogues that take place between teachers interested in the reflective practice of an action learning set. The teachers who belong to this action learning set are, in the main, those with an interest in participation and reflexive practice: their attendance is entirely voluntary. Through the voices of the teachers in this chapter we have seen many concerns re/emerge that we will continue to explore throughout the book: matters of gender, sexuality, race and social class; of power, authority and control; of managerial cultures, audits and funding; and of professional values. No notes of the meeting are taken, and therefore the only records the teachers will take away with them are their memories of the discussions, mediated by their own understandings, experiences, emotions, resistances, identities and subjectivities – issues to which we will return in the final section.

Chapter 7

Retelling the stories of learners

Introduction

This chapter retells the stories of different groups of learners in a range of contexts inside and outside of formal educational institutions. The stories will be presented through the learners' (imaginary) learning journals. Although the learning journals are part of the learners' formal courses, they are encouraged, in some cases, to reflect on their experiences outside of the classroom to make connections between theory and practice, as well as the linkages between personal and public forms of knowledge, meaning and experience. The extent to which the learners are able to reflect on their experiences outside of the classroom is shaped by the kind of courses they are engaged in. For example, one group of students is taking a Women's Studies course, where their personal experiences are explicitly being drawn on to challenge and contribute to the publicly legitimated knowledge within the university and wider field. In contrast, the students who are taking Study Skills on their Foundation Degree Course in IT and Business Studies are also encouraged to consider connections between their experiences outside the classroom, but spending too much attention on personal experiences is strongly discouraged. On this course, writing is constructed as an asocial and decontextualised set of skills and writers are expected to learn the techniques needed to communicate a coherent, linear and evidence-based case or argument. The journal is treated as an opportunity for learners to become skilled at self-evaluation and self-reflection. In this situation, the learning journal entries are formally assessed, and the learners are not invited to reflect on their personal experiences but rather their personal strengths and weaknesses. In the third context, schoolteachers who are undertaking an accredited continuing professional development course within their local education authority on action research are also keeping a learning journal, which will form part of their assessed portfolio. In this context, learners are expected to make connections between their professional experiences and the theoretical literature that they are being introduced to on their courses.

The learning journal entries in this chapter are entirely fictitious in nature and yet reflective of the kinds of entries we have encountered both as teachers and as learners ourselves. The reader is invited to consider some of the key issues being raised in the journals and the kinds of curriculum and pedagogical challenges emerging from their accounts. However, the reader is also reminded that writing a journal is a discursive process involving the production of self, subjectivity and meaning-making, and can only ever be a partial story. The reader is therefore encouraged to consider the constraints around writing a learning journal in terms of what can be written about and what might be risky for the writer in relation to their social and institutional positioning and what counts as legitimate knowledge. We ask our readers to consider the ways that different learners position themselves in their writing and what this might tell us about the struggles around producing such a text in various educational contexts. In what ways are the learners producing a reflective account and does the journal enable the learner to take reflexive approaches to their learning?

Women's Studies learning journals

Gloria, 27 September

Today we looked at different feminist theories of women, family and sexuality. We all got into small groups and selected a text to focus on. Our group chose the text on 'Compulsory Heterosexuality' by Adrienne Rich. This text was a challenge to some of our lifestyles and it made us question all sorts of choices we've made in our lives. I found it really unsettling and difficult to think about. As a happily married woman with two children, I felt slightly under attack. Only a couple of the other women in my group are married. I felt really strange suddenly in a way that I had never felt before. But a lot of what Adrienne Rich said I could relate to. It made me feel ok to feel angry sometimes that my life often is about looking after everyone else. Sometimes I really do want some space for my self. And I'd never before thought about heterosexuality in this way – in fact I never even thought about heterosexuality before at all! It really made me look at things differently. I thought about how my five-year-old son is already so aware of things that 'should be' associated with boys and the ways that he distances himself from girly things – and yet really does enjoy playing with his older sister and her toys sometimes. I don't think I'll ever see the world the same again – it has really made me question all sorts of things that I had taken for granted before. But I don't know what my husband would think of this and in some ways it makes me feel guilty to even be reading this because I don't think I can share it with my husband. It makes me feel quite mixed up. Its really deep stuff and takes a lot of thinking about. A real challenge.

Angelina, 27 September

Our discussion today looked at writing by Adrienne Rich on what she terms compulsory heterosexuality. This was an amazing piece of writing. I really like her point that heterosexuality is made compulsory in our society. As a lesbian woman

I can completely relate to this and feel that this connects with my own experiences. It helps me understand why it was so hard to tell my mum and dad that I was not straight. Of course, I always understood why it was hard but I never thought about it in quite this way before – that heterosexuality is forced on us by society. I feel that this course is going to be so enlightening and will help me understand myself better. Well, this is why I took it.

We had an interesting discussion about the text in our group. Some of the women in my group seemed very defensive about it but this is exactly why Rich argues that heterosexuality is compulsory. When I pointed that out to one woman she got a bit snappy with me. But mostly we had an interesting discussion about this and how it might help us to 'defamiliarise the familiar', which is one of the aims of the course. We also talked about motherhood and what Rich says about the mixed feelings about being a mother. Two of the women in our small group were mothers and they could relate to this part of the text better than the part about compulsory heterosexuality. In some ways it made me think about my mother and what she went through raising me and my sisters. Even though my father is quite liberal, my mum still was expected to do most of the parenting and housework. But this isn't just because my dad expected her to (as well as everyone else in the family) – it's because she expected herself to as well. The idea of compulsory heterosexuality helps to understand why women end up in these positions and what we might do to challenge that – but also that, even now, women are still limited in what they can do or can't do without being ostracised in their local communities. I am really lucky to have a really nice group of friends who see the world in a different way and do not impose this compulsory heterosexuality on others. I definitely want to look at these issues deeper as we go through the course and I think I might write my essay about this.

Carla, 27 September

The readings for today made me feel really angry and I don't know if I even want to continue with the course any more. I felt like my way of life was completely under attack. In the small group that I was in, there was another woman who says she was a lesbian, which made me feel uncomfortable and two women who have children and another one who has children but is divorced. I was the only one who didn't agree with the idea that heterosexuality is compulsory – how can that be if heterosexuality is the normal way of having a relationship? I am not a feminist and I like the way my life is – I like being married and I love looking after my children. No one forced me into that. I'm not sure I agree with what this course is about. I might just keep taking the Return to Study course and forget this one. I will think about it over the week.

Gloria, 18 November

Today we looked at feminist ideas about the public versus the private. I found the session really valuable. It is so true that a lot of our experiences as women get ignored or trivialised because they are seen as private experiences. This also helped me to realise that my lack of confidence relates to not feeling like I have any valuable experiences, because more of my experiences are of things that are not seen as important. When I first came to this course I thought I had nothing to bring. I didn't do well at school and I've never had a career, aside from working in an office for a few years, so I thought I had no relevant experiences. But after today's session, I am beginning to realise this is because of the way society is structured and the way public forms of experience are more highly valued than private forms of experience. So being a mother has never really struck me as something that I could learn from, that other people would ever think was important. Feminists show that being a mother is seen as a natural thing for women to do and so the work that I do everyday to raise a family, keep the household going is not ever recognised as proper work. Some feminists say that society could not operate at all without the work that mothers do, and some extreme feminists even think that women should be paid for the work that they do as mothers. (I don't think I would go that far because I still see being a mother as something I want to do and have a responsibility to do.) It makes you really think about things. Even the way my family reacted when I said I was going to do the course – like why do I need to do a course anyway. And I also realise that I have learned a lot from being a mother. That I should have a lot of confidence because I have been a good mother and I have developed a lot of skills from being a mother. Also, my husband couldn't go to work if I wasn't there to look after the children so my work is as important as his. My work as a mother is actual work and it is important, not just to my family but also in a bigger way.

Angelina, 18 November

Looking at my private life and the way I always have to separate it out from the public because of the structures in society highlights for me the endless work I have to do just to keep them separate. We talked about silencing women and I do feel silenced a lot of the time. At work, I have to keep silent about my private life because my private life would not be acceptable to the others. But they talk about their private lives a lot – what they did with their families on the weekend, their children, etc., etc. This also makes me think again about how compulsory heterosexuality works and is so effective in keeping the status quo and in keeping women like me silent.

But sometimes I do feel that there is some hypocrisy on this course. Although we talk about these things, we are sometimes told not to be 'anecdotal' when we talk from our personal experiences. When we had the workshop last week on writing our essays, we were told we could talk about our experiences in the essay but only if we balanced that out with the literature and theoretical perspectives. I have started writing my first draft and I'm not quite sure what I've written so far will be acceptable, or if I should just take my personal experiences out. We are getting some mixed messages, and this is confusing. I will raise this at the next group tutorial.

Carla, 18 November

Today's session was interesting to me. I never really thought about the divisions between the public and private like that before and it is true that I don't feel I can really talk in public. I always thought that was me – that I wasn't really good enough to talk in public because I don't speak that well and also because I am not that bright really. So who would be interested in what I have to say? But I began to realise that a lot of what we are learning is actually helpful for me at home. Now I have an argument to explain why I feel irritable when everything at home is being left up to me. So it works both ways. I am also feeling like I might be able to say something on my course about what we are learning through my experiences at home. I am beginning to feel better about the course – although some people still make me feel uncomfortable because they are quite posh and also clever. They are really different from me. But they do listen to me sometimes and make me feel I have something to say. Even the teachers. I am not sure that the course will really be able to change my life in terms of getting a job . . . but maybe it will because it's making me think about me differently. Maybe I'm better than I think. Maybe I know more than I think. Well, let's see if I can pass the essay first!

Learning journals for study skills (Foundation Degree in IT and Business Studies)

Abdulla, 18 September

I have been asked to write in this journal and I'm not quite sure what to write. I have never done this sort of thing before. I will start by reviewing what we did today in our study skills class. The teacher was talking about this journal first of all. She explained that the journal would be assessed and that we needed to write in it at least every week. The journal is going to help us improve our skills to help us on our courses. That's good because I am quite worried about writing essays and things. Also taking notes. But we are also supposed to reflect on our personal experiences. I don't like that idea at all. What is personal to me is not my teacher's business to know about. I am not sure what I will do about this but I don't want to be forced to write about things that are private. So I'll see how it goes. We also had a chance to meet some of the other students and that was really good. Everyone seems nice and so I think it's going to be a good year.

Anisa, 18 September

The first week of the course has been good. It has been mainly about meeting people and hearing about the course. I think I am going to like the course. I am a bit nervous about it and being able to do everything I am expected to do but the teachers seem really supportive so that's good. Also, we have had a chance to get to know the other students on the course – there are 17 others. Everyone else seems a bit nervous too, so that made me feel better. I just need to make sure I stay on top of things and I have worked out a schedule already and looked through some of the textbooks we'll be using.

Tom, 18 September

It has been an interesting week and I am excited about the course. I am a little worried that I am going to be able to keep up with everything because there is a lot of coursework to do as well as exams. But my kids will help me! That's quite funny – now I'm a student just like them. But I really want to do this and am looking forward to the year. I have a lot to learn, a lot of challenges ahead, but I am determined to do this.

Abdullah, 5 December

Reflecting back to the beginning of this course, I have found this learning journal very helpful. It has helped me to recognise my weaknesses and try to develop strategies to improve these.

For example, I am not very good at time management and organisation skills. This course has helped me to realise that if I am going to succeed on the course, and it will get harder next year when we move over to the university for a lot of the work, then I had better become more responsible about my time. But the journal has helped me to do that and to organise myself better. I have been able to work out a timetable and keep to it (well most of the time!). This has helped me to get my assignments in on time and not leave things to the last minute. When I am tempted to mess about with my friends I realise that there is work to be done and so I haven't been going out as much.

I have also been able to see what my strengths are. For example, I am good at memorising things and am good at tests. This is my best form of assessment. I am not as good at writing essays – I don't really like writing essays and tend to put it off. But I have realised that if I keep to my time, do a draft for my teacher to read in plenty of time, listen to her feedback, then I should be fine in completing the course. I don't think I'm as lazy as I used to be. But I really want to do well on this course, so I know I have to stick to my timetable and not mess about like I used to at school.

Anisa, 5 December

Looking back over the term, I have learned a lot. In terms of my study skills, I have learned how to write an essay, how to revise, take notes and all the different ways of reading. No one explained that to me before. I still get nervous about these things though but I am a lot better than before. I have more confidence.

My strengths are that I am good at writing essays. I am really pleased with my essay and the grade that I got for that. I have always liked writing and think this is one of my talents. I am also good at writing reports – and now I understand the difference between a report and an essay.

I am not that good at taking exams especially because I get so nervous about them. But I did get quite a high grade for my exam and I was pleased about that. The session we had on revision skills helped a lot. But I don't think my memory is that good and anyway I do get so worried and nervous that it stops me from doing as well as I could. I know that we could use relaxation techniques but that didn't really work for me. I got just as nervous as I always get. I hope that improves next time.

Next term I want to spend more time outside of college on studying. I have made a new timetable, which I plan to follow next term. I think if I follow this plan I will get on even better next term and learn a lot more.

Tom, 5 December

This term has been very hard for me and I am relieved that it's over. I am feeling really tired from trying to study, work and also do my bit at home. I don't think they realise how hard it is for mature students at this college.

I have a lot still to learn in the next two terms. This term has gone so fast in some ways that I can't believe it's already almost Christmas. But at the same time it feels that I have done so much.

I am pleased with the improvement in some of my skills. I take much better notes now. My writing is ok and I did better than I thought I would on my essay. But the exam was a scrape because I had to work the weekend before plus it was my son's 6th birthday so I really didn't have much time to revise. I know I should have started revising a lot earlier but it was so hard to find the time. Anyway, I passed so that's the main thing.

Next term I will concentrate on making more time for my studies. My wife is really supportive so that helps. I need to cut back on some of my hours at work and my wife and I have agreed that I should to make sure I complete the course. So it's a sacrifice for everyone – my wife, my kids and me but in the end it will pay off (I hope). But the main thing is next term, as things get even harder on the course, I need to make sure I have the time set aside to study, to do my writing and reading and to revise for my exams. This is my goal.

Teachers' CPD (continuing professional development) journals

Graham, 6 January

For my action research project I am going to look at teaching and learning in music education. I am very interested in the students' interest in music outside of school and how we can use their own interests and experiences to improve our approaches to music teaching in the classroom.

I have been asked to explore the autobiography of the question, to think about why I am interested in this research and the ways I will go about it. I have been asked to consider why I'm doing it, the social contexts, theoretical frameworks and ontology (who I am). These are new ideas to me, and a bit deep and hard, but I'll try my best!

Why I'm doing it: I guess this is related to my own experiences. I remember when I was younger that I had a wonderful teacher at school who supported my own music interests and valued different kinds of music. I want to give my students that chance and I believe that whatever music they listen to and play in their own time is valuable to their understanding of music in the school context. There are a lot of anxieties about teenagers enjoying R & B, hip hop and rap, but I think that these are legitimate forms of music in their own right. I want to challenge some of the elitism about which kinds of music are acceptable to study at school and which aren't. I want to capture the students' enthusiasm for music and use it to build up their confidence. In this way, I believe that engagement with music of all kinds can be used to raise students' achievement across a range of subjects.

Social contexts: Well, first of all the school that I work in is quite forward looking and I do have a lot of support. I have been encouraged to take this course and my colleagues are interested in what I'm doing. Then there is the national curriculum. This is constraining but I do think teachers have some room to manoeuvre and to bring excitement and creativity as well as kids' own experiences into the classroom.

Theoretical frameworks: I'm not really sure about this yet. I want to look at some of the literature on effective teaching and learning and some of the stuff on curriculum. Maybe after I have the chance to look at this literature I will start to have a better idea of my theoretical framework – I hope so!

Ontology: This is a new word for me but I think I understand what it means. I think it's about the different experiences that I will bring to the research. I understand that this has shaped my interest and once I have refined my research question this will influence the way that I ask the question.

Ros, 6 January

We had our second session today and have been asked to write in our learning journals about:

Why we want to do the research
What the social contexts are
Theoretical frameworks
Ontology

I will do my best but I'm not quite sure if I am doing this correctly.

(1) I want to do research on emotional intelligence first of all because I am responsible for my colleagues' professional development in this area. I have been working with other teachers in the school to help them understand the importance of emotional intelligence in supporting their pupils. I am personally committed to raising the profile of emotional intelligence in the school and believe that integrating certain approaches into our school improvement strategy will raise levels of attainment in the school.

(2) The social context is that in my school the head teacher supports the strategy to integrate emotional intelligence into our overall approach and has therefore asked me to take this forward. In the school I have a lot of support, although many teachers still do not see it as that important compared to their other priorities. Right now I am working mainly with head of years and overall have found them to be cooperative.

In terms of other social contexts, emotional intelligence is still not prioritised by government policy although it is recognised and there is quite a lot of literature about it. I hope this research will allow me to broaden my understanding of emotional intelligence and I would like to do more reading to develop my own skills in this area.

(3) Theoretical frameworks: I will be drawing on the key literature on emotional intelligence, which takes a broadly psychological approach. I am going to have to research this further before I can write much more about it.

(4) In relation to ontology, which I am not quite sure I understand yet, I think it just brings me back to why I'm doing the research. It is linked to my professional work. But I guess that one problem for me is that I do believe it is important and so I already have opinions about it. I am going to have to keep my opinions out of it and be objective. I want my research to be valid, reliable and objective and I am not sure how I will deal with my personal views and opinions but I know that these must be left out of the research.

Aislin, 6 January

I really enjoyed the class today. I love the idea of the autobiography of the question and welcome this exercise. I am quite passionate about my research, which is about helping pupils to formulate their own questions and actively participate in their learning. I am pleased that action research techniques value the perspectives of the teacher-researcher and enable the chance to explore my perspectives and make this part of the study. This is what I bring to the research (well as a starting point anyway).

Why I am doing the research

I am concerned that pupils in the school are often not motivated in their learning because they are not encouraged enough to actively participate. I want them to be able to use their own experiences and to make connections between these and what they are learning in their different subjects. I believe that the pupils can formulate their own questions, and then explore these, and this will enhance their understanding and boost their motivation. For the past year, I have been devising ways to do this in my classes. I would like now to research myself and my students to develop some of these strategies and to share them with the rest of the school. Some of my colleagues have shown an interest and I am excited to have this chance to conduct the research and then disseminate it to others in the school.

Social contexts

I am fortunate that at my school I have a lot of support. My pupils have been enjoying (I think) the approaches I have been drawing on over the last year. Parents have also been interested and encouraging about this. Also, I have the support of my Head, who thinks what I am trying to develop is valuable. If I didn't have that kind of support I don't think I could do it. But in terms of wider social contexts, I don't think the national curriculum is designed to help pupils formulate their own questions. So it is important that teachers find ways to use the national curriculum to get pupils to take more ownership of their learning.

Theoretical frameworks

I am really unsure about this right now but I have agreed with some of the main points made in today's session about dominant forms of knowledge and research privileging scientific and objective knowledge. I will start from the perspective that teachers' and pupils' experiences and perspectives are important to developing educational practices that help pupils to actively participate in their education.

Ontology

My position as the teacher in the classroom will have a very important impact on the research. I have certain ideas that I bring to the research including the belief that pupils' viewpoints and experiences matter and can be valuable resources in their learning. I suppose part of this belief is connected to my own experiences of school, when I often felt bored and lacked motivation because I didn't have the chance myself to participate in what and how I was learning. I want my pupils to have this opportunity.

The session today also pointed out that our social identity matters in research. I agree with this. It matters that I am a woman because I have certain experiences that a man cannot have had. I also relate to the boys and girls in my school as a woman. The fact that I am Irish also is important because I have a sense of what it feels like to be marginalised. In this way I have a compassion for some of my pupils who might also feel that they and their communities are marginalised.

Conclusions

This chapter has presented the fictional journal entries of students on Women's Studies, Business Studies and teachers' CPD programmes. Although the journal writing is imaginary it draws on our own experiences, research and observations in different educational settings. Of course, these are just part of the dialogical relations of assessed work. We have not written in tutor comments, marks or grades, nor have we suggested what the students may say or feel, or how they might act, on receipt of tutor feedback.

The journal entries explore various issues that need to be brought to light analytically and theoretically in order to deepen our understanding of the challenges and opportunities around lifelong learning policy and practice. These include for example, the ways that learner identities get constructed and re/constructed through and against hegemonic discourses; the interconnections between different social positionings and the processes of becoming a learner; the emotional aspects of learning and the ways these are intimately connected with personal experience and social relations; and the complex interplay between identifications and processes of resistances. We will be drawing out and examining these issues in close detail in the next section of the book.

Section III

Revisioning

We created a maze of contradictions. Black and white Americans danced a fancy and often dangerous do-si-do. In our steps forward, abrupt turns, sharp spins and reverses, we became our own befuddlement. . . . We were indeed travelling, but no one knew our destination nor our arrival date.

(Maya Angelou, *The Heart of a Woman*)

In this section we will reconstruct the above stories as analytical rather than narrative accounts. Each of the chapters will draw on the previous section to give an overview of the four (sometimes overlapping) groups of storytellers. They will explore specific themes of identities, differences, power, knowing and knowledge, emotions and resistances. The key aim of this section is to reconsider the narrative section in light of theoretical insights from feminism, sociology and post-structuralism, drawing out emergent themes, issues and debates and critically considering these through making dis/connections with literature in the field in order to develop these further.

Chapter 8

Revisioning identities and subjectivities

Introduction

This chapter explores identities and subjectivities drawing on the stories in the previous section but paying particular attention to gender, social class and cultural differences. The issues that we have already raised in this book about hierarchies of learning and knowledge are shaped and compounded by gendered, classed and racialised identities. We will argue that policies and practices around lifelong learning need to address ways in which identities shape, construct and constrain both participation in and definitions of learning. Whilst this chapter will argue that identities are fluid, multiple and contradictory, it will show that there are also structures in place that reinforce gendered, classed and racialised social divisions, and challenge assumptions around learning identities. We draw on feminist post-structuralist perspectives to consider the ways that learners' identities are both discursive and structural, and are tied to social inequalities as well as cultural mis-recognitions. This theoretical framework highlights the importance of theories of identity for understanding the ways in which learner dis/identifications get made and performed through the hegemonic discourses at play within educational fields and policy texts as well as through the constraints and opportunities presented by the different educational contexts in which learners and teachers are located.

Feminist work reveals the importance of concepts of power for understanding who counts as a learner and who does not. Feminist theory also emphasises the importance of understanding the ways that knowledge is always tied to power. Therefore, in order to transform educational spaces, it is crucial to problematise the meanings constructed by privileged groups by drawing on the accounts and experiences of those from marginalised social positions. Feminist perspectives work towards social justice and revealing the multiple layers of injustices that operate around processes of identity formation. Post-structuralism sheds light on the multiple, contradictory and shifting sense of self that unsettles hegemonic versions of the individual as a coherent, rational and decontextualised self. Such insights are important in understanding the complex processes by which learners and learning get fashioned and refashioned through contradictory policies, practices, and discourses.

Identity as a concept is contested and multiple and there are several useful ways of thinking about identity that help to understand how some people come to take up the position of learner and others come to reject it. For example, Côté and Levene (2002) introduce the concept of identity capital to explain the assets accumulated by some members of society through social environments. Identity capital includes intangible resources such as ego strength, locus of control and self-esteem, all of which can be determined through class consciousness. A sense of identity can be embodied in the occupation of a working-class or middle-class habitus. Although Côté has argued that the development of identity capital enables learners to take control of their own lives, he suggests that young people have tended to 'drift from image to image' rather than become 'pilots of their own destinies' (Côté 1996: 423). However, we will show that identity formation is rooted in complex layers and shifting patterns of contexts, micro-politics and wider struggles over meaning and knowledge. Stuart Hall (2000) conceptualises identity as a continual process of becoming through identifications, a discursive project that is however always linked back to particular social and personal histories and experiences that are connected with deeply embedded social and material inequalities and differences.

Subjectivity and identity

Subjectivity is about our sense of self – our conscious and unconscious thoughts, feelings and emotions (issues we will develop in the next chapter). Subjectivities are experienced in social and discursive contexts, and the meanings attached to these experiences, both by ourselves and others, lead to the formations of identity. By 'identity' we include our positionings as, for example, white, working-class, female, disabled etc., and the meanings attached to these. We are interested in what these identities signify to ourselves and others, and how we develop and name our subjective selves, our sense of who we are.

We shall argue that 'identity' is a negotiated and contested space, and is multi-faceted, fragmented and ever changing. The discursive constitution of subjectivities and identities is located within debates and policies that generate particular understandings of inclusion and exclusion. Notions of self are always tied to notions of the other, and disidentifications and othering are key processes in the formation of self. Concepts of self are never neutral. They are located within constructions of insiders and outsiders, determining who is recognised or recognises themselves as an insider or outsider and therefore who is considered a 'legitimate learner' and who is not. Located within discourses of personal agency, structural inequalities and exclusions are often ignored. In this chapter we shall bring together a range of issues regarding identity and subjectivity, with a particular focus on marginalised identities. This will shed light on the range of social identities as learners and the micro and macro political struggles that take place over the representation of learners. But hegemonic representations inform understandings of what it means to be a learner and define the field and what is possible within it as well as determine policies (and practices) of lifelong learning. They determine what it is possible or impossible to be.

As we argued in Chapter 2, academic knowledge, the privileged form of knowledge within higher education and other educational sites, is constructed as 'objective', 'value-free', evidence-based, rational and produced through reason and scientific inquiry. However, feminist work has argued that academic knowledge is embedded in culturally specific and contextualised epistemologies, which has operated to marginalise certain (feminised) forms of knowing, such as private, emotional, intuitive or experiential knowledge. As a result, particular ontological positions and identifications, for example working-class, homosexual, feminine and disabled, have been and continue to be marginalised within educational fields, although this is often subtle, insidious, implicit and denied. Academic knowledge is partial because it excludes experiences of marginalised identities, but it is also distorted when those who produce knowledge fail to recognise their own social/cultural/historic locations.

> Precisely because identities are constructed within, not outside, discourse, we need to understand them as produced in specific historical and institutional sites within specific discursive formations and practices, by specific enunciative strategies. Moreover, they emerge within the play of specific modulations of power, and thus are more the product of the marking of difference and exclusion. . . . Above all . . . identities are constructed through, not outside, difference.
>
> (Hall 2000: 17)

We turn to the narrative chapters to illustrate some of these points. For example, in Chapter 4, we look at the struggles over identity positions and having a voice in policy-making. Mustafa attempts to represent the voices of support staff in the college and to highlight the important contribution that he and his colleagues can make to policy-formation around issues of student retention. There is a sense though that Mustafa's efforts might be marginalised in the college and this is connected to hierarchical identities within educational institutions and perceptions over who has the right to make important policy decisions. Similarly, in Chapter 6, we see how Aisha feels that her identity has all but disappeared in the new structures in which she finds herself: 'she feels like nothing because she does nothing'.

In Chapter 5, the discussion between educational managers highlights some of the struggles over learner identities in relation to age, with the emphasis currently in policy on younger learners. Some of the managers are concerned to represent the perspectives of mature and older students, as well as learners from under-represented groups. However, the managers must work within the prevailing frameworks of policy and practice, which operate around instrumentalist notions of the value of lifelong learning. Such notions discount and undermine the importance of supporting the development of mature learners' identities because they might be seen as less 'employable' and as having less to offer to the national economy.

Considering difference

Identity is as much about difference as it is about a shared sense of belonging, and considerations of 'difference' will be central to this chapter. Differences are always tied in with wider social inequalities, and the hegemonic discourse of 'diversity' works to conceal the operation of injustices within educational fields. Diversity is often constructed in largely positive terms, for example 'celebrating diversity', and yet the underpinning inequalities are left unaddressed and hidden within the diversity discourse. Simultaneously, those from under-represented groups are often constructed in negative and deficit terms, for example lacking the right values, skills, motivation and aspirations. Recently, with statistics used to point to shifting gender relations in the favour of women, women's success is often perceived and presented as a threat to men's status and place in society, rather than a positive development in the context of a long history of gender inequality. These have important implications for identity formations, with working-class women learners often constructing themselves as undeserving of university access (Reay 2001, 2003; Reay et al. 2001), or men constructing themselves as victims of the feminist movement. However, hegemonic discourses can also be subverted, challenged and rejected. For example, Mirza (2003: 131) talks of identities of refusal in relation to the ways that Black women are able to resist dominant discourses, to redefine the world according to their own values, codes and understandings, although this is far from always being the case. Narinder (Chapter 5) identifies as a Black woman but finds it difficult to redefine the academic world in which she finds herself placed in the lifelong learning managers' network, whilst Aisha (Chapter 6) states that her identity as a Black woman has resulted in her being devalued as a professional educator. Identities of refusal can be difficult and lonely.

Avtar Brah and Ann Phoenix (2004) argue that 'difference' should be conceptualised as social relation, experience, subjectivity and identity. Our discussions will include questions about difference as experience (the ways in which we make sense of the world in which we find ourselves); difference as ideology; structural differences; difference as political; and difference as subjectivity and identity. Drawing on the work of Brah and Phoenix, we agree that intersectionality is a key concept in discussions of difference, so that social class, for example, and its intersections with gender and 'race' is simultaneously subjective, structural and about social positioning and everyday practices.

> We regard the concept of 'intersectionality' as signifying the complex, irreducible, varied, and variable effects which ensue when multiple axes of differentiation – economic, political, cultural, psychic, subjective and experiential – intersect in historically specific contexts. The concept emphasizes that different dimensions of social life cannot be separated out into discrete and pure strands.
>
> (Brah and Phoenix 2004: 76)

However, the different social and political contexts in which we experience our identities means that we do not always recognise intersectionality in the ways in which we perceive ourselves. Jim (Chapter 6), for example, described himself as a gay man, whilst Sally (Chapter 6) identifies as a working-class woman. Neither of them consider 'whiteness' as an aspect of identity. There remains a persistence of unexamined assumptions about disabilities and sexualities, with cultural perceptions based in normalised discourses and unchallenged beliefs (Ware 2001).

Notions of intersectionality are important in making sense of some of these cultural perceptions, including how learners fashion their identities around complex and intersecting social differences. For example, in Chapter 7 Carla's identification or disidentification as a student on Women's Studies is connected to her gender but also to her working-class, heterosexual and white racialised positioning. Her complex identifications make her resistant to the feminist literature she engages with because she does not recognise herself in the texts. Furthermore, notions of intersectionality are important in understanding who is constructed as the ideal lifelong learning subject and who is not. When women begin to participate in university courses in greater numbers than men, then they are constructed as 'taking over' the university (Quinn 2003) and thus threatening men's (natural) social position. Men students become constructed as victims of those women who are seen as 'unfeminine' and unnaturally ambitious, assertive and competitive.

However, in order to make sense of contemporary shifts in gender relations, it is important to address the ways that gender intersects with other social differences. Men, for example, do not equally participate in higher education, and men's participation in higher education is classed and racialised. Despite increased numbers of women undertaking degree level study, there continue to be some groups of women who are under-represented at university. It remains the subject of debate as to whether increased numbers of women students have changed university cultures at all. Another key issue is around the popular notion of lowering standards and the way that it is linked with widening participation. Why, when certain groups of people begin to access higher education, is this seen as evidence of declining standards? This cannot only be understood in terms of gender but also in relation to social class, disability, ethnicity and race.

Identity and power

> All identities are not equally available to all of us, and all identities are not equally culturally valued. Identities are fundamentally enmeshed in relations of power.
>
> (Roseneil and Seymour 1999: 2)

Power is a central concept in understanding the complex formations of identity in relation to social difference and inequality. Power is intimately connected to meaning-making processes, social relations, the ways certain discourses gain hegemony, the formation of policy and the ways certain identities are legitimated, valued and privileged within and across educational contexts. Power operates at all levels of social life; including global, national, regional, institutional, local and individual. Identities are always tied to shifting power relations. Drawing on the insights of post-structuralism, we find Foucault's theory of power useful, conceptualising power as discursive and exercised rather than possessed, and as always in circulation. However, as feminist sociologists we also are interested in the ways that power is linked to wider structural inequalities and tied to complex sets of difference including, for example, age, class, ethnicity, gender, disability, nationality, religion and sexuality. In this way we draw on the concept of intersectionality in relation to power.

Let us turn to the narrative chapters to illustrate the ways that power operates at the national as well as local levels. In Chapter 4, for example, we see that policy-making in the national government context, is regulated by those in more senior positions, and so although there is some space for negotiation, the final text is largely produced through the power relations of the hierarchical structures within government agencies. Those in higher positions in government are, unsurprisingly, occupying more powerful positions in relation to forming policy, and so lifelong learning policy is more likely to reflect the interests of those who already occupy powerful positions. Because the majority of higher-level posts in government bodies are held by white, middle-class men then it is likely that the assumptions, values and perspectives of these groups will be given prominence in policy documents.

In Chapter 5 we see the production of agenda and minutes tied to institutional power relations, including ways in which written documents create their own stories and histories. The first meeting of the lifelong learning managers network is being chaired by a white man in a secure institutional position in higher education, illustrative of the hierarchical positioning of universities in lifelong learning. In addition to Andy, the other key player at the meeting is Stephen, another white man in a secure institutional position. Andy and Stephen both lead much of the discussion, and aim to set the agenda of this and future meetings. Whilst some of the other members of the network try to contribute to shaping the agenda, they are generally unsuccessful. In the main, points made by most of the women (and some of the men outside of traditional educational contexts) appear not to be taken seriously. Some of the women have little to say, including Hafsa, although being a minute-taker can effectively prevent full contribution to a meeting. Although we know that Hafsa agreed to be minute taker, we do not know under what circumstances. When the Chair asked for a volunteer, did Hafsa volunteer? Was she asked or coerced? Did she agree straight away or was there a silence waiting to be filled? Was it her gendered identity that led her to agree to service the meeting? Minutes tell some of the story, but there is much that we do not know.

As both policy and management frame educational practice, assumptions, values and perspectives filter down to local contexts, so that an individual teacher who might want to challenge some of the assumptions of policy and/or managers will be significantly constrained in their attempts. For example, we see from Jim's story (Chapter 6) that he holds a set of professional values that are being constantly challenged by institutional hierarchies derived from centrally determined lifelong learning policies, until they become subsumed under hegemonic meanings of professionalism. Some of the managers in Chapter 5 also face similar issues. For example, discussion about foundation degrees clearly highlights the ideological and real clashes that individuals face when confronted by competing discourses, some of which have the political and financial power that comes from their location in policy. Through these operations of power, the values, perspectives and cultures of privileged groups in society get re-privileged and reinforced and this is beyond the scope of the individual to control or change.

In Chapters 5 and 6 a theme emerges around the identity position of part-time workers in educational institutions and the ways the structures around part-time work significantly reduce the power of such workers to contribute to meaning-making in their places of work. Although Sally (Chapter 6) expresses some of the pleasures of portfolio working, several of the managers express real concern at the lack of political power held by a part-time workforce which consists largely of women, who – as Judith suggests (Chapter 5) – are in the main expected to comply with rather than determine policies and practices. This leads to constructions of identities of part-time workers both by themselves and others in ways which see them dismissed as 'irrelevant' (Chapter 6).

Chapter 7 highlights the important ways that learner identities get constructed through power relations within certain courses. The Women's Studies course uses key literature and the pedagogical tool of learning journals to encourage learners to explore and critique their identity positions in the context of wider gender relations. Although the aim is to empower women, because there are multiple and contradictory differences between women's gendered identities, Women's Studies might be experienced as disempowering and exclusive. As Jennifer Gore (1993) has argued, women might experience feminist pedagogy as yet another regime of truth and disciplinary mechanism.

The Study Skills course (Chapter 7) also regulates the identities of learners so that they can learn to become 'better' students, examining their individual strengths and weaknesses through their learning journals and taking responsibility for improving their study skills. Such an approach does not address complex power relations and the social contexts in which the students are situated. Study skills are seen simply as mechanical skills that are neutral and outside of power relations. On the other hand, the teachers' CPD course uses the journals to encourage the teachers to shift their views from large-scale, positivist methodological perspectives to thinking about research as autobiographical and understanding the importance of ontological questions for constructing classroom-based, practitioner research. This approach recognises power relations and attempts to engage teachers in critically examining the power relations of their classrooms through their research projects, and enabling them to begin to examine their own subject positionings and identities. The autobiography of the question (Miller 1995) encourages the students to narrate the self as a key subject of the research methodology.

Narrating the self

What are the stories we tell about ourselves or others? What stories do others tell of us? In what ways do these stories reinforce or disrupt our identities as learners? Ways in which we narrate the self evidence how we construct and represent ourselves in different locations, and the ways in which meaning is made and communicated. In hegemonic discourses of lifelong learning, the notion of the 'individual' is privileged, reinforcing assumptions around ability, potential, aspiration, achievement, success and failure. The emphasis in policy on the individual learner locates problems of under-achievement, drop-out, low motivation, lack of aspiration, poor skills, etc. in the individual learner and ignores the social structures, relations and contexts, material inequalities, cultural misrecognitions and dominant discourses that reproduce and exacerbate exclusions and divisions.

For example, in Chapter 7, the learners narrate themselves in ways that produce their identities often in relation to deficit discourses. Gloria for example, narrates herself as having the wrong kind of cultural capital: however this is perceived as tied to her own personal weaknesses rather than wider social divisions and inequities. Through engagement with feminist theories she begins to see that her personal experiences are valuable and that she does have a contribution to make, drawing on her experiences of forms of unpaid work such as mothering. However, critical theories also raise uncertainties for learner identities, causing anxieties, anger and distancing from the learner identity, a position expressed both in Gloria's and in Carla's journals. Taken-for-granted assumptions about gender and sexuality are unsettled by feminist literature and this causes emotional reactions from the learners who firmly embrace or reject feminist perspectives in relation to how they know themselves. This could lead learners such as Carla to drop out of their courses, and raises important issues for feminist pedagogy and curriculum. Identities are always tied in with social differences such as class and 'race' and this emerges in the accounts. For example, Carla claims that she does not 'speak that well' and that others in the class are 'posh and clever'. Carla's narrative must be contextualised in relation to wider class politics and particularly the ways that working-class women have been and continue to be constructed as potentially corrupted and corrupting (Purvis 1987; Skeggs 1997, 2004).

In relation to classed identities and the ways that speech is perceived as a signifier of intelligence levels, academic literacies are a key mechanism of reproducing social differences and notions of who deserves to participate in higher education and who does not. The learners demonstrate this particularly when they consider study skills and their supposed lack of these key skills, which are largely conceptualised as mechanical or technical skills rather than social practices, both by the learners and within the educational institutions as well. Abdullah (Chapter 7), for example, is particularly worried about writing essays and Teresa Lillis has critiqued 'essayist literacies' in universities in relation to the ways they keep gendered, classed and racialised identities in place and are highly exclusive practices (see also Introduction to Section II and Chapter 2). Angelina (Chapter 7) has started to realise that there is a 'hypocrisy' in the academy which values literary and theoretical perspectives over experiential ones. Perhaps unsurprisingly, the ways that the learners narrate themselves is often in terms of lack and this reflects wider constructions of 'widening participation students' who are seen to lack the skills required to succeed at university and as contributing to the lowering of university standards. The role of language is key in determining identity, including ways in which some people recognise themselves as learners whilst others do not. The loss of the subjective 'I' in academic writing to a supposed objective and impartial neutrality of language can also lead to a loss of personal identity, especially when being academic appears to be far removed from the realities of lived experiences (Jackson 2004).

As the students in Chapter 7 show, the use of auto/biography in academic work can be one way to reclaim identities and deconstruct the supposed objectivity of academic writing, blurring the boundaries within our learning lives. As Aislin (Chapter 7) shows, she enjoys working through the autobiography of the question which helps her as a teacher to consider and engage with her own professional development. This approach enables her to begin from her own ontological position and the ways that this leads her to particular research and professional interests. Similarly, in Chapter 6 we meet teachers as learners, developing their own reflective practices through narrating themselves, sharing stories told through auto/biography. However, despite the (assumed) confidentiality of the action learning set, the storytellers need to think carefully about what it is they want to disclose about themselves, for disclosure can at times be a dangerous and foolish act (Burn 2001). As Beverley Skeggs (2003) has shown, we should stay alert to the dangers of 'forced telling'. Pedagogies that engage learners in reflexive approaches could be exacerbating positions of marginalisation by forcing those in less powerful positions to narrate themselves and expose their identifications which may carry risks of further marginalisation and exclusion. This has been an issue for many women in the academy, both teachers and learners, including ourselves:

> it has been important to me to locate myself within (my) writing, acknowledging my own subjectivity and identity within language and to include my own voice throughout (my) work. However . . . I have also at times felt denied by academic language, and it has sometimes been hard to find the words. I need to find answers to the questions asked by Audre Lorde:

>> What are the words you do not yet have? What do you need to say? What are the tyrannies you swallow day by day and attempt to make your own, until you will sicken and die of them?
>>
>> (Lorde 1984: 41
>
> (Jackson 2004: xiii)

And yet sometimes we are forced to swallow the tyrannies for, should we not do so, we can find ourselves dismissed as irrelevant, in much the same way as Aisha

(Chapter 6). Diane Reay has argued that: 'The academy has traditionally demonstrated limited tolerance for lived experience which it dismisses as anecdotal or as stories; it is an affront to scholarly sensibilities' (Reay 1998: 15).

We thought very seriously about the implications for our academic identities in writing the previous section, knowing what we may risk in telling the stories as we have.

Working-class academics can find themselves constantly battling with constructions of identities, constantly making decisions about how to locate themselves in which fields. Women who define themselves as working class by birth and/ or community can find themselves having to subjugate their working-class identities to adopt the language and cultural codes that education and work often seem to demand (Jackson 2003; Anderson 2001). 'Naming' takes complex lives which become presented or inscribed as simplistic and/or unitary. Separate narrative constructions of gender, race and class mean the subject is male in racial discourse; white in gendered discourse; and in class discourse race has no place (Mirza 2003: 134).

Women live and produce themselves through social and cultural relations: class, femininity and sexuality all impact on how we inhabit and occupy social and cultural positions (see Skeggs 1997). It is not, then, surprising that many women have contradictory feelings about their class positioning (see Jackson 1998). As Pauline Anderson shows 'I, like many other women of working-class origin, still do not feel that I inhabit the academy in the same way as students and colleagues of middle-class origin' (2001: 141). Location, class, ethnicity and gender all impact on identity constructions.

> The production of meaning is . . . a necessary condition for the functioning of all social practices. An individual's identification with shared social meaning, constitutes identity formation and can be seen as a process of reality construction through which social actors interpret particular events, actions or situations in distinctive ways. It therefore provides the mechanism by which individuals can make sense of their social practices.
>
> (Chappell 1999: 2)

Or not, of course! At times that sense is determined by others, and at times there is no sense to be found. Both individuals and structural conditions impact onto our identities, but so too do our roots, and the routes that we tread.

Learning journeys

Although we move on here to introduce the notion of learning journeys, this metaphor, whilst seeming to introduce notions of choice, growth and development, can also be viewed as problematic: 'Learner as a traveller suggests a certain category of person: an autonomous and enterprising individual, rationally choosing the mode, pace, direction and destination of their learning journey' (Harrison 2003: 4).

Part of the 'work' which the metaphor of the journey does . . . is to provide a discursive context in which related ideas, such as 'ladders of learning', 'routes for success' or 'pathways to opportunity' are easily assimilated, and in which policy developments such as credit accumulation and transfer, targets and learning outcomes are readily understood.

(Harrison 2003: 2)

Harrison argues that institutional structures, funding regimes and qualifications systems all work to ensure that some learning journeys are less stressful than others (Harrison 2003: 4). But so do structures of class, race, gender, sexuality and disability. Learning is a product of social practices and constructions as much or more than it is about institutional structures and/or individual achievements. Whilst Carla (Chapter 7) has started to value her worth and has learned that she may be better than she had recognised, Gloria (also Chapter 7) is feeling marginalised and insecure in her identity within the university.

What then are the multiple discourses that build up our 'academic' or workplace identities? How do teachers (and managers and policy-makers, as well as students) learn who they are? The workplace is both a site of cultural formation and a site where identity is constructed. Writing about raced and gendered workplace iterations, Patricia Parker states:

Power relations are patterned through taken-for-granted often hidden assump-tions about gender and race that are embedded in organisational discourses and that privilege the experiences and interests of dominant racial and gender groups – non-dominant cultural interests and experiences are suppressed, devalued and muted.

(Parker 2002: 1)

It is clear from all the chapters in Section II that hierarchies of identities work in powerful ways, with identities being constructed and reconstructed continuously. For example, as Chapter 6 demonstrated: 'Teachers are faced with renegotiating an identity out of the competing discourses that now insert different and often contradictory meaning-making practices in the institutional life of the organisation' (Chappell 1999: 6).

The teachers in Chapter 6, as well as the learners in Chapter 7, all give personal-ised accounts, although for the learners this may well have involved 'forced telling' (Skeggs 2003). Whilst feminists have long argued for the inclusion of personal experience within 'academic' accounts, the personalised accounts that now pre-dominate are based in individualism rather than the collectivity of feminisms. Today most learners are expected to participate in some form of personalised learning, including personal development planning, portfolios, diaries and logbooks. Whilst these *should*, potentially, be part of a positive inclusion of feminist pedagogies, it has been argued that they are instead part of the discourse of managerialism, performativity and quality assurance, linked to a globalised knowledge economy

(David 2005). The personal is now deeply embedded in learning accounts, but what this means is uncontested. The contrasting learning journals of the Women's Studies and Foundation Degree students serves to highlight the different political, ideological and policy contexts of personalised learning. The individualised personal accounts of today move away from collectivism of feminist pedagogies, with an emphasis on individual rather than collaborative performance.

There is currently a policy language based in individual choice/aspiration which negates sharing/collectivity. Theories of learning styles often assume simplistic models and 'types' of learners. This rests on notions of individual personalities, which can be classified rationally and simplistically, rather than discursively constructed social identifications which are continually shifting, fluid and contradictory. Explanations for retention are based on causal relationships rather than understanding the complexities of learners (and teachers). They are based on the notion that through certain rational educational practices, individual teachers (with the 'correct training' and professional values – see Chapter 6) can control student behaviour and reduce 'wastage'. However, this overlooks complex pedagogical relations and the decisions students make, not only at the individual level but also as a consequence of complicated sets of social practices and relations which are tied to institutional, structural and material inequalities as well as cultural misrecognitions and marginalisations.

Martin Bloomer and colleagues, for example, ask:

> What should you do, for instance, if you discover that low entry qualifications are associated with low retention? . . . (T)he logical response is to raise entry qualifications. Of course, not all colleges can raise their entry qualifications at will; they have classes to fill and are not necessarily able to turn away students in significant numbers. Those that can, might do so, with the result that the displaced students are enrolled by a neighbouring college not able to raise its entry requirements. Through such processes inequalities are exacerbated, ironically at the very time that the government is pinning its educational credibility to notions of inclusivity and the like.
>
> (Bloomer *et al.* 2002)

> (A particular student's) withdrawal is more comprehensively understood as having taken place against the background of continually changing *configurations* of meanings, interests, values and perceptions. It was a particular configuration at a particular time that presented the conditions under which . . . she elected to withdraw.
>
> (Bloomer 2001: 443)

However, whilst we agree with this analysis, it does not show the complexities of relationships (structural as well as individual) between teachers, managers and policy-makers. Nor does it highlight the structural positionings of learners or the implications for learner identities. Classed, raced and gendered expectations impact on the formation of young people's identities, and so also on their occupational expectations and aspirations, and on their choice of learning opportunities. However, they also impact on the expectations of others for lifelong learning (and career) opportunities for both learners and teachers. Some aspirations are sanctioned and others are not, and this is tied to social positioning. For example, Ali (Chapter 7) wants to be a boxer but this is not sanctioned by his parents who want him to be a doctor. Of course, material needs of working-class families are different from those of middle-class families, and aspirations differ for minority ethnic families, and it is therefore not surprising that economic concerns and career opportunities should be a prime concern.

Martin Bloomer and colleagues argue that:

> Little work has been done on the formation of young people's vocational identities and yet there are compelling reasons why it ought to have been done. Over the last forty years there have been significant social and labour market changes contributing to potentially significant changes in young people's horizons for action and vocational identification.
>
> (Bloomer *et al.* 2002)

Helen Colley and colleagues (2003) suggest that although official accounts of learning in vocational education and training emphasise the acquisition of technical skills and knowledge to foster behavioural competence in the workplace, such accounts fail to acknowledge the relationship between learning and identity. They argue that learning is a process of becoming. Learning cultures and the vocational cultures in which they are steeped transform those who enter them. They develop the concept of 'vocational habitus' to explain a central aspect of students' experience, as they have to orient to a particular set of dispositions – both idealised and realised. They use the term 'vocational habitus' to indicate vocation as a calling, and so show how people from certain groupings are 'called' whilst others are excluded. Learning sites shape students' abilities to respond to complex influences and demands within a vocational culture. As we have shown in the previous section, the same is true for academics and other players in the lifelong learning arena. Vocational habitus conveys both the 'sense' and the 'sensibility' (Colley *et al.* 2003: 492) and shows the role of class and gender (and of course race, disability, sexuality, age and so forth) in socially reproductive processes. Predispositions related to gender, family background and specific locations within the working class are necessary, but not sufficient for effective learning. Vocational habitus reinforces and develops these in line with demands of the workplace, although it may reproduce social inequalities at the same time (Colley *et al.* 2003).

Diaspora

Habitus is a concept developed by Pierre Bourdieu (1977), and describes the sense we have both of our own place and that of others. Our perceptions of both place and space (for ourselves and others) affect our actions and interactions, as well as the possibilities for reflexive practices (McNay 1999). Perceptions of place and space are useful for us in considering ways in which we can use 'diaspora' to explore questions of identity. In this final section, we turn to concepts of diaspora to help explain the connection between identity formation across time and space through the experiences of migration (Brah 1996). In extending our understandings of the ways in which learner dis/identifications get made and performed we consider disapora to develop our exploration of learner identities and subjectivities. This is especially important in so-called postmodern times, where 'individuals are held more and more accountable for their own survival in a time where change is the only certainty' (Ball *et al.* 2000: 2).

Diasporan identities are produced through dispersal and homelessness, including the dispersal of learners and teachers in and through institutional and other lifelong learning contexts. This is especially true for those forced to leave behind them identities of, for example, social class or sexuality, as well as identities of politics and ideologies. It is clear from some of the stories in the previous section that this is a difficult and painful process, not just determining identities but also in the ways in which we develop and name our subjective selves, our sense of who we are.

In her work, Avtar Brah (1996) intersperses the concept of diaspora with theories of borders and feminist politics. As Avtar Brah and Anne Phoenix explain:

> The intersection of these three terms is understood through the concept of 'diaspora space' which covers the entanglements of genealogies of dispersal with those of 'staying put'. The term 'homing desire' is used to think through the question of home and belonging; and both power and time are viewed as multidimensional processes. Importantly, the concept of 'diaspora space' embraces the intersection of 'difference' in its variable forms, placing emphasis upon emotional and psychic dynamics as much as socio-economic, political and cultural differences. Difference is thus conceptualised as social relation; experience; subjectivity; and identity.
>
> (Brah and Phoenix 2004: 83)

Many of the characters in Section II cross within and between borders, entering and negotiating diasporan space. This includes borders of home, work and places of learning, differently negotiated for women and for men, as well as borders of identity: gay and lesbian identities, classed identities, identities of 'race', and so forth.

In considering diaspora and cultural identity Stuart Hall (1990) describes:

> the traumatic character of the 'colonial experience'. The ways in which black people, black experiences, were positioned and subject-ed in the dominant regimes of representation were the effects of a critical exercise of cultural power and normalisation. Not only . . . were we constructed as different and other within the categories of knowledge of the West by those regimes. They

had the power to make us see and experience ourselves as 'Other'. . . . [I]t is one thing to position a subject or set of peoples as the Other of a dominant discourse. It is quite another to subject them to that knowledge . . . by the power of inner compulsion and subjective confirmation to the norm.

(Hall 1990: 223–4)

It is clear from the preceding section that gendered, racialised, classed and sexualised subjects are constructed as and/or construct the 'Other', through a sense of un/belonging, of homelessness and of macro- and micro-border crossings, sometimes experienced on a daily basis. Post 9/11 and July 7, identities are also prescribed through anti-Muslim racism, as well as through the racism of colonialism and Eurocentrism. With the creation of the neo-liberal subject, border crossings become confirmed and ever more difficult to transcend or journey around.

Conclusions

We have in this chapter argued that the deconstruction of policies and practices of lifelong learning reveal the multiple layers of injustices that operate around processes of identity formation. Learner identities are discursive as well as structural, tied to social inequalities and cultural misrecognitions. We have shown how power is central to understandings of the complex formations of identity in relation to social difference and inequality, including through the ways we are able to narrate ourselves. We have drawn on some of the learning (and other) journeys and stories told in Section II to show how hierarchies of identities work in powerful ways, with identities being constructed and reconstructed both openly and through hidden operations of power and discursive practices. If learning is a process of becoming, what and who we become is subject to structural and ideological inequalities. Finally we have turned to concepts of diaspora to help develop our understandings of learner identities and subjectivities, including through the sometimes painful processes of negotiating diasporan spaces. In the next chapter, we continue this discussion through a consideration of learning and emotion.

Chapter 9

Revisioning emotions

Introduction

This chapter will draw on Section II to demonstrate that emotion profoundly influences the ways in which individuals and groups participate in and experience learning. It will continue to interrogate the current frameworks of lifelong learning that rest on dichotomies privileging knowledge constructed as objective, scientific and rational and marginalising knowledge constructed as subjective, irrational and emotional. As we have shown in earlier chapters, 'knowledge' is always socially embedded, underpinned by particular values and perspectives. This chapter will argue that current constructions of knowledge undermine the contribution of emotions to learning. We begin the chapter by exploring concepts of 'emotional capital' and 'emotional labour', and move on to explore emotion with regard to identity and 'difference'. Although 'emotion' is excluded from current conceptualisations of lifelong learning, we argue that identities are shaped by emotional as well as rational processes. We end the chapter by engaging in a debate about emotional literacy, and considering the role of emotion in our own professional identitites. We ask for the role of emotion in lifelong learning to be re/visioned, recognising that emotions are constructed, contested, and as much a part of the development of 'knowledge' as supposed objectivity and rationality.

Emotional capital

Bourdieu's economic metaphors of cultural, social and symbolic capital have been enormously valuable for understanding the ways that classed identities are produced at different levels beyond the material and economic. Sets of capital are legitimised in society, enabling certain groups to enjoy their inherited privileges but also reproducing inequalities. In this chapter we extend this metaphor to the emotional and consider the ways in which certain emotional capitals operate within and outside of educational discursive fields in the interests of particular groups. As Diane Reay explains, the concept of 'emotional capital' was developed by Nowotny, who:

> saw emotional capital as a variant of social capital, but characteristic of the private, rather than the public sphere (Nowotny 1981). Emotional capital is

generally confined within the bounds of affective relationships of family and friends and encompasses the emotional resources you hand on to those you care about. According to Nowotny, emotional capital constitutes knowledge, contacts and relations as well as access to emotionally valued skills and assets, which hold within any social network characterised at least partly by affective ties.

(Nowotny 1981: 148, cited in Reay 2002: 5)

Whilst we agree with Nowotny that there is a clear relationship between social capital and emotional capital in relation to networks and trust, we do not agree that social capital belongs to the public sphere and emotional to the private. Social capital is defined in terms of the development of networks, norms and trust and, whilst this is more usually considered part of the public sphere (Schuller *et al.* 2000), social capital is also accumulated by women in the private sphere, although it is not necessarily recognised as such (Jackson 2004b). In the same way, whilst Nowotny and others have argued that emotional capital is confined to familiar and friendship relationships, it is also accumulated, and certainly spent, in the public spheres of work and community. Women are expected to come to work with a pool of emotional capital: resources to be used for the benefits of others. Their engagement in the emotional labour of the workforce (see below) will then replenish those resources.

Reay (2002) suggests that emotional capital is not just gendered but also classed. Poverty, she argues, is not an enviornment in which emotional capital can thrive, whilst economic security and high social status enhance emotional well-being. With regard to lifelong learning, Reay sugests that middle-class emotional investments in learning give higher capital returns in comparison to the emotional investments of working-class people, which are comparatively more risky and insecure. However, Heidi Mirza (2003) suggests that marginalised groups such as Black and minority ethnic women can find new and resourceful ways to collectively network. This can lead to transformative agency by combining social and emotional capital, opening up a 'third space' (between public/private) of strategic engagement, finding other ways of knowing (Mirza 2003: 135). By encouraging her learners to support each other and to network collaboratively to open new social spaces, Hafsa (Chapter 5) tries to enable her learners to develop agency.

Nevertheless, as we have already shown, women are generally capital poor in relation to men. They have less (and/or less valued) economic, cultural and social capital than men, but they do have higher levels of emotional capital. This is because hegemonic forms of femininity rest on emotional, rather than rational, ways of being. Women historically have been constructed as less able to think rationally and as driven to act by their emotions. Intuition, irrationality and feeling have been associated with femininity and women's knowledge has been relegated to the personal, private, domestic realms of social life.

In contemporary society, where industry has shifted from masculinised forms of manufacturing to feminised forms of service, women's ability to draw on emotional ways of knowing has become a valuable (although gendered) commodity for them to possess. Nevertheless, emotional capital lacks the convertibility of other capitals, such as cultural capital and economic capital. The emotional is still seen as separate and as less than the rational, and emotion is not seen as a form of capital that requires sophisticated forms of understanding to acquire. Nowotny (1981) suggests that emotional capital develops in adverse circumstances, responding to barriers rather than to potential possibilities. As Reay explains:

> [Nowotny] asserts that the important question we need to ask about gender differences in capital is 'why women have been able to accumulate only certain kinds of capital and why they have been equally limited in converting the capital they have gained into certain other types'.
>
> (Nowotny 1981: 148, in Reay 2002)

In the home, the workplace and within educational institutions, as learners as well as employees, women are seen as naturally able to work with people and to understand and care for their needs through the emotional labour they are expected to expend.

Emotional labour

The term 'emotional labour' was first used to express the regulation and expression of emotion in exchange for a wage (Hochschild 1983), so showing the relationship between emotional and material capital in ways which are both gendered and classed within patriarchal capitalist states. As Helen Colley explains:

> Feelings . . . are prescribed and learned as powerful norms. However, the expression of these norms differs not only for women and for men, but also between social classes, who inherit different 'worlds of feeling'. . . . They are determined by the specific tasks allocated to each social grouping according to the division of labour within the prevailing mode of production – and that division of labour is gendered under patriarchal capitalism.
>
> (Colley 2003)

This includes the gendered division of emotional labour. Organisations both implicitly and explicitly identify what emotions are required and how they should be expressed, and employees are expected to 'create and maintain a relationship, a mood, or a feeling' (Hochschild 1983: 440) regardless of the sincerity or not of that creation. Emotional labour, then, is organisationally desired emotion (Morris and Feldman 1996), normally given by women. It is undertaken at personal cost to the worker and is a direct result of the commercialisation of emotion (Hochschild 1983). Despite this, the need for emotional labour in the service industries in particular has led to some apparent success for women in the worlds of education and employment, at least in terms of increased numbers. This has shifted attention away from the exploitation of women to a narrative of men being victims of feminism and the evidence that women's situation is improving in developed countries is taken as evidence that women are taking over, including in the fields of lifelong learning (Quinn 2003).

However, what is missing from these definitions of emotional labour and organisations is an account of the emotional labour expended by women in the home, where wives, mothers, partners and daughters also take responsibility for creating and maintaining the 'right' moods and/or feelings required for the emotional well-being of all but themselves. Within families women engage in emotional labour far more than most men, taking responsibility for maintaining the emotional aspects of family relationships, responding to others' emotional states and also acting to alleviate distress (Reay 2002). Linked to the development of networks required of social capital, emotional labour too is expended in friendships and social networking, especially by women. Wherever it takes place, emotional labour is undertaken at personal cost, and this cost is almost always at the expense of women. Women become so used to servicing men that this continues into the workplace. In Chapter 5, for example, when the Chair (a white man) asks for a Minute taker, Hafsa (a Black woman) agrees, although this will be at a cost to her own professional time.

Gloria and Carla's writings in their learning journals highlight the lack of recognition and value given to the emotional labour of women in the home. Mothering is often seen as something that is a 'natural' extension of being a woman and not a form of 'work'. Gloria is struck by the importance of Adrienne Rich's work in theorising the intense pain and pleasure experienced by women in the mothering work that they do. They begin to recognise the important role of emotional labour enacted in the home and how this experience is a valid one that offers insights, understanding and important knowledges that are useful in many other aspects of social life. Nevertheless, learner recognition of this will not alter the value of the emotional capital they are able to accumulate, nor its (lack of) transferability beyond the home.

Yet embedded in ways of being a women is the emotional labour that follows women into all arena, including as workers and learners in lifelong learning. Diane Reay, for example, has demonstrated how the academy conscripts women's emotional labour into service to support the new regulatory regimes operating in UK Higher Education. She shows the connections between class and gender in developing her understandings of both intensification and surveillance in terms of affective aspects of academic labour (Reay undated). Beverley Skeggs describes 'the unremitting emotional distress generated by the doubts and insecurities of living class that working-class women endure on a daily basis' (Skeggs 1997: 167). Indeed, many women, whether or not they identify as working-class, live the emotional distress described by Skeggs, generated by the pressures of balancing work and other demands with the emotional labour required of them.

It is, for example, to another woman that Marianna (Chapter 4) turns to express her anxieties, with women doing the emotional labour in the workplace as well as in the home. Gerri (also Chapter 4), offers emotional support to another female colleague who is concerned about new policies which are part of the surveillance identified by Reay. Although like her colleague, Gerri too feels 'harrassed' by management, the way that she confronts this with her colleague is to suggest that acting professionally is about trying to prioritise higher status work (like publications for the Research Assessment Exercise (RAE)), itself subject to high levels of surveillance.

Hey (2004) suggests that women may be more likely to over-comply, be over-zealous, in anxiety to please. Although Hey refers here to academic work, the same is also true for women students, both in their attitudes to coursework and in their supply of emotional labour. Women students, as well as women staff, supply the emotional labour required to support other learners, including taking on the implicitly enforced role of supporting male learners. Furthermore, moral panics over the state of masculinity often lead to strategies of exploiting women's emotional labour. For example, boys are seen as naturally boisterous and this is identified as a key obstacle to boys' educational achievement. Girls are then seen as a calming presence which can help regulate the boisterous behaviour of boys. As Bourdieu observes, 'women fulfil a cathartic, quasi-therapeutic function in regulating men's emotional lives, calming their anger, helping them accept the injustices and difficulties of life' (2001: 77).

Much of this type of work can be conceptualised as pastoral. This kind of emotional work is gendered and it tends to be women rather than men who carry it out. Women teachers are often identified as particularly 'talented' at this kind of work and therefore get appointed as the person responsible for supporting learners' emotional well-being because they are seen to have the right 'skills' to perform such work. This is tied in with constructions of femininity, where women are seen as more naturally orientated to such work, which is believed to require intuitive knowledge. This is considered less valuable than intellectual knowledge, associated with masculinity. Emotional labour is intensive, time-consuming and emotionally draining for the staff who carry it out, particularly because it is not evenly or fairly distributed across teams. This emotional work is often constructed as less important than other parts of the pedagogical role, and certainly in higher education lecturing is seen as more important than pastoral work, and research is seen as more important than lecturing. As a result of the uneven allocation of emotional labour to women over men, women are often overloaded with such responsibilities, finding it more difficult to build a career and be promoted.

The emotional labour expended in caring work is unrecognised in formal learning institutions unless it goes wrong. It is when students complain about their teachers that the pastoral role becomes visible. Yet, it is often difficult for those who might be expected to carry out emotional labour to do it in the conditions available. Aisha, for example (Chapter 6), is a part-time member of staff, who is not given the space to carry out pastoral work. She still attempts to conduct this emotional work but finds herself doing it in the most public space, the corridor, as she has no other space available to her. This is a slippery path for those already marginalised in their institutions: if they are seen to get it wrong, the fact that they had no private space to ethically conduct the work will not be seen as the key issue. Rather, blame could easily be placed on the teacher who is seen to lack the professional skills to understand the code of conduct expected, most importantly confidentiality. Jim's account (Chapter 6) also shows that emotional labour involves not only the careful regulation of feelings of self, but also feelings of others. He must contain his feelings of stress, which are the result of a bullying line manager, in order to manage the feelings of his line manager towards him. Linked too to issues of identity and sexuality, which we explore below, Jim is not sure how long he will be able to sustain his current role.

Those who display what might be constructed as 'excessive forms of emotionality' are vulnerable to ridicule and undermining and so there is a delicate balance between being respected for having the skills to carry out emotional labour within educational institutions, where it is crucially needed and yet seen as less important, and being seen as 'too emotional' and not rational enough to be a respected member of staff with the potential for career progression and promotion. The teachers' accounts in Chapter 6 illuminate the processes by which certain subjects become associated with being too emotional and how this is deeply tied in with their gendered, racialised and sexualised identities. We do know that when Aisha is ridiculed by one of her male students she finds the experience painful. However, when she seeks some comfort from a colleague, she is told she is being 'oversensitive', leaving her to feel that there is a lack of respect for her as a Black woman without the professional status of a lecturer in a formal educational setting. And so identities are formed and reformed.

Although they are labour intensive, emotional 'skills' are often seen in public discursive fields as less serious work, despite much policy discourse about the need to support learners. Indeed, there is a difficult balance to strike between being seen as the responsible person in charge of pastoral care, or emotional labour, and constructing a professional identity within educational institutions, where professionalism and emotion are seen as antithetical. We go on to explore these issues below.

Emotion, identity and 'difference'

Learning involves the construction of identities, the project of becoming, which is always an emotional process. Feelings of belonging, isolation, exclusion and validation operate around anger, envy, pleasure, desire, satisfaction, frustration and love. However, formal learning is expected to exclude the emotional and engage the rational. Learning is legitimised when it involves particular kinds of knowing, and the emotional is seen as operating outside of learning processes. When it *is* recognised it is silenced as a less important aspect of pedagogical relations, with the cognitive privileged over the emotional. This is related to the gendering of knowledge: knowledge that is tied to feminised ways of knowing (e.g. knowing how to care, 'mother' or love) is seen as natural and detached from serious knowledge pursuits. Masculinised ways of knowing are seen to be detached from emotion and are constructed as scientific, objective and rational ways of thinking and learning. This is crucial to understanding the mechanisms of exclusion for certain gendered, classed and racialised experiences.

The ways in which the emotional has been firmly set outside of forms of knowledge that are socially validated is entrenched in patriarchal assumptions. Being objective and rational is associated with masculine ways of being whilst being subjective and emotional has historical links with constructions of femininity. Learning to control emotions is part of a highly masculinised narrative of becoming a man. Regulating emotion is associated with hegemonic forms of masculinity. However, whilst being told that 'boys don't cry', boys simultaneously learn that some forms of emotion, such as the desire to lead, rule or conquer, is a 'manly' orientation to the world. Some forms of anger are acceptable when used in an authoritarian way to assert a masculine position of leadership over others. On the other hand, it is seen as unfeminine for girls to show signs of anger and particularly to express this through any form of violence, and so most girls learn to control their 'negative' emotions of anger. It is however acceptable for girls to show emotions such as crying, although the dominant emotion for girls is one of caring for others. So emotional expression is always gendered, and learning how to express the right forms of emotion is a type of learning that takes place through the hidden curriculum at school, as well as in other fields such as the home, at work and in college. This contributes to the fashioning of identities as lifelong learners and the kinds of learning in which we participate.

Social class, as well as gender, generates emotional orientations to learning. These are tied in with feelings of intimidation for those not seen to belong to the middle-classed spaces of formal learning, such as the college or university (Burke 2002; Jackson 2004). Skeggs (1997: 167) describes 'the unremitting emotional distress generated by the doubts and insecurities of living class that working-class women endure on a daily basis'. Social class, as well as gender, creates 'structures of feeling' that regulate learner identities throughout personal and social histories.

> Categories of class operate not only as an organising principle which enable access to and limitations on social movement and interaction but are also reproduced at the intimate level as a 'structure of feeling' in which doubt, anxiety and fear inform the production of subjectivity. To be working-classed . . . generates a constant fear of never having 'got it right'.
>
> (Skeggs 1997: 6)

Carla's journal writing (Chapter 7) sheds light on the emotional force of classed positionings. She writes in her journal that she is not very bright and feeling different from the others in her class who are 'posh' and 'clever'. Such feelings of inferiority need to be understood within the context of a British history and cultural common sense in which working-class groups, and particularly working-class women, have been constructed as potentially polluting and pathological. This history has its roots in nineteenth-century bourgeois thinking, and continues to exist today when single mothers are blamed for a variety of social problems and mothers in general (particularly working-class ones) are seen as failing to equip their children with the 'right' skills, attitudes and values to fit the demands of 'the nation'. Such ideas impact upon students' identities and the ways they understand themselves as (not) learners, as well as the way they make sense of what they are learning. Teachers and managers, too, find themselves positioned by social class, believing they need to disguise their working-class identities.

We know from Chapters 5 and 6 that teachers and managers are concerned for working-class learners. However, we need to look beyond what is said or recorded towards the silences and fissures to guess at the class background of the characters in the narratives, and to dis/cover the emotions associated with identities suppressed or reinvented (Jackson 2003). As Stanley articulates so clearly:

> The knowledge/power structures that impact at an individual level are the product of social and economic systems that have for centuries excluded people of my gender, my class and those marginalized by 'race', age and bodily disabilities. Language is used to signify and reinforce class oppression; formal education institutions are just examples of the places where systematic shaming and undermining, posited on notions of superiority and inferiority, are reinforced. That eroding phrase 'working-class thicko' no longer even needs to be spoken, so well is it internalized. It is a conditioned response, quite fixed before adolescence (transmitted through advertising and media as well as through school and social interactions), and one which is useful to a society which wants working-class women to take a usefully low and unchallenging position within it.
>
> (Stanley 1995: 171)

Exclusions from learning are experienced as symbolic violence and at the level of emotion. This penetrates into sensibilities of the self, and self-protection strategies emerge from such experiences. Policy that draws on positivist forms of strategy misses out on these emotional levels. For example, policies of 'retention' might seek to put particular mechanisms in place to improve retention of students, such as induction and study skills support. In Chapter 4 it is clear that college strategy is to look to support workers (who, like Mustafa, are normally low paid and often workers from minority groups) to undertake this work as an add-on to the 'real' work that goes on in classrooms. In addition, workers can be left feeling unvalued and demoralised. Tony's use of language (Chapter 4) includes 'awful', 'ignored', and even 'fatal'. Retention of students can lead to the nonretention of staff. Whilst for institutions strategies for student retention might be effective to some degree, such strategies are never able to grasp these deeper level emotional sensibilities of marginalisation and exclusion. Such exclusions operate at the epistemological level in subtle and insidious ways, ensuring that the those groups who are seen as 'lacking', 'disadvantaged', or 'deficient' are judged as having either no knowledge or the wrong kind of knowledge. They are also forced to prove their 'natural ability' if they want to access education, and this proof has to be given in the currencies of the privileged. Access to knowledge is therefore another realm of emotional conflicts and pain.

The accounts of learners presented as learning journal entries in Chapter 7 help illuminate the power of emotion as a key part of the processes of learning as becoming. For example, Carla, who is on a Women's Studies course, feels angry about the text the class is discussing. Indeed it upsets her to the extent that she considers dropping out of the course entirely. Dominant discourses of retention do not account for the emotional reasons connected to learning that influence whether students might decide to stay on or withdraw from a course of study. Carla experiences the text as an affront on who she is and she writes in her journal about feeling 'under attack'. The classroom discussion, as well as the identities of other women in the room as lesbians, creates a feeling of intense discomfort for Carla, as suddenly she is confronted by ideas that challenge the normalising discourses of heterosexual femininity. Yet she also finds some comfort in the text. The feminist theoretical perspectives challenge who she is but simultaneously give her the tools to articulate her feelings of 'irritability' in the home. Angelina, on the other hand, experiences the text as legitimating her usually 'Othered' identity as a lesbian woman. She describes though the conflicts and tensions the text raises within the group and between the women.

The learning journals of the Study Skills students highlight the dominance of keeping the emotional outside of formal learning contexts and legitimate knowledge. Abdulla expresses his discomfort with writing about his personal experiences in the learning journals, which he sees as private. This is because in hegemonic discourses of lifelong learning, those who are recognised as learners are not encouraged to draw on personal or emotional forms of knowledge, seen as biased ways of thinking. However, Beverley Skeggs (2003) notes that working-class people have too often been forced to 'tell' themselves in particular ways, although the telling often leaves people open to assessments and judgements in which they are viewed as lacking. Forced telling, then, can be a painful emotional experience. However, theoretical explorations of the emotional as part of the process of learning have been written out of research, particularly as emotion is not something that can be observed or measured in any kind of scientific way. Anger, pleasure and desire are to be strictly regulated and controlled and learners need to have disciplined bodies and minds in order to be accepted in educational institutions. The classroom is not a space to explore emotional aspects of learning, and pedagogical relations are also strictly controlled and regulated outside of the emotional. (See Chapter 11 for further discussion of pedagogies.)

As we have consistently argued, current frameworks of lifelong learning rest on dichotomies privileging knowledge constructed as objective, scientific and rational and marginalise knowledge constructed as subjective, irrational and emotional. 'Emotion' is considered the antithesis of 'reason'. This shapes the ways that certain kinds of learning are funded, recognised and legitimated whilst others are not. For example, it is often the case that courses which are said to be for pleasure *only* are often not properly funded and are held in low esteem. As several managers note in Chapter 5 (e.g. Narinder, Edith, Linda and William), this is particularly damaging for groups of learners who do not fit the new policy agenda for lifelong learning, as shown in the Government context in Chapter 4. This then filters into the choices learners (are able to) make about what to study, while simultaneously 'choice' is constructed as rational and freely available to all in society, regardless of age, ethnicity, gender, race and sexuality. Therefore it is, for example, constructed as a free choice that many women do not take up engineering degrees. The experiences of feeling different and isolated as the only woman on an engineering course, or the only man on a nursing course, are not seen as part of scientific understanding of educational choice. However, the complex processes by which an individual identifies as a learner are tied to emotion. Yet although aspirations and choices about what and where to learn in formal contexts are mediated by feelings, making a choice about the kind of learner to become is constructed as making 'informed choice' linked to rational decision-making.

Within educational institutions, because of the subtle gendered interpretations of actions, women walk a fine line within discourses of rationality. If they argue a point, for example, they might be accused of being irrational or even aggressive, whereas a man who argues his point might be seen as logical and/or a strong leader. This is not because of any individual prejudices but due to the deeply embedded constructions of acceptable ways of men and women acting in the social world. This is tied in with unexamined and unreflexive constructions of femininity and masculinity. Although feelings are experienced as natural, they are historically situated and socially regulated. For example, because femininity has historically demanded that women regulate feelings of anger, women need to show a calmness that may not be felt and are caught up in processes of self-regulation to induce or suppress their feelings. Emotions such as feeling confident and strong, associated with heterosexual masculinity, are often valued and rewarded within institutional spaces. Indeed some masculine forms of emotional display might be seen as necessary and productive. Paternalistic postures might be better respected and received than maternalistic orientations, and this, we argue, is linked to deeply misogynistic perspectives that are left to rest and are pretended not to exist.

Professional identities are similarly based on the neutral, apolitical and decontextualised (and masculinist) subject who compartmentalises professional/rational knowledge from personal/emotional knowledge. Discourses of professionalism that rest on specialised and expert knowledge regard the personal as irrelevant to the learning and knowing of professionals. This is illustrated well in Ros's learning journal (Chapter 7). Although she is researching emotional intelligence, she is determined to keep her own opinions outside of the research process and to produce work that is considered valid, reliable and objective. It is expected that professionals make decisions and judgements based on their objective bodies of professional knowledge and experience rather than to respond to intuition or deeper level feelings. This of course operates to make invisible the subjective and tacit nature of professional decision-making.

In addition, decision-making is subject to hierarchical social and cultural positionings. Narinder (Chapter 4), for example, tries to engage her colleagues in discussion and recognition of the experiences of Black women in more formal learning institutions such as further education colleges. However, she finds her views dismissed by Andy, who says that such issues are not the purpose of the Network. Narinder's emotions are not recorded in the Minutes, nor are the emotions of any of the other people present. The Minutes tell us that not everyone agreed with Andy's assessment of the key issues; their feelings at the meeting or on seeing other viewpoints not added to the Minutes remain undocumented. It is clear from looking at the gaps in the Minutes that several of the people appear to have been silenced in different ways, and must during the course of the meeting have been feeling a range of emotions (frustration? inhibition? lack of worth? anger?). However, there is not much in the text that can tell us about these feelings, which by and large go unnoticed. Displays of emotion are unacceptable – especially these sorts of emotions – and are gendered.

It is impossible for professionals simply to step outside of the social contexts, discourses and relations of which they are part. Professionals are social and relational subjects and are not able to disconnect from their feelings, which are connected to their sense of identity, values and perspectives. Yet learners and teachers, whether or not this is conscious, draw on their personal histories, identities and subjectivities to make sense of the world.

For example, Aisha (Chapter 6) feels that her identity as a Black woman undermines her position of status in the college and her chance to contribute to decision-making processes. Jim (also Chapter 6), who identifies as homosexual and empathises with Aisha's story, is concerned that if he raises the issue that he is being bullied by his Head of Department, he will be identified as childish and weak, deemed to be unprofessional and unable to cope. Personal histories by their very nature are full of emotional experiences, sounds, smells, images that resonate with a sense of self in process. Learners have histories of learning, which include moments of pure delight in the processes of discovery, and frustration when learning feels difficult, confusing or uncertain. Such sensibilities trigger emotional reactions, whether subdued or fully expressed, and these colour later experiences of learning and the forming of new pedagogical relationships. Whilst some histories of emotion are damaging to future learning, they can also be enhancing. Graham, for example (Chapter 6) embraces the opportunity to draw on his personal experiences to explore the love of music that he sees as essential to build into the school curriculum. Drawing on his memories of the excitement he experienced at school with a teacher who did not dismiss the kinds of music that inspired him outside of the formal school curriculum, he wants to challenge what he sees as the elitist assumptions that undermine his students' enthusiasm and love of music. Learning experiences are entwined with relationships with other learners, teachers, peers and parents and all relationships include the emotional, tied in with the formation of identification. Despite this, there is a perceived lack of emotional literacy in the various fields of lifelong learning.

Doing 'emotion'

There is a great deal of concern in both policy and practice with regard to literacy. Policy discourses about literacy are often linked to widening participation and focus on individual responsibility, social justice and economic strategy (see policy drafts in Chapter 4). However, primarily discourses of literacy are about 'lack', especially lack linked to class and race. There is an assumption that people with literacy problems have a deficit that needs to be rectified (Crowther *et al.* 2001: 33) and indeed that the 'problem' is one that belongs both to the individual and to their familial and social backgrounds. Emotional literacy is about the ways in which we develop relationships and interact with each other to understand more about the emotions of self and others. Such understandings are then used to shape actions. Emotional literacy, like lifelong learning, is linked to both material and social capital, including the development of nation. *Antidote*, an organisation that sets out to help schools develop emotional literacy amongst their pupils, suggests that 'by attending to the development of our emotional and social skills, we ensure an improvement in the nation's emotional wealth and social capital' (see http://www. antidote.org.uk). This is of course reminiscent of the discourse that surrounds lifelong learning, and feeds into anxieties about controlling 'negative' emotions, building on psychological assumptions around normal and abnormal emotions and behaviour. Likewise, the School of Emotional Literacy has 'found that increasing the social and emotional competence of both adults and children makes a big difference to everyone's learning capacity and behaviour management' (http:// www.schoolofemotional-literacy.com). Doing emotional literacy, then, is more about behaviour management and control than about developing understandings of the role of emotion on personal and professional identities. Mike Radford (2002) argues for a process of self-exploration to develop emotional literacy, encouraging pupils to talk about and explain their feelings, although as we have seen above in relation to Abdullah (Chapter 7), 'forced telling' (Skeggs 2002) works to the detriment of marginalised groups. Radford suggests that the emotional literacy of pupils should be developed by teachers in the context of objective understanding. Such views suggest that the 'right' emotions can be learned as skills, and that

> these skills ought to be observable in the daily interaction of teachers and students if they are part of 'communities that care'. . . . Part of the work of pedagogy then is to train individuals in the proper way to be emotional. This training is currently being provided by human resource managers, staff developers and consulting psychologists whose job it is to reinscribe professionals and academic managers as active, enterprising human resources, so that they, in turn, can develop such skills in their students.
>
> (McWilliam and Hatcher 2004: 181)

As part of the training for the development of skills of and for 'doing emotion' has been the growth of mentoring. Mentoring is now part of the experience of learning, especially for trainee teachers but also for students. It is now a favoured policy initiative within many institutions with regard to students, where mentoring is said to aid retention, and also amongst teacher training agencies. Mentoring has become part of the regulatory practice, for example, of the compulsory training in post-compulsory education and learning endorsed by Lifelong Learning UK. Helen Colley (2004) suggests that the development of mentoring has been used as evidence of an increasing shift towards the more 'feminine' side of learning and work, celebrating emotionality and human connection. However, she argues that the celebratory bias and mythical bias of mentoring should be deconstructed. Applying a feminist Marxist perspective, Colley (2002) argues official concepts of mentoring have shifted from dominant groupings reproducing their own power, to subordinate groupings reproducing their own oppression.

Although we do believe that mentoring can have substantial benefits for marginalised groups in particular, we remain concerned at the emotional labour expended by both mentor and mentee, and we agree with Colley that there is potential for the reproduction of oppression. We are highly concerned that mentoring can slip into individualised, regulatory mechanisms of disciplining the self and others, so shaping the ideal neo-liberal subject. Part of the process of engaging in mentoring, for the mentor and especially for the mentee, is the development of reflective practice. However, being a reflective practitioner too often involves only exploring the individual aspects of experience. It is based on assumptions around self-regulation and self-improvement strategies and undermines politicised approaches to professionalism that would expose power relations at the social and discursive levels. Additionally, we argue that reflective practice is gendered in that women are more self-critical than men, undermining confidence and ability to act.

Of course, reflective practice for teachers and for learners can also help identify the huge pleasures of learning that many of us experience, too often ignored in accounts of lifelong learning, although sometimes this is a guilty pleasure. As some of our earlier work has identified (Burke 2002; Jackson 2004), 'non-traditional' learners in particular who experience pleasure in learning do not feel that this counts as real learning: the work ethic of neo-liberalism dictates that if learning is fun it cannot also be valuable. However, pleasures of learning can also include knowing a job has been done well (although the converse of this is that learners, teachers and managers can all push themselves extremely hard to succeed, and this is related to marginalised identities including gender, race and social class). Issues of identity also bring pleasures to learning, including the pleasures of extending academic and/or learner identities, developing understandings of identities, or even leaving old identities behind. They may be about the anticipated pleasures of new careers or about new ways of thinking about 'self'.

Conclusions

We have in this chapter drawn on the narratives in Section II to consider ways in which emotions are both written out of lifelong learning, and yet are part of the formation of identities, knowledge and understanding. From a consideration of the gendered biases of emotional capital and emotional labour, we have demonstrated ways in which emotions form and are formed by (marginalised and dominant) identities and hegemonic practices. We have ended by considering ways in which lifelong learning 'does' emotion, and in particular how this is tied to the construction of neo-liberal subjects, in their gendered, racialised and classed positionings. This is certainly something which has continued to interest us with regard to our own emotions and professional academic identities whilst writing this book. Writing, especially academic writing, is normally considered a rational and scientific project. However, in the main we have found (are finding) writing this book to be an emotional project.

We described in the introduction to this book something of the pleasures of working together on this project of reconceptualising lifelong learning, and they have been considerable. However, our emails to each other indicate that the overriding emotions in writing this book are not only pleasure but also pain! We have loved the pleasure of working with each other, and of producing creative work. We have found the work painful for much of the time, including the pain of trying to be creative, and the pain of trying to write a book with little or no relief from other aspects of our work. Additionally, there has been the strain of knowing that we need to have the book published in time for the RAE. We have been surprised to recognise of ourselves that we play into neo-liberalism and want to be seen as 'good' academics. We have also been surprised to recognise of ourselves that we are ambitious in our career aspirations. Despite that, we have both given time and emotional labour to the other, and have been grateful to have received it. If we were sometimes also resentful of the cost in doing so we have not told each other so.

In exploring something of our own emotions we also invite you, our readers, to explore your own emotional responses to reading the narratives and subsequent analysis. Of course, in writing we have shown something of our own emotions – we have told our stories in the order that we want you (our readers) to know us – first as people excited by ideas; last as aspirational careerists, turning ourselves into ideal neo-liberal subjects! And that in itself elicits emotional responses from us, including resistance to what we have been forced to recognise of ourselves. We go on to explore resistances in the next chapter.

Chapter 10

Resistances in lifelong learning

Introduction

This chapter focuses on the theme of resistances in lifelong learning to consider how they are played out, in what contexts and by whom. We conceptualize resistances as counter-hegemonic practices that operate at the micro-level of everyday experience and attempt either consciously or unconsciously to challenge and subvert hegemonic regimes of truth and privileged discourses and identities. As hegemony works by consent rather than force, a key question running through this chapter is what happens when consent is not given to hegemonic discourses of lifelong learning. However, we also want to account for the complexities of resistances in this chapter. We recognise, for example, that compliances, acceptances and resistances can happen simultaneously and are not clearly delineated in practice. We acknowledge the emotional dimensions of acts of resistance, and the risks and pleasures associated with such acts. Foucault argues that resistance is carried out at a local level, with a constant shifting in the exercise of power, and with pleasure coming through the challenges of resistance:

> The pleasure that comes of exercising a power that questions, monitors, watches, spies, searches out, palpitates, brings to light; and on the other hand, the pleasure that kindles at having to evade this power, flee from it, fool it, or travesty it.
>
> (Foucault 1980: 45)

Foucault theorises that 'pleasure is to be found in both resisting and trying to maintain discourses of power and powerful discourses, and power is more than simply a form of repression' (Jackson 2004a: 105). Yet Jackson argues that 'it would be wrong to argue that those who exercise power and those who challenge it are engaging in a game of hide and seek, as Foucault seems to suggest' (ibid.). There are material risks attached to acts of resistance such as loss of career opportunities. Therefore it is important to understand that resistance is not simply an act of pleasure; indeed resistances often take place despite fear of reprisals. Resistances take place within unequal power relations, where some identities carry power, authority and privilege, whilst others are despised, ridiculed and subject to derision (Skeggs 2004). The point we are making is that although resistances occur at the emotional level, they are simultaneously caught up in the politics of identity and attached to deeply embedded structural inequalities and discursive misrecognitions.

Of course, acts of resistance take place in a range of different lifelong learning contexts apart from formal educational institutions. For example, resistances take place within workplaces, families and community settings, and these acts shape and reshape learning processes and experiences. Processes of identification, which involve the ongoing project of becoming (Hall 1992), are a key part of learning. Such processes are shaped by doing as well as being (Youdell 2006), thereby constituting self as (not) learner. This is key to understanding the subtle and almost invisible operation of exclusion, which involves resistances. This is illuminated by classic ethnographic studies such as Willis's *Learning to Labour*, in which he argues that working-class masculine resistances at school feed into the reproduction of classed divisions and differences in the labour market (Willis 1977). Although his study made a significant and valuable contribution to theorising reproductive processes, it has also been critiqued as overly deterministic (Coward 1977; Aggleton 1987). Rather, Aggleton (1987) argues that reproduction is contested and so it should not be assumed that educational institutions are always reproductive sites:

> Male and female students often expressly reject or contest the overt and covert messages of the institution. Reproduction and contestation go hand in hand. Therefore one cannot always assume that institutions are always successful in reproduction. No assembling of ideological practices and meanings. And no sets of social and economic arrangements can be totally monolithic.
>
> (Apple 1982, cited in Aggleton 1987: 121)

Drawing on feminist post-structuralism, we argue that resistances are more fluid than these early studies would suggest, and although resistances contribute to the reproduction of social inequalities, they are also sites of struggle and instances where subversions and small changes might take place. Resistances are not only counter-hegemonic, they are also recuperative and involve the contestations of counter-hegemony. Resistances are tied in with complex sets of subjectivities and positionings and are interlinked with the construction and reforming of learner identities. Resistance should be understood as grounded within relations of inequalities (Archer 2006: 81). They happen in unexpected spaces and are made by individuals and groups in a range of different subject positions. As we have demonstrated in the previous section, teachers, learners, parents, managers, young people, undergraduates, policy-makers all participate actively in resistances, as well as contributing to the re/privileging of hegemonic discourses. We want to highlight here that resistances are usually not large and dramatic acts; they are often subtle and implicit and take place in everyday routine practices. They might not always be conscious acts and they take place often at the emotional and discursive level – shifting and contesting meanings, feelings, identifications and understandings through everyday interactions and relationships. They are always, however, deeply embedded in complex power relations and are about the negotiation, politics and contestation of representation, recognition, marginalisation, authority, silencing and legitimisation. Therefore, an analysis of the working of resistances in learning must be understood within a framework of power and the complex micro-politics of identity formation and knowledge construction.

In this chapter we re-visit the narratives of Section II to uncover and analyse the operations of resistance within complex relations of power. Whilst we recognise that these narratives are fictional accounts, they are also embedded in and reflective of the discourses currently at play in the field of lifelong learning. As the authors of these imagined narratives, we are also constrained in our narrative writing by the competing discourses available to us. In this way, our re-working of these narratives into an analytical focus sheds light on the nature of resistances, particularly by making connections with insights from the theoretical literature. Our analysis is organised around four key themes: resistance, micro-politics and subjectivity; social position, power and (counter/ing) hegemonic discourses; writing resistance; and knowing, meaning-making and resistance. We focus on the subtleties of resistances that take place in unspectacular ways to consider the differences these small acts make for experiences and constructions of lifelong learning.

Resistance, micro-politics and subjectivity

Micro-politics is a powerful concept for understanding the ways that resistances play out in different discursive fields of lifelong learning. The micro-politics of personal lives help expose power structures at all levels of experience. The concept brings to light 'hidden meanings' and 'gendered processes of power' (Morley 1999: 5) at play through processes of resistance and compliance. These processes are 'subtle, elusive, volatile, difficult to capture, leaving individuals unsure of the validity of their readings of a situation' (ibid.). Resistances are deeply entangled in the micro-politics of social relations across difference and inequality and require attention to the micro-politics of context, subjectivity and struggle (Mohanty 2002: 501, in Mojab 2006: 164). The concept of micro-politics helps to understand the ways that power is used and structured into social relations so that it does not appear to be used at all. It helps to understand the ways that subjects influence others to protect themselves and create networks of support to achieve their ends (Morley 1999: 5). The concept helps to expose subterranean conflicts and the minutiae of social relations. A micro-political analysis uncovers the social significance of a single instance of resistance which might on the surface appear trivial and unimportant (ibid.).

Resistances involve struggles over identity and status, and the meanings associated with different subject positionings, including 'professional' and 'learner'. Youdell (2006) usefully develops theories of subjectivity by pointing out that the naming of certain subjects is also the making of certain subjects.

And in so far as to name is to make, it is also an action, a doing, that is speech and action come together in discursive practice. Furthermore, that 'there is no doer behind the deed' insists that there is no pre-existing subject, who, in her/his rationality, chooses a course of action and embarks on it. Instead, it suggests that while there may be intention behind actions, it is the discourses in which these actions are embedded that gives them meaning and which need to be considered in understanding their effects. It is not good or bad intention, then, that determines the outcome of action, but the discursive frame in which the action is located.

(Youdell 2006: 75)

Youdell explains that 'the doer' is produced through her/his own practices, 'not because of her/his desire to be so, but because of the discourses that are called up by his/her deed' (Youdell 2006: 76). Through acts of resistances, then, subjectivities are made and re-made, and this process is discursive and entwined with the complex micro-politics of learning sites. Those who perform acts of counter-hegemonic resistances and occupy marginalized positionings, are likely to be re-made as 'Othered' subjects. It is not surprising then that those in marginalized positions might consciously choose not to act in counter-hegemonic ways.

However, feminist scholars such as Skeggs demonstrate how although those in marginalized positions are aware of their marginalisation and seek to act in ways to distance themselves from the classifications of others, they are often unable to escape those classifications. In her study of working-class women participating on caring courses, she explains:

The women in this study are aware of their place, of how they are socially positioned and the attempts to represent them. This constantly informs their responses. They operate with a dialogic form of recognition: they recognize the recognition of others. Recognitions do not occur without value judgments and the women are constantly aware of the judgments of real and imaginary others. Recognition of how one is positioned is central to the processes of subjective construction.

(Skeggs 1997: 4)

Her analysis sheds light on the complexities of resistances in relation to subjectivity and subjective construction. The women of Skeggs' study, 'live their social locations with unease' (ibid.). Their attempts to resist the classifications they recognise as derogatory result in the reclassification of subjectivities of derision (ibid.). This sheds light on the ways different subjects navigate complex micro-politics and choose (not to) perform acts of resistance in their everyday encounters.

For example, in Chapter 6, Jim presents to his colleagues in the learning set the issues that are causing him an immense level of stress in his job. He speaks about his identification with Aisha's story, which is about occupying an Othered position in his institution. Aisha makes a direct connection between her struggles to contribute to the curriculum and to engage her students in the work of marginalised authors and her identity as a Black woman. Her struggles to introduce the perspectives of misrecognised Others into her classroom reconstitute her identity as an 'Othered' subject and she is warned by her colleague to take up the hegemonic discursive practice of selecting mainstream literature for her course.

Jim empathises with Aisha's struggles suggesting that he experiences similar difficulties as a gay man. However, he wants to distance his narrative from his homosexual identity and focus on his professional self. This speech act is another illustration of the discourses at play in struggles over recognition and misrepresentation (Skeggs 2004). Jim's narrative highlights that 'normative heterosexuality is promoted, sustained and made to appear totally natural' in educational institutions (Epstein *et al.* 2003: 2). Jim takes part in his own marginalisation by denying the importance of his sexual identity. Rather, he attempts to constitute his identity around higher status representations of the professional and thus focuses his discussion around being a professional.

Jim's fictional narrative highlights some significant points for theorising resistances. This narrative brings to light the struggles over what it means to be a 'professional' and how this is tied in with complex and shifting subjectivities. It highlights that misrecognised selves make careful decisions around their positions of Otherness and attempt to re/construct their identities around legitimated subjectivities such as the professional. Yet, the construction of 'the professional' is itself (middle) classed, (masculine) gendered, (white) racialised and (hetero)-sexualised. Jim and Aisha take different strategies of resistance against this; Aisha attempts to build her professional identity around being a Black woman, whilst Jim attempts to construct his professional identity through the absence of his homosexual identity. Neither strategy seems to work, which supports Skeggs's conceptualisation of the dialogic nature of mis/recognition and subjective re/construction.

Jim's story also highlights the ways that Other subjects might be placed into a position of authority (such as managing institutional audit) without authority over resources. He therefore has little space to manoeuvre any kind of resistances to the approaches taken in his institution yet he is given the visible and public position of authority in this area as 'manager'. It is only through the space of the action learning set that he is able to express his frustrations and anxieties about his situation in the workplace. This space then is one in which resistances to the everyday work practices of formal learning institutions are played out. This enables different professionals to make connections between what might be seen as individual experiences and begin to recognize patterns. Through a process of consciousness-raising, such spaces contribute to re-thinking personal experiences, shedding light on their social and political nature. A micro-political analysis of Jim's account raises questions about Jim's position in the institution and the legitimacy of his status as manager. It highlights that personal identities are not separate from professional ones because these are shaped by and against the multiple and contradictory identities that subjects bring to their practices. However, it also demonstrates that resistances within formal institutions are at times impossible and that professional identities are discursively constructed within the micro-politics of organisations. The analysis also illuminates that resistances are tied in with complex positions, power relations and competing discourses.

Social position, power and (counter/ing) hegemonic discourses

Resistances are deeply interconnected with social position and power. The ways that resistances play out is linked to questions about status, authority and position. Individuals make decisions about resistances, subversions and compliance in relation to these and consider the level of risk and danger attached to not conforming to hegemonic regimes of truth. We argue that this has become intensified with new managerialism, which actively creates workplace situations that restrict democratic processes (Rowland 2002). This is particularly evident in Chapter 4 with the introduction of time sheets and other mechanisms to tightly regulate the ways that individuals use their time at work. The strategies of new managerialism are highly effective in containing levels of resistance within institutional spaces. This is because the emphasis is on performativity (Morley 2003) and rests of the assumption that managers must continually police and regulate the performance of their staff. The overwhelming focus on these kinds of concerns, connected with discourses of quality and accountability (Morley 2003) and the sheer pace of daily work (both paid and unpaid), constrains the opportunities for resistance, particularly because there is increasingly little space for collective action (Burke 2002). Currie *et al.* argue that the effects of performativity are gendered:

> Scholars are competing against each other in a performativity culture that tends to benefit men more than women. This competitive atmosphere reduces the sense of community within institutions and is likely to emphasize those aspects of the male culture that are seen as most hostile to women.
>
> (Currie *et al.* 2002: 36)

We also argue that resistances play out against hierarchical positionings established in institutional spaces, which are tied in with the privileging of some forms of learning and education above others. To illustrate this we examine in Chapter 5 the (imagined) minutes of a meeting of educational managers representing a range of different contexts. These included adult, further and higher education, older, community and 14–19 learning, and learning through volunteering and in libraries and museums. It is of interest that those managers in positions with arguably more status were white, middle-class men and those in managerial positions carrying less status were mainly women and from minority ethnic backgrounds. This fictionalised situation is supported in the literature, which shows that men continue to occupy the most powerful and senior positions in formal educational institutions (see, for example, Anderson and Williams 2001; Currie *et al.* 2002; Cotterill *et al.* 2007). In our analytical discussion, we pay attention to the politics of resistance in relation to social positioning and complex and shifting power relations within lifelong learning fields.

How do different participants have authority and voice at different moments in a formal meeting and in what ways is this resisted? In our fictionalised account, each participant speaks in direct relation to their institutional/professional position, and this is also linked to the kind of status they have in the meeting. We argue that this is common practice and that institutional position is the primary way that educational professionals are recognised in formal meetings as well as seminars and conferences. Indeed, not belonging to a formal institution is a marker of difference and makes positioning oneself particularly difficult. In the imagined meeting, the higher education manager is also the Chair while the manager for asylum and refugee learning was asked to service the meeting by taking the minutes. This highlights the ways that different positions in meetings and committees are usually allocated around institutional position and status. We point out that it is not easy to contribute to the discussion while simultaneously keeping notes of the meeting, and therefore the minute-taker is working at a disadvantage. Furthermore, the connection between voice and position is closely made throughout the formal meeting, so that the power relations entwined in institutional status (higher education versus the education of asylum and refugees) play out in ways that are not immediately noticeable. How these power relations then shape processes of resistance becomes a matter of interest in shaping the agenda and the outcomes of the meeting between educational managers.

For example, in the imagined meeting, Narinder, Hafsa and Edith perform subtle acts of resistance by arguing for the value and importance of non-accredited forms of learning. This is supported by their colleague Linda. However, all of these women occupy positions that are themselves marginalised in the hierarchy of institutional status, where it is probable that the concerns of higher and further education are prioritised and privileged above the concerns of learning for asylum seekers and refugees, older and adult learners, learners in libraries and museums. This is not only connected to institutional status but also to the status of the learners themselves and therefore the subjective construction of those learners. This is also tied in with wider questions around standards, admissions and selectivity, with entry to higher education the most selective of all the different forms of learning represented in our fictionalised meeting. The acts of resistance in arguing against the hegemonic discourses of lifelong learning which prioritise accredited learning are thus entangled in the hierarchies of different forms of learning. However, it is important to note that resistances do not only come from those occupying high status institutionalised positions. Feminist scholars argue that resistance can come from marginalised women, who can 'demonstrate a high level of political and social consciousness on issues of patriarchy, equality and social justice' (Mojab 2006: 170).

> Marginality is a central location for the production of a counter hegemonic discourse – it is found in the words, habits and the way one lives. . . . It is a site

one clings to even when moving to the centre . . . it nourishes our capacity to resist. . . . It is an inclusive space where we recover ourselves, where we move in solidarity to erase the category colonizer/colonized'.

(hooks 1991: 150, in Mirza 2006: 149)

Indeed, the marginalised women in our imagined meeting act collectively to demonstrate their resistance to the hegemonic assumption that accredited learning is the most important. Yet resistances can be met with authoritative challenges. Thus in our story, Sarah who supports her women colleagues is asked by the Chair to produce a defence of their argument in writing. In this way, small resistances in the meeting are met with acts of resistance from those occupying higher status positions. The point is that the alternative or 'Other' view will only be heard if it is produced in a specific way – argued logically and rationally to be recognised by those who have the authority to demand their need to be convinced. bell hooks argues that those occupying positions of power, privilege and status shape language 'to become a territory that limits and defines, . . . they make it a weapon that can shame, humiliate, colonise' (hooks 1994: 168). And yet, she says, those in marginalised and misrepsresented positions can *use* this language, which needs to be 'possessed, taken, claimed as a space of resistance' (hooks 1994: 169, cited in Jackson 2004a: 116).

The struggles over the discourses of lifelong learning presented in the imagined meeting highlight the ways that resistances play out, showing the possibility of individuals rejecting hegemonic versions of learning. Yet, they also highlight the ways that discourses get recuperated through social position and power and how difficult it is for those in lower status positions to make their perspectives heard. These kinds of struggle are important in understanding resistances at the level of practice.

Writing resistance

In this book, we have argued that academic forms of writing, and particularly the essay, operate as practices of exclusion, contributing to the hegemony of privileged identities and epistemologies. However, writing is a social practice embedded in contested power relations and different social contexts and therefore can be a practice of resistance as well as exclusion. Mary Evans conceptualises writing as a 'survival strategy' which has 'allowed individuals to occupy a conventional private space while constructing a radical world of the imagination' (Evans 2004: 129). She explains that:

Charlotte Brontë and Jane Austen are just two examples of the women who remained entirely dutiful at the same time as they were writing works of radical challenge. Writing is not just about the conscientious fulfillment of professional expectations; it can also be about protest.

(Evans 2004: 129)

However, writing does not only act as a form of resistance, as Evans acknowledges. Writing can be a key gate-keeping device ensuring that particular forms of epistemology are continued to be privileged giving legitimacy to certain knowers (Burke and Hermerschmidt 2005). Writing as a social practice is inextricably connected to complex relations of power and politics of identity (Lea and Street 2000; Crème 2003; Ivanic 1998). As we have argued above, the essay is a privileged form of literacy practice and as a 'gendered practice-resource' operates around a binary framework, which 'provides particular ways of meaning-making' (Lillis 2001: 129). The binary framework of essayist literacy 'privileges particular dimensions of meaning making over "others"' (ibid.). Lillis explores, through an analysis of her interviews with women students from 'non-traditional' backgrounds, the desires of women writers and their longing for connection and involvement.

> It is no accident that these categorizations of 'other' – for example, emotion, evocation, informality – are precisely those dimensions of meaning that those historically constructed as 'others' should desire. The women writers seem to accept the dominant conventions in constructing their texts, but resist them in their thinking about what their texts are, or might be.
>
> (Lillis 2001: 129)

In our narrative section, we offered the (imagined) writing of policy-makers in forms other than the essay. This was a deliberate attempt on our part to resist the conventions of the academic voice and to present our ideas in forms other than the essay. It also enabled us to show the different literacy practices that subjects engage in within formal educational contexts. For example, the policy-makers were engaged in processes of policy formulation through the everyday practice of composing email communications. Emails have their own conventions; often they are seen as informal, yet there is a certain social etiquette about ways of writing an email in professional contexts. The email written in the work context is usually structured, organised around key points, polite and considerate and written for a specific purpose, with a key theme identified in the subject heading. Furthermore, emails often appear on the surface to be intimate and private communications, but can be forwarded to others and used as a legal document. Although emails are not usually assessed in the ways that essays are, they are open to judgment and contribute to the construction of the writer's and readers' identity and social positioning. In considering these characteristics, in what ways might resistances operate through email as a social practice?

In the further education context we see in the fictionalised emails that the student support workers are mobilising themselves against new policies that they feel are not in their interests. The appointment of a new manager to oversee the work of the support staff has the potential in their view to change the nature of their work and to overlook the important contribution they make to the learners' positive experiences. Email is used to communicate their perspective and maintain a sense of control over their work. In the different kinds of emails that are generated around this key issue the different forces and resistances at play come into view. Mustafa takes a lead to mobilise his team in contributing to a policy of student retention. His Head of School supports their desire to meet; however formal procedures are put into place so that their voices have to be filtered through the appropriate channels. Although they have their meeting and Mustafa feeds back their key points through a rather formal email text, he has no control over how his message will be taken forward to the senior management team, who have the final control over decision-making. Email messages are also used more informally amongst the team to express their anxieties in more intimate ways; there is a strong sense of trust and collegiality between colleagues shown through these kinds of more intimate messages. These imagined emails highlight the ways that email as a literacy practice provides new sites of resistance but also shows that these can be overshadowed by the same institutional hierarchies as discussed above in the context of formal meetings.

In the national policy text, we see a different kind of email communication in operation. The emails here are directly contributing to the formation of national policy. However, what we learn from these email exchanges is that the text is re-written and rewritten again by different individuals moving up the hierarchy to the (final) decision-maker. There is no one author of national policy – it is in a sense a post-structuralist exercise of blurring different voices together to create the final version which is seen to represent the 'true' voice of the government. Policy-making is a complex process of reformulation of text to produce the version that author-ises the agenda of the key government players (Ball 1990). The email exchange provides new sites of policy-making and the opportunities for different voices to be written into the process. Yet, again, final decisions rest with those occupying senior positions and who are able to edit out and select the different voices parti-cipating in the exchanges. Resistances are possible but are likely to be silenced and overshadowed.

We have also created imagined spaces for learners to engage in practices other than essay writing. In Chapter 7, different groups of learners created writing through learning journals in a range of formal learning contexts, which highlighted the contested nature of learning and knowing in educational institutions. The learning journal could be seen in itself as an act of resistance against essayist literacy where the 'Other' dimension of the binary that Lillis refers to is valued. However, we can see from the writing of the learners that this is not the case in all the contexts being explored, and in some instances writing the emotional or personal is heavily discouraged. However, in the learning journals that were written for the Women's Studies course, the learners were able to contest the binary between the rational and emotional and explore in some depth their emotional responses to the course materials and discussions.

There is always the possibility of resistance, which for Foucault starts from the bottom and permeates upwards. Such resistance comes through an oppo-sitional politics that takes the form of a critique, that moves from a suspicion of universal truths to a criticism of the workings on institutions which appear natural and neutral. The non-totality of the exercise of power is a crucial and determining point: women's studies, for example, is set up to offer a resistance to dominant academic discourses, although the extent of any success of such resistance is arguable.

(Jackson 2004a: 104–5)

Indeed in the imagined Women's Studies course, some of the learners wrote about intense feelings of anger in relation to the Women's Studies curriculum and related to this feelings of not/belonging and marginalisation. The women used the journals to develop their responses to the core texts on the course and to consider their feelings about the theoretical ideas underpinning those texts. This provides a space of less subtle forms of resistance, for example when Carla describes her anger at the theories and materials introduced on the course, and how these lead her to consider dropping out of it altogether. Yet these feelings of anger were often in response to counter-hegemonic discourses of feminism and lesbianism, which challenged hegemonic regimes of truth and the comfort of these in relation to taken-for-granted formations of femininity. As the women found their sexuality being challenged by the feminist theories explored on the course, they used their journals to talk back and reassert claims to being 'normal' women. This is not a straightforward narrative of counter-hegemony; the learning journal provided a space to resist feminist discourses and therefore to recuperate normalising discourses of heterosexual femininities. This highlights the complexity of sites of struggle over meaning; these are often conservative as well as radical resistances (Epstein 1997). In this way, there is a question about whether or not these were expressions of resistance or recuperation – the women seemed to be recouping the hegemonic discourses of 'normal' versions of femininity against 'abnormal' versions of feminism (Burke 2002).

Similarly the students express resistances to the learning journal approach on the Foundation Degree in IT and Business Studies. They question the notion of writing the personal on their course. This kind of response by learners is supported by research by Burke and Dunn, which explores the learning journals of science students (2006). Although their questioning of the personal is a form of resistance, it is also about holding up hegemonic practices. Their resistances represent a concern not to move away from traditional approaches in formal education and to write in ways that are understood as valid, rational and logical. These acts of resistance operate to maintain rather than subvert the existing order. However, they also reveal the struggles that take place in formal educational contexts and the power of students to resist change and counter-hegemonic practices (Walkerdine 1992; Gore 1993; Burke 2002). Although learning journals have often been constructed as a transformative method of writing and supporting learners' development, in the context of this (imagined) Foundation Degree course it is used by the participants in recuperative ways. Reflection is left at the individual level and learners are encouraged to use it as a way of identifying their strengths and weaknesses rather than reflexively interrogating their socially contextualised perspectives, values, positions and assumptions (Burke and Dunn 2006).

Yet the teachers engaging in CPD write their journals in ways that might be seen as resistant to hegemonic discourses. They embrace the opportunity to write in ways that explore beneath the surface to consider social context, autobiography and ontology. This writing allows them to resist the hegemonic regimes of truth within their schools and classrooms and use their research to investigate their practices as teachers. However, this cannot be understood as a simple process of 'resistance'; rather they are small steps towards transforming relationships and practices within classrooms and are not anticipated to have radical effects on educational institutions.

Knowing, meaning-making and resistance

In this section we argue that the production of knowledge is always a space of struggle, involving resistances that both work for and against hegemonic regimes of truth (Gore 1993). We look to the narrative section to explore the processes by which meaning is produced, challenged, reconstructed and recuperated by subjects engaged in the discursive fields of lifelong learning. The struggles over meaning are always linked in with processes of identification, and although the assumption is that knowledge is made through rational processes, it is also produced at the intuitive level, involving feelings, emotion and subjectivity. The politics of knowledge come into focus through the examination of resistances in this context; resistances are connected to the micro-politics of social spaces, relations and contexts and are risky and dangerous acts. Thus, engagement in resistance, particularly in the formal field of lifelong learning, is often subtle and even manipulative and demonstrates the complexity of power relations (Morley 1999). Knowledge and power, as Foucault theorises, is inextricably linked, discursive and generative. Therefore, meaning-making involves the complex re/negotiation of power, silence, voice and author/ity (Hernandez 1997).

Let us first reconsider the imagined email communications of policy-makers, in Chapter 4. In the further education context, the support workers, led by Mustafa, are challenging new policy around the management and control of their work. Emailing as a social practice provides a space for the support workers to construct a voice and assert their experience and position, which they are arguing must be recognised as a legitimate source of professional knowledge. Indeed, underpinning their emails is the message that their knowledge is specialised and in this way they have the understanding to maintain their autonomy and to manage themselves (Freidson 2001). This is against the understanding of the senior managers in the college who do not recognise the support workers as having the right level of knowledge to manage themselves. Professionalism then is a struggle over who has the right to claim to know, and how this is connected to the legitimacy of the label 'professional'. The email messages are polite and formal between Mustafa and Kimberley but are about subtle struggles over the legitimisation of the knowledge of further education support workers within an institution that operates around hierarchies of knowing. Although these are imagined subjects, they are constructed out of the discourses available to us around who is seen to have legitimate knowledge and who can be a professional and a manager.

The imagined stories of the support workers' attempt to claim a position of recognition illustrate that emails provide spaces of informal resistance, giving opportunities to voice discontent when there might not normally be such opportunities. This is because emails can be sent at any time and to some degree by anyone. Of course, this does not mean that the author of the email has control over the ways in which the email is received and read. Indeed emails can be ignored and can be used in ways that the author did not anticipate. Yet, they represent a document that has legal status. In this way, emails provide a tool for those in marginalised positions to be heard, to at least some extent, by those in positions of authority. Emails create a range of different spaces then, both formal and informal, for the struggles around authority and knowledge and who gets recognised as having expertise.

The imagined learning journals of Chapter 7 highlight other kinds of processes of resistance from the perspectives of learners engaged in formal courses. For example, the learning journals offer the teachers engaged in continuing professional development a chance to explore their interests in the research questions they are developing. This allows them the possibility of challenging hegemonic epistemologies and to consider the methodological approaches they might want to take and why. Graham is able to emphasise that his interest in the research project is connected to his own experiences as a music student. As a result, he wants to place greater value on the knowledge of music that his students bring to the classroom and to broaden the curriculum in order to recognise the value of their experiences and understanding. Similarly Aislin wants to interrogate motivation in the classroom in relation to the importance given to students' experiences and interests. Although the teachers are struggling with their theoretical position, the learning journal helps them to explore contestations of epistemology and to begin to think critically about this in relation to their own practitioner-based research for CPD.

Of course, as the authors of these imagined narratives, our own subjectivities are embedded in their construction and in the kinds of meanings we generate through them. Therefore, our own resistances against particular forms of knowledge underpin the telling of these imagined stories.

Conclusions

This chapter has explored resistances with particular attention to formal institutional spaces. We have drawn on the narratives from Section II to shed light on the complexities of resistances and to demonstrate that resistances can be challenging to hegemonic regimes of truth but also recuperative and conservative. Using concepts such as 'micro-politics', we have considered the subtle nature of resistances and that these often take place in ways that are almost invisible in the daily life of institutions. We have seen how power is struggled over, how resistances are im/possible, pleasurable and risky and how some spaces allow for louder resistances than others. We have also paid attention to the discursive level of resistances and the ways that meaning-making is entwined with resistance and compliance. We have argued that resistance operates within complex power relations and involves intricate negotiations, networking, manipulations and manoeuvering. Hegemonic regimes of truth are deeply embedded in institutional spaces and are difficult to shift, and resistances often support rather than contest hegemony.

In this section we have returned to our narrative stories to analyse the emerging themes of identities and subjectivities, emotions and resistances. As we move into our final section we look towards practices of and for lifelong learning.

Section IV

Reconceptualising practice

> The more education becomes empty of dreams to fight for, the more the emptiness left by those *dreams* becomes filled with technique, until the moment comes when education becomes reduced to that. Then education becomes pure training, it becomes pure transfer of content, it is almost like the training of animals, it is a mere exercise in adaptation to the world.
>
> (Freire 2004: 84, original emphasis)

In the book so far, we have critiqued neo-liberal constructions of lifelong learning embedded in a hierarchical individualism. In this section, we re-visit those critiques to draw attention to the different kinds of constraints and exclusions these conceptualisations generate. We will argue for the need to challenge hegemonic discourses in order to shift and reconstruct the frames in which learning takes place. However, we will primarily argue that if (re-)conceptualisations are to make a difference, they have to be grounded in practice.

We have chosen to consider four key areas of practice: pedagogies, curriculum, assessment and quality. These are not of course discrete areas, and readers may prefer to engage with these chapters in an order which is different from the one we offer you here. In this final section we ask our readers to read between and alongside our chapters, looking out for what we have not said, challenging our presentations and constructions of the issues we raise, but joining with us in an attempt to reconceptualise our own practices (as learners/teachers/managers and/ or policy-makers).

In our previous sections we have attempted to reclaim the possibilities to challenge the boundaries of current fields; to tell in different ways and in different voices some of the stories of learning, learners and (apparent) non-learners; to find alternative visions. In this final section, we re/turn to key issues raised in the previous sections, not so much as a summary but in an attempt to demonstrate a cyclical, rather than linear, organisation of the book. In doing so, we offer both our critiques and our recommendations for practice of, in and for lifelong learning.

Throughout the book, we have grounded much of our arguments within feminist post-structuralism, arguing that post-structuralism helps us to understand the fluid, shifting, multiple, and contested nature of knowledge and meaning. Yet in this final section we highlight a dilemma for the book, for lifelong learning and for us, the authors (and maybe for our readers too). In arguing for the reconstruction of knowledge(s), we face a theoretical dilemma embedded in an equality versus difference debate. How do we find ways of reconstructing 'knowledge' that are democratic and that validate and recognise different knowledges equally, without imposing sets of shared assumptions that are embedded in classed, gendered and racialised values and experiences? There are huge social implications for the validation of different knowledges in society and what we count as valuable knowledge. How do we make recommendations for changes in practice that do not involve power relations, either implicitly or explicitly?

This final section of the book confronts our struggles, raises questions and suggests some answers for a range of issues, although we also invite our readers to search for answers and raise questions of their own. These questions include: who determines what should be validated and recognised; how can we intervene in processes of meaning making and power relations; and why is it currently so difficult to do? If we simply reconstruct lifelong learning – take apart and put together again in a different way – thinking 'outside the box' becomes impossible. However, if we continually deconstruct and recognise never-ending multiple, shifting knowledges, how can policy ever be written and, even if it can, who should participate in its writing and which of the multiple possible readings are ones which will inform hegemonic practice(s)?

What, then, are the challenges ahead for reconceptualising lifelong learning? We have set out to challenge current hegemonic discourses of lifelong learning, including who counts as a learner and what counts as learning. In our final chapter of this book we will point to strategies for change and suggestions for ways forward, and invite our readers to do the same. Whilst suggesting our own alternative visions from our specific standpoints, we invite our readers to participate in considering the questions we have raised in this book, and the issues that we will consider in this final section, and to take forward in their local communities the processes of participatory discussion and decision-making.

Chapter 11

Pedagogies for lifelong learning

Introduction

In writing about pedagogies for lifelong learning, we are interested in those pedagogical approaches that most facilitate lifelong learning. We will explore the politics of pedagogies for lifelong learning, outlining our own epistemological frameworks, but also outline some practical strategies which we believe will facilitate the development of these pedagogical approaches.

Pedagogy literally translates (from its Greek routes) as the art and science of teaching children, but is commonly used synonymously with teaching and facilitating learning with and for adults. We could instead have written about andragogy, related to adult learning, but its routes more precisely indicate an interest in and for men. We do not have an appropriate gender neutral term for facilitating (lifelong) learning for adults, nor one which is not routed in Western thought and ideas. In some ways, 'pedagogy' is a useful term, indicating that teaching is both an art and a science. However, that too is not sufficient. Other pedagogical approaches that we have found useful in informing our thinking – feminist, critical, liberatory, radical pedagogies – all start from an epistemological and political base, embedding theoretical and conceptual frameworks. Pedagogies for lifelong learning do not seem to do that, suggesting rather a list of teaching methods that will enhance lifelong learning. Indeed, there *are* teaching methods that we do believe facilitate lifelong learning, methods that encourage group work, that develop reflective practices, that promote collaborative learning.

However, we are concerned that current discourse means that in the main teachers in both formal and nonformal contexts are more likely to be considering learning and teaching styles than pedagogies. Teacher training courses, whether those endorsed by Lifelong Learning UK (the non-university sector), or accredited by the Higher Education Academy, are concerned with modules on learning, teaching, curriculum design and assessment (see below for further discussion), rather than pedagogical approaches. In addition, most post-compulsory educational institutions have learning and teaching committees: we do not know of any examples of pedagogy committees. We will go on to show below why we think a focus away from learning and teaching methods and towards pedagogy will help enhance lifelong learning agenda for all learners. With regard to formal learning, policy-makers in Lifelong Learning UK, the Higher Education Academy and within educational institutions would be well advised to move to giving pedagogies a high profile. However, this will not be sufficient unless quality assurance procedures and practices also support and indeed encourage this development, an issue that we explore in depth later in this chapter. As we show below, our arguments are political: pedagogies for lifelong learning are likely to recruit more students from informal and nonformal learning environments to formal ones, and to improve retention through developing the values that all learners – however defined – will come to place on learning.

In our discussion of pedagogies, then, we want to move beyond a focus on methods. It is our view that to talk about 'learning and teaching' is to enter into the hegemonic discourse of skills (here skills and tool-kits for teaching). It is peda-gogies, rather than learning and teaching methods, that both inform and transform practice. We therefore use 'pedagogies' politically and our concern is with trans-formative action and practice. In other words, in this section we want to engage in praxis, defined by Freire amongst others as a cycle of action-reflection-action which creates critically conscious human beings, and is central to transformative learning. We do not see theory and practice as distinct from each other: rather they inform each other and enable critical reflection. Whilst we begin with epistem-ology and move on to consider practice, there is an interconnectedness between the two.

Situating learning

Our own theoretical framework for pedagogies for lifelong learning starts from considering the underpinning epistemologies and our own political positionings. Always important, we see these as vital to developing our pedagogical approaches. Epistemology is the study of knowledge, and therefore has to be fundamental to pedagogies of lifelong learning. Like pedagogy, it has its routes in Greek (*episteme*, meaning knowledge, and *logos*, meaning words or speech). It is often taken as stemming from Western philosophy, but that in itself begs an epistemological question. Why is primacy of attention given to Western thought when questions about routes of knowledges can be found in Eastern and other world philosophies? Epistemological concerns ask questions about constructions of knowledge, i.e. Whose knowledge? What enables truth claims to be made? How do we know what we know? and so forth. They also question whether knowledge is acquired through the senses (an empiricist viewpoint) or through 'reason' (a rationalist claim). However, we argue that neither senses nor reason can be considered discretely, nor can they be taken as given: rather both are mediated through complex interactions of the social, cultural and political with our multiple lived experiences.

Key elements of pedagogies for lifelong learning, then, are the recognition of diverse and contested knowledges and situated learning. By this we mean that pedagogies for lifelong learning should make explicit ways in which human knowledge develops in the course of relationships with others and their social contexts. It includes understanding and encouraging ways in which people both create and interpret social meaning. Diverse knowledges are created through our communal interactions, through which we continually construct and reconstruct what it is we (think we) know. Situated learning is concerned with everyday or lifelong learning, which it places, or situates, within our positions and identities as community members. This is not to say that the only learning, or the only worthwhile learning, takes place with others, with a community of learners. Rather, it is about recognition of ourselves as social beings, as members of a community, and that learning is always tied to social processes, relations and practices.

Situated learning has its routes in the work of Vygotsky (see e.g. Vygotsky 1978), who believed that social interaction plays a key part in learning and understanding. More closely associated with situated learning are Lave and Wenger (see e.g. Lave and Wenger 1991). Lave and Wenger say that learning takes place in social relationships or situations of co-participation. Participation 'refers not just to local events of engagement in certain activities with certain people, but to a more encompassing process of being active participants in the *practices* of social communities and constructing *identities* in relation to these communities' (Wenger 1999: 4).

Learners become involved in a 'community of practice', formed by people who engage in a process of collective learning in a shared domain of human endeavour. Such learning embodies certain beliefs and behaviours which are to be acquired, although this suggests a more passive acquisition rather than the political engagement that we will go on to suggest is a key component of pedagogies for lifelong learning. It also takes little account of power structures in such a community of practice, which we also explore below. Nevertheless, despite our criticisms we do think that pedagogies for lifelong learning should be concerned with facilitating communities of *reflexive* practice, and that such practice should include engaging with political processes, including the political processes of power relations.

What this means in practice is that far greater movement needs to be facilitated through all contexts of learning. Successful learning – by which we mean learning that enables learners to think through ideas, relate them to their own contexts, and make the links to wider societal and political concerns – can best take place when both learners and teachers are able to de/re/construct 'knowledge' and create and interpret social meaning through understanding local and global political contexts. For example, understandings of gender politics can be transformative in situating learning in wider social, cultural and political contexts. If these understandings are developed in formal educational institutions, in the workplace, and in community centres, then diverse knowledges are brought to bear on interpretations and potential future actions.

This can happen through the curriculum and through assessment, both of which we explore in more depth below, but also through the learning environment that is created in the 'classroom', whether that classroom is in a college, a virtual space, the workplace, a university, a community centre or ideally a combination of several classrooms. Such an environment would enable the crossing of physical boundaries, but other boundaries too need to be crossed or indeed transcended, including academic boundaries, so that learners come to also see themselves as teachers, and teachers as learners. However, we want to move beyond Bakhtanian dialogical pedagogy which calls for the co-construction of knowledge between student and teacher, to shared and reflexive multi-de/re/constructions of knowledges. We recognise, for example, that community leaders, caregivers, employees/ers, activists, the young and the old are all both learners and teachers, and have much both to give and to gain through working in and with communities of reflexive practice. Therefore, learner and teacher identities are shifting and fluid so that learners are teachers and teachers are learners.

Partners and citizens

In our considerations of communities of practice, we have argued that pedagogies of lifelong learning, at their best, recognise the learning that takes place in a range of contexts and settings, and facilitates the crossing of boundary walls so that learners in the community, in the workplace, in further, adult and higher education institutions, can learn with and from each other. However, examples of this happening are difficult to find, especially in ways which have become formalised and supported through funding. Changing classroom practices is not enough. Learning within and between communities can never happen whilst funding is attached not just to assessment but to completed assessment aligned with teacher-determined learning outcomes, issues which we consider in greater depth later in this chapter.

Such initiatives though cannot take place without the necessary policies and structures in place, including funding. There *are* some examples of current policies which could potentially support communities of practice. At the time of writing, for example, in the UK the government is keen to facilitate knowledge transfer partnerships, which it supports through funding. However, whilst knowledge transfer partnerships may be assumed to help develop communities of practice, it is clear that the 'partnership' is limited to key players and to clearly defined (economic) goals and targets. In addition, this is not an equal partnership: the transfer of knowledge is uni-directional – from formal learning institutions, primarily universities, to the business sectors. The Department for Trade and Industry's website regarding Knowledge Transfer Partnerships has this to say:

- Knowledge Transfer Partnerships enable Higher Education Institutions to apply their wealth of knowledge and expertise to important business problems.
- A Knowledge Transfer Partnership can help a business to develop and grow by accessing the wealth of knowledge and expertise in the UK's universities, colleges and research organisations.

- Knowledge Transfer Partnerships enable staff in Further Education Colleges teaching at NVQ Level 4 to apply their expertise to important business problems.

(http://www.ktponline.org.uk)

This is a far cry from our communities of reflexive practice where diverse experiences and knowledges are shared for the development of new knowledges and understandings. Ivan Illich showed how community education can be used as a critical and radical tool of collectivity and critical action (see e.g. Illich 1976). An engagement with pedagogies of lifelong learning enables facilitators to work with some of the tools we have described above to find ways to rebuild solidarity and encourage the development of social movements.

Active citizenship in these conditions can start to take on new meaning. Citizenship has long been associated with lifelong learning (see e.g. Schuller 2001), with an expectation that the more we engage in lifelong learning the more we are likely to engage as active citizens. However, being a good citizen is often more about compliance than about critical action and is currently, in the UK at least, inexorably linked in both policy and discourse to economic concerns: 'good citizens' are those who add to the economic benefits of the nation state. Citizenship is not of course an uncontested concept (see e.g. Lister 1997; Crick 2000; Evans 2001; Field 2001), and for disadvantaged groups questions of citizenship are neither straightforward nor unproblematic. Democracies are full of some individuals and groups claiming privileges over others, and the democratic right for individuals to be able to participate guarantees neither equality of opportunity nor equality of outcome. Indeed, it might even guarantee quite the opposite, with the more privileged having the means to achieve greater access to limited resources (Jackson 2004b). As Kathleen Weiler (2001) shows, women's exclusion from public spheres 'has meant that men alone had access to the resources that allowed them to become socially respected and acknowledged intellectuals. As a result, men have claimed authority to speak for all' (Weiler 2001: 1). The same is of course true of and for other marginalised groups.

In addition, active citizenship has more usually been associated with the public worlds of (mainly) white, middle-class men. Citizenship as participation has been defined as 'equal opportunity for participation in legal, socio-economic and political activities' (Fuwa 2001: 2), with active citizens who are 'willing, able and equipped to have an influence in public life' (Crick 2000: 2): definitions which ignore our private lives in their emphasis on the public (Jackson 2004b). Ignored, too, is an analysis which shows that despite being 'willing, able and equipped' to influence public life, participation in political and public life remains limited, gender-defined and unsupported (*Gender Research Forum* 2002).

Whilst pedagogies for lifelong learning are concerned with active citizenship, the type of citizenship that we argue should be espoused in such pedagogies is one which may also be about civil disobedience. Certainly we see engagement with lifelong learning to be about developing political awareness, regaining criticality, and acting as an active trigger for sites of struggle, and aim to develop pedagogical approaches which support these struggles. We recognise of course that governments are highly unlikely to fund or support in any way pedagogic approaches which purport to be about civil disobedience. However, governments *are* concerned about increasing participation in political activity, including voting. It is this in part that has prompted the development of citizenship education as a compulsory national curriculum subject for pupils aged between 11 and 16. The three key pillars of the curriculum include:

- *Social and moral responsibility*: pupils learning – from the very beginning – self-confidence and socially and morally responsible behaviour both in and beyond the classroom, towards those in authority and towards each other.
- *Community involvement*: pupils learning about becoming helpfully involved in the life and concerns of their neighbourhood and communities, including learning through community involvement and service to the community.
- *Political literacy*: pupils learning about the institutions, problems and practices of our democracy and how to make themselves effective in the life of the nation, locally, regionally and nationally through skills and values as well as knowledge – a concept wider than political knowledge alone.

These are not dissimilar to some of the key concerns within pedagogies for lifelong learning, which includes social, communal and political awareness and engagement, and we argue that learners and teachers in all contexts of lifelong learning should be engaged with all three. However, by situating learning in communities of reflective practice, new meanings, interpretations and knowledges of what these mean will develop, with outcomes very different from the state proscribed and compulsory citizenship education for schools.

Pedagogy and power

It is not possible for us to leave a discussion of pedagogies for lifelong learning without turning to questions of power. In considering pedagogy and power, feminists have long paid close attention to the power relations within classrooms, especially between teacher and taught (see e.g. Jackson 1997). We agree that this should be a key concern in developing pedagogies for lifelong learning. In particular we have argued that all of us occupy multiple positionings, including learners and teachers. Moreover, this extends beyond the classroom so that though we may, for example, be teachers as parents or within our communities, yet we come to the post-compulsory classroom as learners, albeit learners with our multiple and complex experiences, knowledges and understandings. We have argued throughout this book that knowledge is always tied to power. As Basil Bernstein has shown in his work on *Pedagogy, Symbolic Control and Identity*:

> Different knowledges and their possibilities are differently distributed to different social groups. This distribution of different knowledges and

possibilities is not based on neutral differences in knowledge, but on a distribution of knowledge which carries unequal value, power and potential.

(Bernstein 1996: 8)

According to Foucault:

Power produces knowledge. Power and knowledge directly imply one another. There is no power relation without the correlative constitution of a field of knowledge, nor any knowledge that does not presuppose and constitute at the same time power relations.

(Foucault 1980: 93)

The possessors of power, individually, institutionally and structurally, are able to determine what counts as 'truth' and therefore also to determine dominant/ hegemonic discourse. However, according to Foucault, this power is not total, and hegemonic discourses are sites of contestation. There is always the possibility of resistance, and so the possibilities for new discourses to become dominant and it is this resistance that we place at the centre of pedagogies of/for lifelong learning, although we do also recognise that resistance itself takes place in structures and conditions of power. In her book *Killing Thinking*, Mary Evans (2004) argues that for far too long academics have acquiesced to the demands of policy-makers and that teachers need to learn to resist. In particular she is concerned with resistance to 'quality assessment' such as the Quality Assurance Agency and the Research Assessment Exercise. However, the price for individual resistance is likely to be high. A report in the *Times Higher Education Supplement*, for example, notes that 4 in 10 academic staff believe that their freedom to express controversial opinions is under attack, with 'controversial' meaning that which is critical of institutions and policy-makers (Shepherd 2006: 1). As Foucault (1977) suggests, in the end the discipline becomes self-regulatory: almost a quarter of the academics surveyed admitted self-censorship. However, if personal resistance is difficult, then the individualism currently embedded in academia and within neo-liberal discourse makes collective resistance even more so.

Foucault argues that there is a constant shifting in the exercise of power, with resistances being enacted locally (Foucault 1984), through the micropolitical terrain of practices of resistance. Subversive acts by both learners and teachers occur in many classrooms and learning environments, and the development of pedagogies for lifelong learning increase these acts. Shared meaning-making and knowledge creation are political acts of resistance. Rosemary Deem *et al.* (2005) define micro- politics as 'a concept which focuses on the ways in which power is relayed in everyday practices. A micropolitical perspective can reveal the subtle and sophis- ticated ways in which dominance and discrimination are achieved in academic organisations' (Deem *et al.* 2005: 61).

There is a continuing struggle over meaning at both micro and macro levels and Foucault's concern is with the institutional fields in which particular discourses gain power and control. Deem *et al.* (2005) argue that the micropolitical terrain is perhaps the most challenging, the most sensitive, and the most contingent of all aspects of the conduct and implementation of equality and diversity policies. Institutional macropolicies can be sabotaged and undermined by intense subjective struggles at the micro level of the day-to-day experiences of staff, struggles over stakes and interests specific to the academic game (Bourdieu 1988). This disconcerting backstage micropolitics highlights the 'disjuncture' between cultural/normative engineering, the official normative culture that the institution's policies try to enforce and the actual embodied and enacted norms, tactics, concerns, allegiances and priorities, on the other.

(Deem *et al.* 2005: 67)

However, as some of our stories indicated, in the neo-liberal environment within which staff at universities and colleges of further education are working, the macro-political terrain can be difficult to sabotage. As Jean Barr (2002) has shown, adult educators are working in a state of permanent anxiety formed by the reification of audits and managerial control, and risk becoming the deliverers of the political and business dealings of education management. We have argued through much of this book that lifelong learning has become part of a discourse that supports and maintains globalisation, neo-liberalism and patriarchal capitalism. We have shown that educators in all lifelong learning contexts do risk becoming the pro-ducers and reproducers of compliant subjects who always strive to do better, living in a cycle of training to participate in and develop the global economy, believing it is for personal enhancement, and that self-aggrandisement is the key to success.

Conclusions

Although transformative pedagogical practices, coupled with theoretical and experiential challenges to constructions of power/knowledge, have led to resist-ances to constructions of truth and knowledge claims (Jackson 2004a), we have argued in this book that such resistances are limited in their ability to challenge constructions of learning and learners. A clear example is the way in which Women's Studies became incorporated in the academy, leading to its demise, rather that being able to incorporate the academy into the politics of Women's Studies. This is not to say that we are suggesting that it is not possible for resistance to be enacted through challenges to pedagogy in (trans)disciplines such as Women's Studies, and we have shown throughout the book ways in which pedagogies *of* lifelong learning are concerned with deconstructing classroom dynamics and power relations.

As we showed in Chapter 3, much of this work has arisen from that already developed for feminist pedagogies. Although there have been different attempts to define feminist pedagogies, they have been described as having three overarching principles:

- to strive for egalitarian relationships in the classroom;
- to try to make all students feel valued as individuals;
- to use the experience of students as a learning resource (Welch 1994: 156).

However, although we support these principles, we are also keen to explore here the macro-political terrain. We do not believe that these principles alone are enough to challenge existing structures and, as we have shown above, are unlikely to lead to transformative action. Egalitarian relationships *are* important in the classroom, but of themselves do not challenge structural inequalities beyond the classroom walls. Making students *feel* valued as individuals does not mean that they are in fact valued, particularly outside of the classroom. We are wary of some of the practices which aim to develop student confidence through egalitarian practices in the classroom without also considering the political contexts of gender, social class, ethnicity, sexuality and so on. It is only by understanding that the personal is also political and the political personal that new knowledges can be situated both locally and globally. The development of pedagogies for lifelong learning, then, means the creation of learning environments in which critical political awareness is linked to the development not just of personal but also of communal and social transformative action.

We are, then, also critical of constant focusing on individuals, which can mitigate against social action. Henry Giroux, for example, has said that empowerment comes with 'social betterment . . . the necessary consequence of individual flourishing' (Giroux 1992: 11) but has little to say about communal flourishing. We want to move from pedagogies that support individual and personalised modes of learning to those that support social and collective ones. In practice, this means dismantling boundaries to share ideas and experiences through invited speakers, visits and classroom exchanges, as discussed above, through teaching methods which encourage group work, and through curriculum design and assessment practices.

Finally, we want to re-emphasise the point that whilst we do wholeheartedly support and practice experiential learning, we believe that this must be situated and contextualised within a socio/political framework. Whilst important, the writing and telling of experience, even reflectively, is not enough. We have argued here that pedagogies for lifelong learning have an imperative to move beyond the classroom and even the institution, and deconstruct the power relations that are embedded in societal, cultural, political and structural definitions of knowledge. Paulo Freire has said that from reflection by the oppressed on their oppression and its causes 'will come their necessary engagement in the struggle for their liberation. And in the struggle this pedagogy will be made and remade' (Freire 1972: 25).

In this section we have called for the re-making of feminist and other liberatory pedagogies into pedagogies for lifelong learning through both the policies and practices which will enhance and develop communities of reflective practice and transformative action.

Chapter 12

Considering curricula

Introduction

In Chapter 11 we outlined our epistemological frameworks as well as some practical strategies which we believe will facilitate the development of pedagogical approaches in lifelong learning. In this chapter we extend that discussion by exploring ways in which such pedagogies are both informed by and inform the curricula of formal and informal learning environments. By curricula we mean both the sets of courses that make up a programme of study, and the content of those sets of courses, including the content of individual sessions. However, we go beyond that to include hidden and ideological constructions of curricula. Our main argument in this chapter is our view of the curriculum as a powerful ideological tool. In so arguing, we recognise 'the curriculum' as contested, complex and multidimensional. Although viewed as objective, neutral and apolitical, curricula offer partial and selected knowledge and serve the interests of particular and sometimes competing groups.

We ask questions here about what knowledge gets validated as part of the curriculum, about why this is, and about whether curricula are differently designed according to hierarchical constructions of who counts as learners. Constructions of knowledge are produced and reproduced through the curriculum within hierarchies of learning and learners, and through value judgements about what constitutes knowledge and who the knowers are able to be. However, whilst the curriculum can be formal, intentional, planned and officially sanctioned by institutions and teachers, alongside this there is also a hidden curriculum, differently experienced, determined and received in different contexts and by different groups and individuals, most especially by learners, but also by teachers. Michael Young (1998) describes the curriculum as socially organised knowledge, and sees curriculum debates as always about alternative views of the future. We therefore argue that the curriculum must be reconceptualised in ways which enable participatory learning and which challenge pre-determined ownership of knowledge by teachers through the authority of institutions.

In this chapter we explore the curriculum: first as the transmitter of skills, leading to the production and reproduction of skilled workers; second as the transmitter of knowledge, including what we know of ourselves; and finally we turn to our own alternative views of the future as we explore ways in which the curriculum has the potential to operate as a developer and facilitator of lifelong learning. In considering curricula in a range of lifelong learning contexts – especially formal institutions of learning – we begin with a critique of current practices, arguing that many curricula support the continuation of exclusionary practices, and move on to point to ways in which curriculum development could lead to innovation and change in reconceptualising understandings of and practices for lifelong learning.

Learning to do (and learning to be): the curriculum as transmitter of skills

Over a decade ago Jacques Delors, former president of the European Commission, published his report to UNESCO's International Commission on Education for the Twenty-first Century, *Learning: the Treasure Within* (Delors 1996). In this report Delors outlined what he described as the four pillars of lifelong learning: learning to know, learning to be, learning to live together and learning to do. We shall use these pillars to support our discussion of curricula for lifelong learning, discussing learning to do, learning to know, and learning to live together. Throughout this book we have argued that we all continually 'learn to be', and this theme will thread through this chapter. We have chosen to start with the final pillar, learning to do, as we argue here that within current lifelong learning polices in the UK and beyond, it is 'learning to do' that dominates curriculum development, with its primary focus on learning to do the skills that are required for the knowledge society/economy, both of which construct learners and workers as gendered, racialised and classed. We also argue, therefore, that we cannot learn to do without also learning to be. Although the knowledge economy/society are used in a seemingly interchangeable way they are constantly linked with different types of learner: 'knowledge economy' is used when referring to those who work in high-tech manufacturing or knowledge intensive sectors; 'knowledge society' when referring to 'low skilled', long-term unemployed adults or early school leavers (Brine 2006).

Our discussion begins with a critique of the curriculum as the transmitter of skills, teaching students to learn to do and to learn to be in ways which are gendered, racialised and classed. We have chosen to use these pillars at the start of our discussion as calls for the development of key skills seen as linked to employment and to the knowledge economy have been central to lifelong learning debates and to a host of policies (e.g. DfES 2006, 2005, 2003b, 2003c). These skills have variously been called key skills, transferable skills and/or core skills. However, although meaning differs in the discursive fields of policies and practices, the skills that matter are the skills that are required for employability. Within this is an assumption that skills are there to be learned and developed in ways which are perceived as value free and decontextualised, with little explicit recognition that the ways in which the learner-worker is placed in the knowledge economy are gendered, racialised and classed (Webb *et al.* 2007, forthcoming). Despite dominant discourses to the contrary, both 'education' and 'employment' are subjectively constructed and contested and reproduce classed, racialised and gendered divisions of labour.

Traditionally the further education sector has concerned itself more with a curriculum for vocational learning than have other sectors. It is not surprising then that the government has looked to further education to specifically expand its curriculum for skills for employability. In recent years, three White Papers have enshrined this expansion in both policy and the practice. In 2003 the Government published *21st Century Skills: Realising our Potential* (DfES 2003b). Its subtitle 'individuals, employers, nation' means it may not be immediately clear who 'we' are, nor who needs to realise 'our' potential. However, once it is seen that the Paper is jointly presented by the Department for Education and Skills, the Department for Trade and Industry, Her Majesty's Treasury and the Department for Works and Pensions, it becomes very clear what potential further education colleges are expected to realise. Read on and it can be seen that 'we must put employers' needs for skills centre stage' (DfES 2003b: 6).

Two years later this Paper was followed by the *14–19 Education and Skills White Paper* (DfES 2005) and then the following year came *Further Education: Raising Skills, Improving Life Chances* (DfES 2006), stating:

> We have put in place major reform programmes for 14–19 year olds and adult skills, backed by substantial investment. . . . But there is a long way to go to raise skills and qualification levels for young people and adults to world standards. We must set a new ambition to tackle once and for all those skills weaknesses. The colleges and training providers that make up the Further Education sector are central to achieving that ambition. . . . But at present, Further Education is not achieving its full potential as the powerhouse of a high skills economy. This White Paper sets out the reforms needed to realise that potential. . . . Our reforms will renew the mission of the Further Education system, and its central role in equipping young people and adults with the skills for productive, sustainable employment in a modern economy.
>
> (DfES 2006: 3)

If there was any doubt that a skills agenda set by the State is expected to lead curriculum development in further education, then that doubt must by now have disappeared.

However, it is not just in further education – more traditionally the transmitter of skills for employability – that the curriculum as transmitter of skills for employability has become embedded in policy discourse. A discourse of lifelong learning for employability was eagerly seized by Sir Ron (later Lord) Dearing when preparing his Report of the National Committee of Inquiry into Higher Education published in 1997, the year following the Delors report and right at the start of New Labour's term of office. The focus of the Report revolved around the dilemma of what is meant by education, the role played in vocational training, and the development of lifelong learning. In the Report, Dearing stated that one of the main purposes of universities is 'to serve the needs of an adaptable, sustainable, knowledge-based economy at local, regional and national levels' (Dearing 1997: 5.11).

As part of this agenda, and spanning both further and higher education, the UK government has been very interested in showcasing foundation degrees, launched in September 2001, and designed to equip students with the technical skills needed by employers. The current curriculum for lifelong learning is about developing the skills necessary for learners to take their place in a (racialised, classed and gendered) global economy. This means for foundation degrees at least that much of their curriculum is intentionally and explicitly employer-led. Although foundation degrees are located within a policy context of widening participation for 'non-standard' students, they are discursively placed within the context of the knowledge-economy and, more specifically, within the demand-led skills agenda of local labour markets (Webb *et al.* 2007, forthcoming). 'Skills', then, are being taught in further and higher education institutions but also in the workplace, where of course employers again set the agenda for curricula development.

As we have argued earlier, so-called key skills for employability embody gendered, racialised and classed positionings, and there is clear and often explicit delineation with regard to which groups of learners are expected to develop which skills. Despite a discourse of transferability, there are different expectations of and for working-class and middle-class students and for women and men with regard to the transferability of their cultural capital to the workplace which, for working-class students and women, is seen as 'lack'. As Morley (2001) argues: 'there has also been only a limited critical debate about the role that power, hegemony and ideologies play in determining what is "core" at a particular political and economic moment' (Morley 2001: 135).

We have here aimed to open that debate, exploring connections between learning to do and learning to be. We go on to outline ways in which we learn to know.

Learning to know (and learning to be): the curriculum as transmitter of knowledge

In the previous chapter we argued that each student approaches their subject and their study of it from their own (multiple) perspectives, identities and subjectivites, including their past and current experiences and their understandings of themselves and others. Their identities are influenced by gender, race, culture, ethnicity, social class, sexual orientation, age, geography, past educational experiences and so forth. How we learn to know is filtered through how we have learned to be, and we learn to be through what we come to know of ourselves and others, and of the social structures within which we live. There is increased student diversity in most lifelong learning contexts, and it cannot be assumed that students have common purpose in what they hope to know and to achieve through their learning experience.

We focus our discussion of the curriculum as transmitter of knowledge by considering learning outcomes, which state precisely what outcome the learner will achieve, including what they will know, at the end of a learning event. Purported to be learner centred (see e.g. Light and Cox 2001; Hillier 2002), learning outcomes, we argue, are in fact teacher centred. They are usually deemed to be objectively set by the teacher, who has both the knowledge and the authority to determine not just what the student should learn and know, but what the student *will* learn and know, by the end of the learning event. Although the language of learning outcomes centres on the learner ('by the end of this session/module/programme/course learners will be able to . . . ') learners have no say in the skills and knowledge for which they are expected to demonstrate achievement.

In formal learning education institutions which receive State funding, such funding is attached to the successful completion of assessment, demonstrating achievement of learning outcomes. Learning outcomes, then, must be both achievable and assessable (see Chapter 13 for more detailed discussion of assessment). Institutions demand of teachers that learning outcomes are set in advance and publicly documented. Many institutions, following demands of quality assurance agencies and assessors, ask teachers to publish what are seen as four distinct types of learning outcomes: subject specific, intellectual, practical and personal and social. We have considered the practical outcomes of learning to do, and go on to discuss the social and personal outcomes of learning to live with others. Here we are concerned with the subject specific and intellectual outcomes of learning to know. For learners to be told at the outset what it is that they are expected to know can be helpful and can enable them to measure their own progress and sense of achievement. However, we also argue that such a rigid approach to learning outcomes mitigates against the independent and reflective learning that we believe should be integral to lifelong learning. The outcome of learning becomes a product, not a process.

There are several assumptions deeply embedded within the ideology of learning outcomes which privilege the power/knowledge of teachers and their institutions. First of all learners are expected to come to learning with the cultural capital to know what academic action is required by the verbs of those learning outcomes, privileging middle-class students at the expense of those who are first generation post-compulsory formal learners. As Bourdieu (1973) has shown, access to cultural capital resides with the past and current social habitus that learners inhabit. The development of cultural capital also resides in places and spaces (physical and ideological) that learners feel they have a right to inhabit and in which they gain a sense of belonging. Nevertheless, learners are expected to understand what the end product must be, and to clearly demonstrate that they can reproduce the outcome. If they do not, they are seen as lacking: at best they can hope for remedial study skills to try and achieve the outcomes, and at worst they will not demonstrate that the learning outcomes have been achieved (whether or not they have been, or whether or not they have learned from participating) and will not formally pass the course.

Second there is the assumption that teachers and their institutions are and should be the determiners of the knowledge that is transmitted in the classroom. We argued in Chapter 2 that some knowledges are legitimated and some voices (here, the combined voices of teacher and institutions) are heard louder than others. The selectivity of knowledge creation and meaning-making is embedded within complex politics about the kinds of knowledge that are seen as valid and worthwhile in ways which we demonstrated are highly classed, gendered and racialised. Constructions of knowledge represent the interests of those in more powerful positions, and the transmission of knowledge through the setting and enforcement of learning outcomes is one more example of ways in which this operates in practice.

Third, then, is the assumption that learners are not able to determine for themselves what it is they want to achieve through their participation in a learning event. We argue that a more learner-centred, participatory and potentially transformative practice would be one where learners are able to negotiate and/or determine the learning outcomes that they would like to achieve, based in reflective practice. Whilst some learning outcomes are rightly bound to be individual, learners could also be encouraged to consider learning outcomes for the group, linked to wider social contexts, including engagement with constructions of gender, social class and race. Whilst some might object to the apparent politicising of learning outcomes, we argue that they are in any case politicised, although they are expressed and often regarded as though they were logical, neutral, apolitical and value free. Learning outcomes, however, have legitimacy for those by whom they are determined, and this is currently not the learner.

Finally we argue that learning outcomes are linked to the fragmentation of knowledge that seems such an integral part of postmodernity. We have increasingly seen the commodification of knowledge, and modularity in learning means that learners (and teachers) work on a production line to produce and reproduce required outcomes. Learning outcomes set for each module of work that students undertake ensure carefully orchestrated portion control over access to knowledge, termed 'McDonalisation' by George Ritzer (1995). The concern of education institutions is to ensure that students accumulate a series of credits which, added together, constitute an award. This concern is in part understandable, as it is linked to State funding. However, what this means in practice is that students are not encouraged to build on and develop the knowledge that they acquire through the curricula of each module so that they can take a more critical and/or holistic view of the learning that they are acquiring. Nor are they able (at least formally) to experience opportunities that move beyond and between the different aspects of lifelong learning that they encounter daily, and as discussed in the previous chapter.

It is this that has led to suggestions that universities (and other formal education institutions) are killing thinking (see Evans 2004). Although more subjects are now on offer than ever before, with greater numbers of students participating in formal education, Mary Evans argues that 'a broader curriculum, and a broader intake . . . has done very little to shift either the nature of the British class structure as a whole or the location of significant academic power and resources' (Evans 2004: 20). While the curriculum remains the transmitter of privileged knowledges, determining what and how students learn to know, this will inevitably remain the case. However, that it must remain the case is, we argue, not inevitable. We move on to consider ways in which the curriculum can take on a social and participatory aspect, becoming a developer of lifelong learning.

Learning to live together (and learning to be): the curriculum as developer of lifelong learning

In this part of the chapter we want to return to some of the issues that we raised above, arguing for ways to use curriculum development to enhance and facilitate communities of reflective practice and transformative action. In particular, we argue that learners need to inhabit a space (or multiple spaces) for learning which they experience with a sense of new possibilities, spaces which are open, creative and potentially transformative. One way in which this can happen is through a negotiated curriculum and there are currently some good examples of ways in which this can happen, although in the main not within formal educational institutions. We return here to some of the examples we gave in Chapter 3, to point to ways in which the curriculum can be successfully and collaboratively negotiated between learners in order to develop lifelong learning, although we recognise that there are constraints that face the providers we describe.

We start with the University of the Third Age (U3A), whose philosophy is to capitalise on the accumulated knowledge, skills and interests of its own members, who are both learners and teachers. No qualifications are necessary to teach other than an interest in doing so, and there is no formal assessment of learning and no qualifications gained. There are however, study support networks and subject networks so that learners and teachers can work together and support each other. Their 'Objects' state that the U3A aims:

*   To provide for amongst the retired the resources for the development and intensification of their intellectual, cultural and aesthetic lives. In this way to help them to make effective and satisfying use of their freedom from work at the office, shop or factory.
*   To devise methods of doing this which can be afforded in Britain.
*   To create an institution for these purposes where there is no distinction between the class of those who teach and those who learn, where as much as possible of the activity is voluntary, freely offered by the members of the university to other members and to other people.
*   So to organise this institution that learning is pursued, skills acquired, interests are developed for themselves alone with no reference to qualifications, awards or personal advancement (Manley 2003).

However, and especially in villages, groups often meet in each other's homes, and the need to offer a suitable learning space may well mean that middle-class people are more likely to occupy these spaces. Currently in the UK there are around 150,000 people learning with the U3A in almost 500 local groups (http://www.u3a. org.uk), although the U3A extends far beyond the UK, including Europe, China, Australia and the USA. Of interest to us here is the fact that members of the groups are responsible for choosing and setting the curriculum and for selecting and/or offering themselves as teachers.

The WEA (Workers Educational Association) is another major lifelong learning provider, with a membership actively involved in curriculum planning, development and delivery. However, unlike the U3A, the WEA comes under the control of Lifelong Learning UK and therefore has to concern itself with State funding and the requirements that go with it. Its website sets out its epistemological and political concerns, whilst alluding to some of the current difficulties it is facing. It states the characteristics of WEA provision:

- Effective WEA programmes built on students' experiences and interests and linked them both to a wider social and critical understanding and to social and civic action and involvement.
- An emphasis on people who missed out on education first time round so WEA offered potentially a route back into a sometimes life-changing educational journey.
- The development of educational processes that built a democratic relationship between tutor and students, building the curriculum together, and encouraged students to go on to become active WEA members.

However, it continues:

Today, as we renew our own vision and values in a changing and unpredictable world, we need to think about translating these into a modern context. We are proposing to set out our defining characteristics to provide benchmarks for our own work and to enable students and others to assess us.

(http://www.wea.org.uk)

Today the WEA is straddling the formal and nonformal sectors of lifelong learning, inevitably concerning itself with some of the same issues we have considered above, and that we will go on to explore in the next chapter, whilst trying to find ways to hold onto and continue to work with its founding principles.

A main provider of active learning opportunities for older women is the NFWI (National Federation of Women's Institutes). The NFWI currently has over a quarter of a million members, the majority of whom are over 50, and offers a wide range of choices and learning opportunities for its members. However, like the WEA the NFWI is trying to find its way between formal and nonformal learning. Each Women's Institute sets it own curriculum of informal learning, including a range of invited speakers and other nonformal learning opportunities. However, although this is a participatory curriculum, in practice it means that all too often the learning that takes place is amongst 'like-minded people' assured of their positions in the world embedded within middle-class (white, English and rural) feminine respectability (Jackson 2006).

However, the NFWI also has a substantial number of formal courses franchised with further education colleges, under the auspices of Lifelong Learning UK. In part the reasons for this are financial: like other providers of adult and continuing education, the NFWI has had problems with public funding, especially with regard to non-accredited courses. Accredited courses are eligible for Learning and Skills Council funding, and more and more courses are now being accredited. Although the NFWI has an active campaign to lobby Government on widening participation within a lifelong learning agenda, they are experiencing real problems in getting students to complete coursework, which also severely affects funding. These issues do of course have serious implications for learners (Jackson 2006).

Given these constraints, how can curricula for lifelong learning be developed? In considering this, we should like to explore issues for policy-makers and for teachers, as well as of course for learners. To enable learners to succeed means not just that they have to recognise themselves and their potentiality within lifelong learning, including formal, nonformal and informal learning, but they also have to have the opportunities to move towards the realising of potential. We believe that policy-makers and teachers, as well as managers, should concern themselves with the two key areas outlined above.

First there is the question of the skills agenda, and learning to do. We have been critical of ways in which classed, gendered and racialised constructions of 'skill' have become embedded in the development of curricula within both higher and further education. This is inevitably also linked to workplace learning, and in all arena employers are determining what is taught, and to whom. Current constructions of 'skill' are likely to result in working-class people being constrained in a never-ending cycle of skills-based training to enable them to go from one short-term job to another, whilst skills developed by, for example, women in the home remain unrecognised or valued. Instead we should like to see the development of curricula that both critique constructions of skill, and that embed skills development for work, learning and participatory citizenship within wider contexts of learning. However, this requires policy-makers to engage with setting a broader curricula agenda for lifelong learning than is currently happening. In making this case, we argue that to do so will more greatly develop skills that are required for the workplace, but also within communities, thus enhancing social cohesion and active participation by wider communities of citizens.

Likewise, we also argue here for learning support skills to be embedded within curricula rather than being viewed as add-on remedial work for those who enter learning institutions in lack. Widening participation should not merely consist of enabling less able learners to participate as best they can in current structures. Rather learners should be able to participate in learning environments that recognise different ways of knowing and of being. Planning for effective curricula should not assume remedial activities of learning support to bring all students up to acceptable levels, but should instead assume that all students are engaged in learning development processes, finding ways to enable students to recognise their own learning needs and to find strategies to meet them.

Finally we turn to the transmission of knowledge, and learning to know. Currently, as Hussey and Smith have indicated:

> The teacher is stuck in the middle between tight adherence to achieving pre-specified outcomes, on the one hand, and optimising the opportunities for development and support of independent, autonomous and lifelong learners, on the other.
>
> (Hussey and Smith 2003: 358)

Teachers need to be supported by managers, policy-makers and training providers in considering a range of ways to develop curricula which will encourage active and participatory learning, to make subjects relevant to the lived experiences of their students, and to draw on and develop their accumulated knowledges. Teachers need to adapt and change the curricula to include and value the diverse experiences of their students. This includes encouraging and enabling the use of personal experience in theoretical and analytical approaches (Jackson 1999) and integrating learner experience into the conceptual structure of subject matter (Withnall and Percy 1994). This means taking account of ways in which constructions of sexuality, disability, age, gender, race, social class and so on affect how we learn to be. The curriculum needs to be more explicitly political, enabling challenges to be made to constructions of knowledge and to claims of apolitical neutrality. Both learners and teachers need to participate in the development of a curriculum which makes explicit the ways in which our own experiences of power, privilege and discrimination in learning and teaching affect our practice.

We have then argued for the development of approaches which enable the curriculum to be used to challenge social exclusion and inequalities, showing how some lifelong learning providers, such as the WEA, have an explicitly political agenda. All learning environments need to take account of changing social contexts, and there will be very many more external factors that influence people's learning than those that go on inside educational institutions. Although many groups of disadvantaged learners are currently largely excluded from the production of knowledge, especially in formal educational institutions and in the workplace, knowledge gained from and through our cumulative experiences is a valuable addition to current curricula for lifelong learning, producing new knowledges and ways of knowing.

In the last chapter we called for pedagogies for lifelong learning that move from only supporting individual and personalised modes of learning to those that support social and collective ones. We believe that curricula for lifelong learning should be engaged with Jacques Delors' call for us all to be learning to live together. It is our view that this means the development of curricula that take account of local, national and global contexts, and that engage politically with constructions of difference. The ways in which curricula are determined, and the practices for curricula design and delivery, need to be reconceptualised to recognise, value and open opportunities for transformative practice. Many of the possibilities for new curricula are currently being fulfilled outside of formal educational institutions. However, a start to these processes within formal education institutions would be via a negotiated curriculum between learners and teachers which allows for learning outcomes to emerge so that learners and teachers engage together in new possibilities and de/re/constructions of knowledge. Additionally, we would like to see curricula that extend beyond traditional boundaries of both discipline and space, enabling the development of social practices and participatory and critical citizenship.

However, whilst knowledge remains fragmentary; whilst gendered, racialised and classed constructions of 'skills' dominate policy recommendations of what learners needs to know; and whilst pre-determined learning outcomes define the assessment of successful learning, this remains a challenge. We continue to explore these issues as we move on to the next chapter in which we consider assessment.

Chapter 13

Assessment practices

Introduction

This chapter focuses on assessment frameworks and the ways that current practices privilege particular epistemologies and ontologies. This theme has been central to all sections of the book and here we focus on the specific effects of assessment practices in light of our earlier arguments. In examining assessment practices, we are interested in uncovering the implications of current frameworks, and the assumptions behind them, for lifelong learning. We argue that the contemporary emphasis on outcome-oriented assessment instruments operates in ways to re-privilege certain identities and knowledges. Therefore, a dramatic shift is required that refocuses assessment on negotiated processes of recognition to challenge and dislodge the exclusive assessment frameworks that permeate lifelong learning. We need negotiated, creative and fluid practices that are collaboratively constructed to recognise those identities and validate those knowledges that have historically been Othered, misrepresented and misrecognised. In this part of the chapter we uncover the complex and subtle ways that certain identities are favoured by the hegemonic forms of assessment in formal educational institutions and the ways these perpetuate wider social divisions, exclusions and inequalities.

Hegemonic assessment practices

Our discussion begins with an interrogation of essayist literacy, which is the hegemonic assessment practice in contemporary Western educational institutions (Lillis 2001). We have already highlighted the problematic nature of essayist literacy earlier in the book, raising the issue of the dominance of the essay in our opening discussion of Section II and in Chapter 2. We have argued that essayist literacy is a social practice that is exclusive of certain voices and author/ises particular selves. The narratives in Chapter 7 help to illuminate the ways that essay-writing conventions penetrate other literacy practices such as journal writing, where personal experience and emotion are often discouraged and seen as outside the realm of legitimate learning. In this chapter, we begin our interrogation of the problematic practices of assessment in educational institutions by critiquing the essay. We start with a focus on universities because this is the discursive site where the most highly valued learning takes place, and as a result, other learning spaces and practices are significantly shaped by what happens within universities. Our key argument is that the essay is tied to certain epistemological frameworks, which privilege academic and positivist forms of knowledge. The essay as the privileged form of assessment in universities sets the scene for who has access to the most highly valued kind of learning – the honours degree – and thus plays a key role in the stratification of learning, which kinds of learning are recognised and which are not counted as 'real learning'. Learner identities are constructed within these struggles over what kind of learning can be socially recognised and validated.

In higher education there are two dominant assessment instruments: the examination and the coursework essay. Indeed, the examination often involves writing an essay under exam conditions. Essay writing is often seen as a skill, and as such as something which can be taught and learnt in a rather straightforward way – 'how to' write an introduction, 'how to' reference, 'how to' structure an argument and so forth. This way of conceptualising essay-writing, as a set of mechanical skills, ignores that essay-writing is a social practice, situated in particular contexts and communities and embedded in taken-for-granted assumptions about the nature of knowledge and knowing (Burke and Hermerschmidt 2005). As a social practice, essay-writing requires particular kinds of cultural capital and ways of doing 'learner'. Essay-writing involves struggles at the intellectual and emotional levels and it is ultimately about author/ising the self; the production of an authorial and authoritative voice. It involves complex selection processes, which are deemed to be 'objective' and are talked about simply in technical terms of 'referencing' and 'editing' but are actually about meticulous processes of 'orchestrating the voices' of the field (Lillis and Ramsey 1997), while also crafting an authorial voice that is recognised as authoritative by (legitimated) others in the field. Audience is central in the process and assumes an ontological link between self and other. However, only certain selves and others can be recognised through the practice of essay-writing, and this demands conforming to the conventions of the essay (Lillis 2001). Essay-writing requires complex decoding of tacit understandings and conventions and as such remains mysterious to those on the outside of academia. Essay-writing therefore is a highly exclusive practice; it serves as a gate-keeping mechanism to ensure certain (contaminating) identities are kept out.

Teresa Lillis, drawing on Gee (1990), explains that the features of the essay include: linearity, a particular kind of explicitness, making a central point or argument, and the standard form of a language. These features are embedded in particular literacies and ways of constructing knowledge and they operate to exclude other literacies and ways of understanding, including the personal, practical, emotional and creative. There is a fictionalisation of both writer and reader, the reader being an idealisation, 'a rational mind formed by the rational body of knowledge of which the essay is a part' (Lillis 2001: 38). Furthermore, Lillis argues that the essayist literacy serves to privilege 'the discursive routines of particular social groups whilst dismissing those of people who, culturally and communally, have access to and engage in a range of other practices' (Lillis 2001: 39). Her points help to uncover the subtle ways that certain personhoods get excluded from formal learning, particularly those forms of learning that carry high esteem and status. Indeed, essayist literacy is a key mechanism by which some groups become excluded from full higher education participation, even after they have secured entry to degree level study. The recognition that essayist literacy dominates assessment practices further supports the argument we have made earlier that access to formal lifelong learning is as much about the cultural and discursive practices within institutions as financial and material barriers. As Lillis states:

> The conventions surrounding the production of student academic texts are ideologically inscribed in at least two powerful ways: by working towards the exclusion of students from social groups who have historically been excluded from the conservative-liberal project of HE in the UK and by regulating directly and indirectly what student-writers can mean, and who they can be.
>
> (Lillis 2001: 39)

Essayist literacy practices serve to exclude certain social groups at both ontological (who can claim authority and to know) and epistemological (what kind of knowledge is seen as worthy of public and institutional recognition) levels. This form of assessment constructs authorship in specifically gendered, racialised and classed ways as the objective, scientific, neutral and rational subject who is uncovering the truth rather than fashioning a particular way of seeing and knowing the world. The relations by which knowledge gets produced are perceived as apolitical and/or irrelevant in such practices and other ways of writing, for example fictional or poetic, are not recognised as legitimate or valuable for the serious pursuit of knowledge. If we consider this in relation to attempts to widen participation in higher education, and acknowledge the different epistemological perspectives students bring to their studies, then we might be able to understand why this issue is so central to developing strategies within lifelong learning for equality, inclusion and social justice (Burke 2006).

This discussion draws attention to the major strategy currently adopted within higher education to support 'non-traditional' students, namely study skills provision. The study skills approach constructs writing as a set of techniques that are separate from methodological, epistemological and ontological concerns and that can be straightforwardly taught to those individual students seen as having poor literacy skills or problems with their reading and writing (Lea and Street 1997). It is embedded in a deficit construction of students seen as 'Other', 'non-standard', potentially contaminating of university standards and lacking the right kind of cultural capital, ways of being and ways of doing 'student' (Bowl 2003). Those who struggle to express their understanding in the privileged essayist literacy are often labelled as 'weak' by their teachers and often identify themselves as 'unable'. Study skills approaches are unable to address the ways that some writers have author/ship and author/ity whilst others are seen as outside of the realms of meaning-making (Burke and Hermerschmist 2005). By trying to teach a set of techniques for essay-writing, the power relations of those who are un/able to write become reinforced. Those learners who, even after being taught 'how to' write, are left unable to express themselves through the essay are seen as lacking potential, talent and ability and therefore are not able to position themselves as a 'real learner'. The current frameworks of assessment work to ensure that certain subjects, those who do not have access to the cultural tools to decode essayist literacy practices, are not able to identify themselves as learners.

The approaches to teaching writing for assessment vary in different countries: the USA has 'composition' classes; the UK offers 'study skills' support, albeit in a rather fragmented way; Australia, South Africa and the USA often provide 'writing centres'. All of these approaches take place in centrally provided writing support outside of the disciplines. In other words writing is seen as a mechanical process that simply reflects knowledge and understanding, rather than as being part of the construction of knowledge and understanding. The conceptualisations of writing embedded in all of these different kinds of approaches are rooted in the same kinds of assumptions and share a common frame of reference (Lillis 2001: 22). Lillis identifies three prominent characteristics in relation to this:

> Firstly, both the 'problem' and the 'solution' are constructed/perceived as being overwhelmingly textual. That is, they are construed as being locatable and identifiable in the written texts that students produce, rather than in any broader frame of reference which includes, for example, questions about contexts, participants and practices. This is manifested not least in the continuing widespread belief in the possibility of teaching writing skills or 'good academic writing' outside mainstream disciplinary courses. [. . .] The second characteristic is what can be refered to as the institutional claim to transparency; that is while the language of students is made visible and problematised, the language of the disciplines and the pedagogic practices in which these are embedded usually remains invisible, taken as a 'given'. [. . .] Thirdly, both the 'problem' and the 'solution' are conceived as being, whilst annoying, relatively straightforward to identify and resolve.
>
> (Lillis 2001: 22)

What Lillis argues in the above quotation is important to our considerations because it demonstrates that educational institutions construct the written text as separate from methodology and epistemology. The production of text is a discursive act and is constitutive of knowledge; knowledge about the social world and knowledge about ourselves and our position within it. Modes of assessment that rely on written text and yet assume that student writing is decontextualised and separate from social practices and relations play a significant role in re/producing exclusions and inequalities.

Therefore, it is crucial that the dominant assessment practices in educational institutions are significantly reconceptualised to draw attention to the key contribution they make to narrowing what can count as learning and who can count as a learner. Once attention is paid to the ways that certain assessment practices, such as the essay, play a central role in the production of knowledge, we can begin to see that assessment is not simply the rational, objective and scientific measure of ability that it is constructed to be (Gillborn and Youdell 2000). The process of assessing a piece of writing is always tied to value judgements and these are made within contested discursive sites. Critiques of lifelong learning must involve the deconstruction of the ways that essay-writing privileges particular ontological positions through 'academic conventions', which are taken-for-granted as the preferred way of writing in formal educational spaces (Burke and Hermerschmidt 2005). By taking this approach, study skills would be replaced with studies in writing, so that the assumptions underpinning essayist literacy can be deconstructed and problematised. Studies in writing would engage students in critical interrogation of different writing methodologies and the effect of these on knowing and knowledge. This would give learners, and their tutors, the opportunity to carefully re/consider and re/negotiate the kind of contribution to meaning-making they want to make through their writing, and it could also contribute to challenging hegemonic academic practices within educational institutions that serve to maintain privilege and exclusion. Furthermore, we argue that writing itself as the preferred medium for assessing learning must be contested. There are other ways of representing understanding and knowledge emerging from learning processes; for example visual, musical and dramatic representations. The development of lifelong learning opportunities that address issues of social justice would enable a range of different representations of understanding to be valued and legitimated.

Complex exclusions from lifelong learning

In the current framework, however, essayist literacy practices are embedded in middle-classed, white racialised and masculinised ways of constructing knowledge and meaning. Therefore children from middle-class, traditional (nuclear) white families are more likely to develop the cultural capital and ways of doing and being that is legitimated and recognised in schools, colleges and higher education institutions. Because all learning is not equal but is implicated in social divisions, hierarchies and inequalities, those children who are encouraged to follow the 'standard' route through to higher education are those whose learning will be most highly valued and rewarded in wider society. Access to the professions, for example, is dependent on being recognised as a particular kind of learner; one who is seen to be 'able' to express themselves through the dominant literacy practice privileged in and through the education system.

Indeed, we argue that academic knowledge, and more specifically the essay, serves as a gate-keeping mechanism to the professions. Because essayist literacy practices are embedded in taken-for-granted academic conventions and are the dominant way of measuring 'ability', it is those who are able to learn the rules of the essay-writing game who are ultimately most likely to have access to the highest levels of the labour market hierarchy. Those who are seen as unable to write an essay effectively are more likely to end up on the bottom rungs of the stratified work order. Of course there are exceptions to this. However, overall, because 'success' equals career success and career success often depends on academic success, those with the right kinds of habitus and cultural capital will be more likely to 'succeed' academically and professionally.

This level of unequal access to high status learning opportunities does not stop at entry to the professions. Access to accredited continuing professional development also depends on having the right kinds of cultural capital and habitus. Gaining access to CPD at masters or doctoral level rests on the 'ability' to write essays 'effectively'. The conventions of academia are embedded in academic-oriented assessment criteria, seen to be transparent and objective instruments of measurement (Orr and Blythman 2005; Shay 2005). Yet these criteria are constructed through certain assumptions about knowledge that privilege academic forms of meaning-making. These are not value-free but are inextricably tied to middle-classed, white racialised and masculinised dispositions and subjectivities. Examiners similarly are subjects that are constituted through classed, racialised and gendered discourses; they are context-bound and situated knowers who make judgements based on what is seen as 'rational', 'scientific', 'objective', 'critical', 'coherent', 'logical', 'reasoned' ways of constructing knowledge.

As we have explained above, we have launched into our discussion of assessment practices by focusing on the context of higher education, because it is important to understand that the assessment practices of higher education set the scene for lifelong learning more generally. Because essayist literacy is the preferred practice within higher education, secondary school education also privileges essayist literacy.

> The practice of essayist literacy is enacted and maintained through formal institutions of schooling and in many ways is synonymous with formal schooling: to do schooling successfully means doing essayist literacy successfully.
>
> (Lillis 2001: 53)

In the UK, for example, those pupils who demonstrate the 'ability' to write well in this kind of way are more likely to be encouraged by their teachers to follow the traditional 'A' level route, setting them up for their future participation in undergraduate level studies. Those pupils are most likely, as well, to come from white, middle-class backgrounds, where their parents have focused on developing their child in the 'right' kinds of ways (Reay 2001). Those pupils who are not seen as 'able' will be encouraged to follow 'Other' kinds of learning paths, or to leave school at 16 to begin work (Reay 2001). These pupils are more likely to come from working-class backgrounds. Furthermore, assessment practices themselves produce real problems for conceptualising learning outside of institutional spaces. The very practice of assessment creates a rigid set of structures around the recognition and legitimating of learning. As long as assessment of formal learning exists then learning in life outside of institutions continues to be overlooked as a key source of understanding and knowing. Accredited learning is further privileged through funding mechanisms; this point was highlighted in Chapter 5 through the managers' narratives. Although Narinder, Hafsa, Edith and Sarah all articulated their commitment to non-accredited learning, the attachment of funding to accredited courses made this particularly difficult to argue.

The privileged status of essay-writing has implications for learners early on in their school experiences. Gillborn and Youdell (2000) examine the effects of what they call the 'A–C economy' in General Certificate in Secondary Education (GCSE) selection processes in the context of UK schools. Drawing on the notion of 'triage' from the medical field, they argue that current policy has placed teachers in a position where they are making decisions about who to, and who not to, support. In the educational market and the context of league tables, such decisions are informed by concerns about the survival of the school that they work for. Gillborn and Youdell (2000) explain that in the medical context, doctors make decisions about how to use scarce resources in terms of which patients are most likely to survive if they are given treatment. Those who are most likely to die, in a crisis situation, will be least likely to receive treatment. Similarly, in the school context, those who are seen as unlikely to benefit from 'treatment' will be least likely to receive scarce educational support and resources. They explain:

> The extraordinary demands of the A–C economy are such that both our case-study schools are seeking new ways of identifying suitable cases for treatment – pupils who will show the maximum return (in terms of higher-grade passes) from receipt of additional resources of teacher time and support.
>
> (Gillborn and Youdell 2000: 199)

However, they further argue that, because of the racialised ways that 'ability' is constructed, it is Black students who are 'significantly over-represented in the group of pupils deemed to be without hope' (Gillborn and Youdell 2000: 200). Access to formally recognised lifelong learning, therefore, is dependent on social positioning from early on at school through to later years of continuing professional development. The dominant forms of assessment, seen as objective and value-free, operate to construct certain social groups as having, or not having, academic ability.

Bourdieu's concepts of cultural capital and habitus help shed light on the ways that classed and racialised divisions are perpetuated through educational systems and assessment frameworks and practices. Those individuals with the social habitus to develop the 'right kinds of habits' for learning are more likely to participate in the learning that is socially legitimated and held in high esteem (Reay et al. 2005). Those who feel less comfortable in the institutional spaces where learning that is socially validated takes place are more likely to be seen as 'non-participants' in learning. We could argue however that all individuals are lifelong learners, whether or not they learn in formal institutional spaces. Learning in life happens on an every-day basis, in a range of social contexts, including for example community centres, domestic sites, voluntary work, libraries and so forth. However, because 'lifelong learning' is understood as learning that can be accredited and transferred across different institutional spaces, assessment practices become central to the validation of some learning above and to the deletion of others.

Practices of recognition

We are not arguing that accredited learning is the only kind of learning that matters. Lifelong learning does not only include learning that takes place in educational institutions. Learning that takes place outside of institutions, for example in the home or community centre, through friendships and travel, is important and must be recognised and valued in society. We have given some examples of this in Chapters 3 and 12, where we looked at organisations like the National Federation of Women's Institutes and the University of the Third Age. Many problems in relation to community learning come to light though when assessment is interrogated. How can learning in informal and nonformal contexts be recognised? Can educational institutions participate in the recognition of learning that takes place outside of the school, college or university? Are there other bodies that can recognise such learning processes? If we want to stretch the boundaries of assessment frameworks and practices, what kinds of assessment instruments should we be developing?

We want to explore the possibilities for transforming assessment practices in a way that opens up the possibilities for representing, valuing and recognising different kinds of learning, both inside and outside of formal institutional spaces in a way that challenges well established hierarchies and power relations. The first step, we would argue, is to understand the political nature of assessment and to reject the notion that assessment is a rational and scientific instrument that if designed in a transparent and logical way can objectively measure learning outcomes. Rather, we must understand that assessment is tied to wider social inequalities and power relations and is caught up in struggles over who has the right to claim authority and knowledge. The claim that assessment is apolitical and outside of wider power relations in itself operates in the interests of privileged groups.

Assessment should be collaboratively re/designed with learners to support learning processes across a range of discursive sites. A key problem with the current assessment framework is that as a result of quality assurance mechanisms, learning outcomes are the key focus of assessment approaches. We will explore this further in the next chapter, but we want to argue here that this undermines the creativity of learning and the uncertainties and surprises that learning can bring. The setting of fixed and predictable learning outcomes immediately narrows what it is that can be learned and this is decided before the learner even arrives on the scene. This makes the unpredicted nature of learning an impossibility and imposes a rigid framework on the learner. Again, the learner is constrained and undermined by the values and perspectives embedded in the pre-conceived framework set by the teacher and is unable to move beyond this. Mary Evans powerfully articulates the limitations and rigidity of the current assessment frameworks, which operate around fixed learning outcomes:

> The skills necessary for technical competence are not the same as those necessary, indeed essential, for intellectual creativity or understanding. Moreover, it is a basic misunderstanding that learning in these subjects necessarily follows a mechanistic pattern. The sad truth is that the authors of assessment want the world, and indeed everything we might possibly know about it, to be organised into the bite sized portions of mass catering. The standard potato chip becomes the standard idea, it has measurements and it has contours and nobody will be given one that is a peculiar shape or made of different materials. Goven that mass catering also depends upon 'portion control' we can also expect that no one will receive more (or less) 'knowledge' than anyone else.
>
> (Evans 2004: 71–2)

Learners need to learn within a flexible space in which the unexpected, exciting, imaginative, creative, uncertain and iterative processes of learning are embraced and made possible. Assessment, or as we prefer it, practices of recognition, should offer the pedagogical tools to support learning as a journey of unanticipated insights and understandings. This approach supports learners in formulating their own lines of inquiry and following the autobiography of the question (Miller 1995). This means that learners start from their own interests to formulate questions for learning and then, as part of the learning process, map these onto wider histories, contestations and meanings, making connections and disconnections, so that they participate in wider debates and discussions. This process moves back and forth between the personal and the social, the emotional and the rational, the subjective and the objective, breaking down the boundaries between these constraining binaries to fully explore meaning and develop new understandings. The learning project is collaboratively designed within learning communities rather than institutionalised and individualised and in the control of educational managers. Learners then begin to take control of their learning from the positions, values and perspectives that they start from. Learning, taking this approach, involves critical transformations, which are unpredictable, uncertain, challenging and impossible to anticipate and audit.

It is through transforming practices that are shaped by a reconceptualisation of lifelong learning that assessment practices can be re/developed to recognise different epistemological perspectives and to challenge the assumption that rational, objective, scientific, positivist and value-free knowledge is the only kind of legitimate knowledge that deserves to be assessed and accredited. This transformatory approach places value on learning processes rather than on measuring the pre-set outcomes of learning. It values the complex insights and understandings that emerge from participation in learning in a range of social sites, including but not only formal educational institutions. It does not assume a particular ontological position but enables a range of learner identities to be valued, transformed and recognised to learners across multiple and diverse social spaces. Personal experience is valued alongside professional and academic experience and 'being critical' involves not only making connections with literature in the field but also with the insights emerging from the personal, subjective, creative and emotional. However, such transformatory practices are not straightforward to develop because, as sociologists such as Skeggs (2004) have shown, who is seen as having legitimate experience is again classed, gendered and racialised. What counts as experience is always tied to value judgements and usually the experience that is socially valued is the experience of over-privileged groups.

In the current frame, the only resources we have to draw on to assess learning outside of formal institutions is through AP[E]L – the Accreditation of Prior Experiential Learning. This is a useful beginning. However, we would argue, it is also hugely limited because it is still embedded in particular assumptions about knowledge. Therefore, to take an example, it is unlikely that the learning that a mother experiences in the home will be accredited by a college through AP[E]L. If her learning were to be considered under AP[E]L, it would also be required that the learner write about her experience drawing on the academic conventions we have already critiqued. In other words, she would have to understand the expectations attached to academic forms of writing in order to re-present her knowledge in a way that could/would be recognised by a formal educational institution. AP[E]L therefore is a recuperative mechanism that serves to maintain the current order and keep the privileged forms of knowledge and learning in place.

Conclusions

It is no coincidence that as authors of an academic book we are writing within the very frameworks that we have critiqued and challenged in this chapter. Although we are not being assessed as learners, our book will be assessed by colleagues in the field of lifelong learning and crucially through the Research Assessment Exercise. It seems ironic that our writing falls into Lillis's essayist literacy practices. However, in order for our book to be recognised as legitimate we must attempt to meet the expectations of the academy. We have also attempted to subtly subvert the conventions of academic writing by presenting part of our argument through narrative in Section II. These are the contradictions that we are confronted with in this project – writing a book about lifelong learning that challenges hegemonic discourses, epistemologies and ontologies whilst simultaneously attempting to produce a book that will be recognised as 'academic' and 'RAE-able'. This sheds light on our key argument – that these struggles do not take place at the individual level, and although individuals do have agency, they are always implicated in the social relations and discourses at play at that moment in time and it is almost impossible to move outside of these. We are subjects of the same regulatory discourses as everyone else. Like the learners we are writing about, we too are subjects of the current regimes of truth and have only small spaces to manoeuvre around these. Indeed, we are currently subject to a particular disciplinary regime in the form of quality assurance, which ensures that we as authors position ourselves in the 'correct' ways for the RAE, just as learners are disciplined by the discursive practices of educational institutions.

Lifelong learning and assessment are inextricably tied together in policy and in the ways we conceptualise learning. Indeed it becomes difficult to imagine a policy of lifelong learning that is able to move beyond assessment and accreditation to recognise nonformal learning processes. This is exacerbated by the quality assurance frameworks that now tightly regulate what kinds of learning is recognised and validated, and it is to these mechanisms that we now turn.

Chapter 14

Quality assurance and lifelong learning

Introduction

In Chapter 13, we discussed the serious implications of current assessment practices on learners and on learning. We focused our discussion on the formal assessment of those learners participating in accredited courses in educational institutions. In considering the effects of these on inclusion and exclusion, our key argument was that particular identities and epistemologies already privileged in over-developed Western societies are re-privileged through current assessment frameworks and, most particularly, through essayist literacy practices. We raised the issue of how these assessment frameworks make it almost impossible for learning outside of formal institutions to be valued and recognised.

In this section we turn again to a critique of assessment practices but this time we consider the broader assessment practices of quality assurance regimes operating in educational institutions. We will interrogate current practices of quality assurance to highlight the effects of this audit culture on learners', teachers' and managers' practices and subjectivities. Quality assurance and enhancement has become a permanent fixture of educational institutions in most Western societies; a force that is near impossible to reckon with. The language of quality assurance is particularly powerful, with key icon words being transparency and accountability. In this chapter we argue that the current regimes are repressing creativity in learning and are a key mechanism of regulation and control over the kind of learning that is available to differently and hierarchically positioned subjects. We begin the chapter by critiquing the current quality frameworks in order to expose the problematic assumptions that construct meanings around 'quality' and 'accountability' in lifelong learning. We then consider Foucault's notion of the panopticon to theorise the impact of quality assurance regimes on subjects and to expose quality assurance as a complex mechanism of regulation. We end the chapter with our thoughts on a different vision of quality for the future and our ideas for transforming the current framework into one that is able to support reflexive and creative pedagogies.

Problematising 'quality'

Teachers are subject to quality assurance and enhancement regimes, which are designed to make judgements about the effectiveness of the teaching and learning for which they are responsible in their institutions. In this section, we will examine the practices attached to these regimes and consider their effects on teaching practices. We will deconstruct the key discourses of quality assurance and their implications for pedagogies and equalities within the different discursive sites attached to lifelong learning.

We begin our discussion by exploring the contested nature of 'quality' and the different understandings it represents to those being held accountable: teachers and managers in schools, colleges and universities. What does quality assurance mean for teaching practices and the ways that learners experience their courses? A key focus of this section is to understand the operations of power within quality assurance regimes and how this constrains and creates opportunities for teachers and learners. 'Quality' is often assumed to have a universally shared meaning, and appears to represent something good that we would all want to work towards. Policy discourse presents quality assurance 'as an exercise in "information" and accountability'; for many working in schools [and other educational institutions] however, surveillance and control are more adequate descriptors' (Gillborn and Youdell 2000: 21). 'Quality' is a contested concept that has multiple meanings and is tied to hegemonic discourses of what counts as learning and who counts as a learner. Although, it is directed by central government agencies, it is also enmeshed in the micro-politics of local sites; including for example school meetings, classroom spaces and examination boards. Such local sites are embedded in wider power relations across differences that make a difference; age, class, ethnicity, gender, nationality, race and sexuality, for example. However, these sites, and the subjects within them, are constructed as neutral, apolitical, transparent and value-free sites that are regulated in order to assure fairness, equity and high standards. Quality assurance then is represented as a mechanism that operates outside of the micro-politics of institutional spaces.

Yet, in order to account for the quality of their teaching, teachers must justify their professional decisions and practices in ways that are often narrowly defined, are linked to local and macro-politics and are embedded in the assumptions of hegemonic discourses. For example, detailed course documents must be produced with specific descriptions of key areas in order for a course to be validated and accredited. The specific areas that must be described include course aims, learning outcomes, content, reading lists, assessment tasks, rationale, students to be recruited and risk assessments. Although we would not argue against the careful design and thought of a new course, we are concerned that there is currently little space for negotiation, collaboration and reflexivity within such quality systems. For example, a teacher might find that as she discusses an issue with the students, her understanding changes and she would like to re-develop the learning outcomes in light of her, and her students', changing understanding. However, this is not possible; the validation document exists and in order to make such changes, the teacher would have to resubmit these formally for consideration to the validation panel. This privileges bureaucratic rather than educational processes to the detriment of reflexive pedagogical practices. Our conceptualisation of pedagogies, curriculum and assessment as processes that are relational and negotiated and that must change as a result of reflexive practices is unable to be supported in the current framework. On this basis, we must ask whether this current system is supporting or deterring 'quality', as such flexible and reflexive approaches are at best constrained and at worst not possible.

There is a growing literature on quality assurance that helps expose the complexity of 'quality' and other connected discourses, including 'accountability' and 'excellence' (Broadfoot 1998; Morley 2001, 2003; Evans 2004). This literature reveals that the construction of quality assurance as a rational, transparent and neutral system is discursive. Yet, the lived practice of quality assurance involves subtle and complex power struggles. Indeed this literature suggests that quality assurance is a technology of surveillance and control. Morley, for example, argues that quality assurance is 'a system of coercion and domination', constructed as neutral and able to transcend social background and context:

> Quality assurance is producing docile bodies as the consequences of resistance are too high. There is a powerful rhetoric of inevitability, or a TINA effect ('there is no alternative'), and a ludic engagement with quality assurance (Morley 2001). Walkerdine (1989) argued long ago that femininity is performance. I argue that quality assurance too is performance.
>
> (Morley 2001: 476)

Much of the literature on quality assurance represents the growth of quality procedures as an inevitable outcome of the increase in post-compulsory educational participation, and the changing nature of teaching and learning as a result of 'massification'. Quality assurance has also been linked to the marketisation of education and the construction of students and their parents as consumers of education. The marketisation of education has led to concerns to assure high quality educational products which represent 'value-for-money' (Tapper and Salter 2003: 5). The move towards marketisation has led to a 'retreat from welfare states, public expenditure constraints and scepticism about public service professions' (Henkel 1998: 291). Henkel describes quality assurance as a 'new theology of quality, efficiency and enterprise' in which: 'there is an imperative to manage all resources as efficiently as possible, including higher education to incorporate it more fully into the polity as a key institution for national economic prosperity' (Henkel 1998: 291). The theology of quality assurance is connected to assumptions about a 'knowledge economy', which requires citizens who are lifelong learners, to continually capitalise on (formal) learning opportunities to improve their employability and transferable skills.

However, Morley (2003) explains that the momentum behind quality assurance is linked to powerful images of loss and destruction at play within discourses of expansion of higher education, including for example 'the university in ruins' (Readings 1996), 'the university in crisis' (Sommer 1995) and 'the death of autonomy' (Dill 2001). Such images contribute to the assumption that particular modes of regulation are an absolute necessity in an era of 'mass education'. It is through the discourses of derision (Ball 1990) at play within educational policy that anxieties about the lowering of standards have come to be so potent. The formation of mis/recognised identities is central to understanding these anxieties and the policing of self and other contributions to the regimes of surveillance and self-governance in educational institutions. As 'Others' have gained entry to higher education, the fears that the university is in ruins have deepened. The discourse of quality is intermeshed with the discourse of expansion, because the opening up of higher education to Other groups has been associated with the potential con-tamination of universities (Morley 2003). As we have argued earlier in the book, widening participation is always connected in policy to the potential damaging of standards. Quality assurance, in this context, has been identified as a mechanism of defence against the unknown dangers of Other groups achieving traditional qualifications including GCSEs, 'A' levels and higher education degrees.

Thus, quality assurance discourses are embedded in assumptions about who should, and who should not, have access to certain kinds of learning. The media is full of examples of discourses of derision in a range of sites, including for example, the improving level of achievement in GCSE examinations. Rather than constructing such improvements as an indication of the development of good educational practices, it is often taken as an indication of 'dumbing down' and the lowering of standards. For example:

> Newspapers also reported that some independent schools were now consider-ing ditching the exams completely arguing they had been 'dumbed down' to meet government targets. The GCSE results come a week after exam authorities said the pass rate in this year's A-levels had reached a record high, prompting similar accusations from critics that the tests were becoming meaningless.
>
> (Reuters 2005: 5)

Indeed, discourses of derision are not only about anxieties regarding the lowering of examination standards but also about the quality of teachers themselves, as this example demonstrates:

> One of Scotland's leading educationalists has called for teachers to be forced to face professional 'MoTs' every three years to ensure they are fit for the classroom. Douglas Osler, the former chief inspector of schools in Scotland, believes teachers should undergo mandatory assessments to prove they are developing their skills and knowledge.
>
> (Nutt 2006: 6)

These narratives from the media expose the ways that quality assurance regimes are connected to struggles over access and authority and the assumption that greater participation means poorer quality. Indeed, quality assurance instruments are not designed to challenge social inequalities and do not address the inherent contradictions of the quality and equality discourses. Quality assurance regimes overlook the politics of meaning-making and struggles over knowledge that we have discussed above. Furthermore, learners, often constructed as 'consumers' of lifelong learning, are treated as a homogenous group in quality practices, undifferentiated by age, class, dis/ability, ethnicity, gender, race and sexuality. Issues of equality and misrecognition are left outside of quality assurance systems. These absences and mis/understandings exacerbate the inequalities that already exist within educational institutions. Thus, quality assurance practices reinforce norms and standardisation and work against diversity, equality and a politics of recognition (Morley 2003). They are also about regulating those selves that are seen as a threat to educational quality.

Disciplining selves: quality assurance as panoptic regulation

Similar to the essayist literacy practices critiqued above, quality assurance practices have established normalising and standardising practices that thwart the possibility for the recognition of diversity, difference, fluidity, flexibility and contestation. Although the quality movement might have torn down some of the certainties of those in privileged institutional positions, new mechanisms of unequal power relations are in operation. Foucault's concept of the panopticon as the ultimate regulatory device is valuable in conceptualising quality assurance practices, which work to regulate and discipline the subjects of lifelong learning policy (including, of course, policy-makers themselves).

Foucault draws on Bentham's architectural device, the panopticon, to shed light on the complex operations of power within institutions that are no longer tied to an individual person in authority but rather 'a certain concerted distribution of bodies, surfaces, lights, gazes; in an arrangement whose internal mechanisms produce the relation in which individuals are caught up' (Foucault 1977: 202). Foucault explains that 'whenever one is dealing with a multiplicity of individuals on whom a task or a particular form of behaviour must be imposed, the panoptic schema may be used' (Foucault 1977: 205). We would argue that quality assurance in educational institutions is a form of panoptic regulation. The concept of the panopticon helps shed light on the insidiousness of quality assurance in contemporary educational institutions and the reason that it has the TINA effect that Morley refers to above. The panoptic regulation of quality assurance has created an environment where all subjects, regardless of social and hierarchical positioning, are mired in self-regulatory practices and, despite resistances and subversions, are ultimately exposed to these operations of governance. There is no one to blame, no one individual or group, and so there is little manoeuvre for resistance and struggle.

The quality assurance gaze is fixed on all subjects in educational sites; students, teachers, managers, administrators, researchers, inspectors, policy-makers, external examiners and moderators and even quality assurance officers themselves. Indeed, as part of the quality assurance machine, subjects within educational institutions continually experience the 'reconfiguration of space', as new systems are continually developed to 'enhance quality'. It could be argued that the constant reconfiguration of space is part of a wider agenda of regulation and control, optimising space so that the subjects within it remain under surveillance and control. It is a common experience of those working within educational institutions that an ongoing hot issue is that of 'rooming'. Who gets placed where and the spacialising of subjects across institutional spaces is a central issue within educational discourse. Yet, the ways that subjects within institutions engage in spacialising practices is often left unobserved as part of the regulatory regime, although it is paramount to its effects. Such spacialising practices include, for example, the positioning of the lecturer in the lecture hall or the teacher in the classroom, the use of offices and teaching rooms (and particularly the move towards open plan spaces), the spacing of students in examination situations, the ways that meetings get organised spatially, the spaces used for VIP visitors, the ways that the auditor uses the space during the institutional inspection or audit, and so forth. This also includes the architectural design of educational institutions and the ways that different subjects are in/visible and are positioned within it. Quality assurance practices ensure that all subjects will be made visible in regulatory ways through the systems in place, operating as a 'permanent, exhaustive, omnipresent surveillance, capable of making all visible' (Foucault 1977: 214).

Let us take the example of the move in many contemporary educational institutions from personal office space to open plan offices. Such a move is often justified in terms of bringing people together in teams in their daily work. We would not argue against any strategy to support collaborative practices. However, the move away from individual office space to open plan rooms deserves some critical attention and examination. The subjects within open plan spaces are positioned in particular ways, and are continually visible to others in the routine of their work. All subjects are open to regulation, not only the regulation of managers but also the regulation of peers. The daily visibility leads to the self-disciplining practices that Foucault refers to; subjects regulate themselves in case they are being observed by others. Furthermore, the move away from 'private' space to 'open' space has micro-political implications; managers decide who will be put together and in which room. Managers make decisions about who will be kept separate. Such decisions are made in a similar way to the teacher deciding the seating arrangements of the classroom. Workers who are unable to work well with their colleagues in such environments are identified as 'trouble-makers' and the subtle politics of social relations at the micro-level creates tensions, alliances, potential for bullying, antagonisms and networks. Power relations are always interlinked with spacialising practices and the effect includes self-governing subjects.

Ethical issues also need to be considered; for example issues of confidentiality. The discourse of widening participation is a central theme in the development of quality assurance practices, and part of that discourse is the growing importance of pastoral support. Yet the move into open plan rooms does not take that aspect of professional work into account and teachers are likely to be confronted by distressed students with no space to support them in a confidential and ethical way. The gendering of space also needs to be considered, particularly as women are more likely than men to use their office as the place of solitude where they are able to develop their thinking and intellectual work.

What are the consequences of panoptic regulation vis-à-vis quality assurance for teachers and learners? We have already critiqued the imposition of pre-established learning outcomes in Chapter 13. A key point is that even though many teachers reject the value of predetermined sets of learning outcomes, due to the great machine of quality assurance, individual and groups of teachers must conform to the practice of setting learning outcomes. Similarly the development of innovation in pedagogical approaches and assessment practices is unlikely in the climate of panoptic regulation; there is always the possibility of a disapproving eye looking over the subject's shoulder and as a result teachers are less likely to adopt potentially controversial practices attracting unwanted attention their way. Innovation is a risky business for those subjected to panoptic forms of regulation and 'tend[s] to advance or enhance the position of certain groups and disadvantage or damage the position of others' (Ball 1987: 33). The power of the quality assurance machine is that it creates self-governing subjects, who regardless of their individual and political perspectives, are caught up in the force of panopticism.

> The panoptic mechanism is not simply a hinge, a point of exchange between a mechanism of power and a function; it is a way of making power relations function in a function, and of making a function function through those power relations.
>
> (Foucault 1977: 206–7)

The effects of panoptic regulation through quality assurance are significant for understanding the current field of lifelong learning, the subjects within that field and the discursive practices attached to it. This is particularly intensified in formal institutional spaces but extends to the recognition of learning that takes place outside of formal spaces. When teachers are forced through such disciplinary mechanisms to design their courses around fixed and defined aims and objectives long before the students appear in the classroom, there is little space for the collaborative construction of knowledge and meaning through critical learning processes. Rather, the teachers and learners are forced to squeeze their experiences of learning into the pre-determined framework of the course, which will be subject to the panoptic gaze of QA systems.

Moreover, quality assurance regimes tend to direct the energies of teachers into bureaucratic tasks rather than into pedagogical concerns – for example:

- filling out the course proposal form in a way that will meet the expectations of the validation panel;
- writing the course handbook to make 'transparent' the aims and learning outcomes of the course;
- determining the course materials and readings before the students even sign up to the course;
- setting the assessment task in a way that ensures the pre-existing assessment criteria and learning outcomes will be met;
- creating the evaluation form in a standardised way to ensure that the students have a 'voice' in measuring the 'quality' of the course.

Where are the learners in these processes? As the learner is not present and is unable to negotiate these key decisions about her learning, she is constructed in the teacher's mind as a particular kind of student. The course then is designed for the imagined student, not the living breathing learner who brings to her learning complex identities, experiences and expectations. Epstein (2003) has argued that the project of creating pre-determined learning outcomes is always a pedagogic failure, because the act of creating these is not located in the complex lived pedagogic relations between teacher and learner. Quality assurance then creates a situation where learning is designed in a systematic way without connection to pedagogic relations. Teaching and learning and 'modes of delivery' must be considered in the course documentation but this is not grounded in the practices and experiences of teachers and learners. Rather it is an exercise of surveillance and regulation to ensure that 'standards' are maintained.

We argue that quality assurance has led to a 'tick-box' culture in which learning is reduced to sets of pre-determined bullet points. Mary Evans develops the argument that quality assurance is about 'killing thinking' and 'learning how to organise pre-packaged information' (Evans 2004: 44). She says of quality assurance:

> This creature from the depths of hell is curriculum and discipline blind: the content, the substance of a discipline is reduced to a resource through which students can acquire the means of demonstrating the 'key' or 'transferable' skills which will then be apparently 'useful' to the labour market.
>
> (Evans 2004: 46)

Mary Evans argues for learning that is firmly separated from the market economy and that helps learners develop 'the ability to recognize the relationship between ideas, and how to evaluate them' (Evans 2004: 46). Evans's work highlights the effect of QA practices, which validate particular kinds of learning within formal institutional spaces to the marginalisation of lifelong learning that takes place outside of schools, colleges and universities. Since only the learning that has been stamped with approval through quality assurance systems can be validated, then informal and nonformal learning becomes increasingly marginalised and lumped together with other 'personal experiences' that are seen as disconnected from 'real learning'. This has serious implications not only for how learning is recognised and conceptualised but also how learner identities are constituted and validated. Exclusions from learning are thus intensified by quality assurance practices.

We have argued earlier that pedagogies for lifelong learning necessitate the transformation of quality assurance practices. The current regime is embedded in a teaching and learning 'styles' framework that conceptualises teaching and learning as mechanistic skills and methods rather than socially embedded pedagogic relations. Indeed, many of the radical ideas developed by critical and feminist pedagogues have been expropriated by the quality assurance machine in a way that has lost all original meaning. For example, the concerns of critical pedagogues to shift learning from the individual to the social level, and to highlight the importance of collaborative rather than competitive learning cultures, has been taken over by the mainstream teaching method of 'small group work'. Such approaches assume a separation of teaching methods from teaching methodologies, so that 'small group work' in itself will assure 'quality' and 'effective' learning.

We argue that putting learners together in small groups does not create an 'excellent' learning experience; indeed it can be used as another way to transmit information in order to meet the sets of pre-determined learning outcomes for that session. Small group work is merely a tool, it is the pedagogy behind the way that it is used by the learner and teacher that is significant. However, the current quality assurance systems are unable to account for the complexities of different pedagogical approaches and relations. This is because they are embedded in a framework that conceptualises teaching as a toolkit for learning; again teaching is reduced to 'how to': how to lecture, how to make a handout, how to create a powerpoint presentation, how to give feedback, how to use small groups, and so forth. These tools are assumed to be meaningful in themselves, rather than understanding that it is the pedagogical approaches that make the tools meaningful or not.

Morley (2003) has pointed out that there is a problem with a quality assurance framework that draws on largely quantitative methodologies to measure what is actually a qualitative problem. Understanding what 'quality' means to different subjects in different contexts would entail complex methodological approaches that would explore and scrutinise pedagogical relations and experiences. Indeed, we would argue that 'quality' is not measurable, because what is valuable to one learner might be experienced as oppressive to another. The instruments used to evaluate learning and teaching are again pre-determined, with imposed categories that learners tick off on a scale of 'poor' to 'excellent'. Such approaches can tell us nothing about the complex experiences of learning, which we argue is an uncertain process of exploration, deconstruction, refashioning and interrogation. This process will not straightforwardly be experienced as simply 'excellent' or 'poor' because learning will usually involve moments of discomfort and uncertainty, even pain, as taken-for-granted assumptions get challenged, questioned and contested. Indeed, a key site of understanding that is missing from the current framework is the emotional aspects of learning; the joy, pleasure, pain, anger, delight, frustration that are all tangled up as part of learning experiences (Rowland 2002; see also

Chapter 9). The evaluation forms distributed to students on the last day of their course are not designed to capture such complex and emotional processes and experiences. Rowland argues that evaluation forms serve only as another mechanism of control over teachers and learners:

> Standardised evaluation forms modelled on customer satisfaction surveys, are now commonplace for this. A recent in-depth study (Johnson 2000) has shown how students often view such feedback with cynicism, that it in fact undermines the communicative relationship between teachers and learners, and that far from empowering students, it serves the bureaucratic function of controlling both teachers and students.
>
> (Rowland 2002: 56)

Quality assurance then appears to be functioning more as a form of regulation over teachers and learners than it does to be enhancing quality within educational institutions. Indeed, as we pointed out above, quality assurance is such a time-consuming set of endless tasks that it seems to take up the majority of the teacher's energy and time. This makes the development of pedagogical practices for lifelong learning almost impossible, not least because such pedagogies require the time and space for learners and teachers to think and to reflect.

The construction of knowledge itself has not escaped the panoptic regulation of quality assurance regimes in higher education institutions. As we have seen above, the regulatory frameworks of quality assurance keep concerns with knowledge construction outside of the picture and rather place emphasis on bite-size chunks of information that are acquired as an outcome of learning. As Morley has high-lighted, this ensures that questions of diversity are left outside of lifelong learning fields, because the politics of meaning-making are hidden away. Knowledge itself is largely tucked away as learners are required instead to demonstrate their competencies and skills.

The Research Assessment Exercise (RAE) is another instrument of panoptic regulation that takes place in higher education. Academics no longer engage in intellectual activities for the sake of contributing to ideas and meaning but are judged largely on the number of outputs and the nature of the publication itself. Indeed, in the current RAE, publications in 'prestigious peer-reviewed journals' are the most highly valued of outputs and entire books are treated as the same weight as single articles. This again is tied in with assumptions about assessment; books are seen as too easily accepted by publishers without 'rigorous' systems of peer review whereas peer-reviewed journals are seen as sites where rigorous and valid judgements are made. All academic staff are expected to produce at least four outputs in the assessment period of the RAE and where this expectation has not been met, the higher education institution must produce a detailed explanation for this anomaly. No academic, regardless of positioning, can escape the RAE panopticon, and all subjects must be self-regulating in order to meet the rules of the system.

Rowland argues that the quality assurance machine has led to the fragmentation and commodification of knowledge:

> Policy documents on research typically emphasise how knowledge is needed to fill gaps in knowledge rather than offer new interpretations; to discover how to do things, rather than question why such things should be done; to find out how to execute policy, rather than develop critiques of it.
>
> Such commodification of knowledge leads inevitably to the appearance of an enormous increase in the quantity of knowledge and consequently to fragmentation as it becomes increasingly impossible to familiarise oneself with more than a small fragment of the total.
>
> (Rowland 2002: 60)

We have discussed earlier in the book the impact of particular methodologies on how we conceptualise lifelong learning. Add to this the impact of the fragmentation and commodification of knowledge, to which Rowland refers, and we are able to build an understanding of the limitations for developing pedagogies for lifelong learning that are embedded in critical knowledge and understanding. Again, we find ourselves in the centre of the practices that we critique but as we have explained we are not outside the current frameworks of lifelong learning, and our critique can only be offered from the perspective of critical insiders in the field.

Conclusions: Where do we go from here?

We are highly critical of the current quality assurance regimes at play within formal educational institutions. However, we also argue that there should be mechanisms in place to support the development of pedagogies that account for, and challenge, unequal power and social relations. We argue for the need for theorised practices around quality that reveal and challenge, rather than hide, the workings of power around wider social inequalities and misrecognitions in lifelong learning fields. The current frame of quality assurance and enhancement privileges ideas around 'excellence', 'effectiveness' and 'accountability' without a critical understanding of what these mean for lifelong learning and particularly for issues of equality and recognition of diverse learners and courses. Processes that are developed to support quality must challenge discourses of derision that hide the politics of classed, gendered and racialised identity-making and epistemologies. In the previous sections of this chapter we have tackled some of these issues, in order to deconstruct and expose the problematic notions behind the key icon words of quality assurance. We have also theorised the current quality regimes as panoptic regulatory mechanisms that produce particular relations of power around spacialised and spacialising practices.

In this concluding section, we explore how we might *re*construct quality practices to support teachers, managers and learners to work creatively and collaboratively towards critical and reflexive pedagogical approaches. As we have argued before, this is no easy task; reconstructing involves taking a particular position and our position is embedded in the particular ontological and epistemological perspectives we bring to our work, as teachers, researchers and writers of this book. However, we are going to attempt, in this final section, to work towards reconceptualising quality assurance in a way that works against the marginalisation of misrepresented selves and knowledges and towards a quality framework that engages different learners (including managers and teachers, who are also always learning) in critical and ethical considerations about their practices.

In this chapter so far, we have argued that quality assurance practices are technologies of regulation that are entrenched in bureaucratic practices. We are concerned, as we have shown, that these practices disempower teachers and learners, by creating endless and often meaningless tasks that are part of a bureaucratic and disciplinary regime. The tasks that teachers and learners find themselves caught up in involve the production of documentation to meet certain 'tick-box' criteria, yet do not contribute to the enrichment of learning experiences, identities or practices. Rather than enhance quality, we argue that such tasks create a formal learning environment that is superficial and unable to address deeper level pedagogical issues and questions. Quality assurance practices create problems for the recognition of learning outside of formal spaces. Further, we have argued that the current quality assurance framework creates forms of panoptic regulation that are more about disciplining selves and less about pedagogical approaches.

Quality must be reconceptualised to account for in/equality, so that those involved in developing formal lifelong learning opportunities are held accountable to issues of social justice. Quality assurance practices must be designed to support the development of pedagogical approaches that are reflexive in a way that can account for the values, assumptions and perspectives that teachers bring to their work and that involve learners in reflexive practices. A reflexive pedagogy involves teachers in thinking and planning their teaching in a way that is sensitive to difference and diversity and that challenges hegemonic regimes of truth. Reflexive teachers negotiate the pedagogical approaches with learners, enabling active participation of learners from different backgrounds, engaging them in challenging taken-for-granted assumptions within the field of study. Teachers taking a reflexive pedagogical approach will seriously consider the ethical dimensions of their pedagogical relationships with their students, drawing attention to the ways that knowledge is always tied to context and is located within particular (classed, gendered, racialised, sexualised) epistemologies.

Drawing on the learners' experiences and perspectives, reflexive teachers will be responsible for fostering an environment that enables learners to openly discuss ideas but also to challenge the underlying assumptions of these ideas. Quality assurance mechanisms will ensure that teachers work with their students to demystify and deconstruct the academic conventions and discourses that operate against diversity and equality. Teachers operating within this reconceptualised framework will examine the underlying values, assumptions and perspectives that they bring to their teaching and research in relation to wider social inequalities and power relations. Teachers and learners who are accountable in this way will engage in critical examination, with students, of the assumptions behind certain 'truths' and the ways these might operate in the interests of particular social groups. Teachers will be responsible for identifying ways of ensuring that all members of the class can contribute to developing understanding from different, and sometimes competing, perspectives. This might for example, involve students working with a particular text to construct a response that makes connections with their personal or professional experiences and/or interests, then sharing those to value and recognise the diverse ways of working with the course materials. Such an approach understands knowledge as situated and political and as tied in with the construction of identities and subjectivities.

We would therefore like to see the development of a quality framework that supports critical and reflexive pedagogical practices. This would involve a structure that creates new critical spaces, challenging the spaces of panoptic regulation. New approaches would need to be developed engaging teachers, learners and managers in negotiated, reflexive and critical practices supported through collaboration, sharing and accountability within communities of learning. The focus would be on ethical practice to challenge misrecognition and inequality and to critically reflect on pedagogical relations rather than on individual accountability. Reflexive spaces would enable teachers and learners to think carefully about their practices not as individuals but as socially positioned subjects. Reflexive spaces would allow teachers to create, then recreate, pedagogical approaches following the negotiation and collaboration with learners. This would involve a dialogic approach to lifelong learning, where learning communities engaged in deconstructive discussions to expose the problematic assumptions behind their experiences, identities and understandings.

Chapter 15

Reconceptualising lifelong learning?

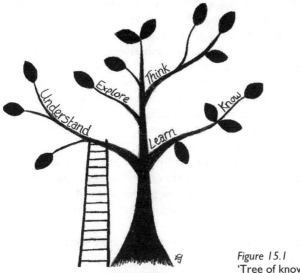

Figure 15.1
'Tree of knowledge' by Liz Jackson

In this final chapter we want to create spaces for reflexivity, resistances, subversions and possibilities for change, creating a new terrain of possibilities. Those possibilities may be small, or appear small, but possibilities added together, united, argued with, developed, reconstructed can start to bring about individual, collective and structural challenge and change.

In writing this book, we have engaged with lifelong learning as a site of struggle. In doing so we have taken up our position within that site as feminist, but we have invited our readers to also engage with the struggles and find their positions and their voices, and to create spaces of resistances, subversions and new possibilities. Here we are thinking about the spaces and silences, asking where the spaces are for reflexivity, for exploring positionings of ourselves and others, for reflecting back and moving forwards. This chapter aims to create spaces of silence in order to interrupt the current obstacles to thinking that are created by engagement with lifelong learning that is solely about economic progression, or by the new managerialism which keep people so busy that they have no opportunities for reflexivity.

We want to offer our own observations of what the key issues are around struggles over learning and being a learner but we also want to challenge the certainties around scientific claims to knowledge. Some of the silences are our silences, deliberately made to destabilise our own positions as the authors of this text. Rather than contributing to the formulation of new regimes of truth, we hope this book will open up the spaces to interrogate the problematic assumptions of lifelong learning. In previous chapters we have critiqued essayist literacy practices to expose the exclusionary nature of this social practice, whilst often drawing on the very practices that we are critiquing. In this final chapter we will include some different ways of representing knowledge through the inclusion of the visual as well as the textual, and through the creation of empty spaces on the page to allow reflective moments for our readers and to silence our own voices. Here we are taking a post-structuralist approach, using different kinds of texts (e.g. visual images, narratives, sociological analysis) to represent these struggles and to re-emphasise our point that text and discourse is not linear and certain, but messy, contested and constructed.

We are offering visual forms of representation in order to create a space of silence without words and ask our readers to engage in their own reflections. In his work on 'Visual Imagery, Lifecourse Structure and Lifelong Learning', Tom Schuller argues that 'critical understanding of lifelong learning and its social context is radically enhanced if we bring images into the equation' (2004: 72). He says that images can be used as illustration, as evidence and as heuristic. Here the third meaning comes closest to our intention. We are using images in this chapter as triggers to enable our readers to draw on their personal and political experiences to de/re/construct conceptualisations of lifelong learning, whilst at times offering some of our own deliberations.

For example, a 'tree of life' image, such as that with which we open this chapter, could stand as a metaphor for lifelong learning. However, whilst a 'tree of life' appears affirming, the image above also suggests particular ways of conceptualising lifelong learning (through literacy; through the meanings attached to the words at the centre of the tree . . .). It could also suggest the struggles, journeys to the top and/or hierarchical climbing for achievement that we critiqued in Chapter 3; and will suggest different ways of considering lifelong learning to each of us consuming the image, including maybe the alternative landscapes that we also discussed in Chapter 3. We could have chosen other 'tree of life' images (see, for example, Figures 15.2 and 15.3).

We also present textual images: the stories of learners in different social contexts through (partially) fictionalised vignettes, again offering our own observations and interpretations, whilst leaving the spaces for our readers to construct their own. We do this to return to our point at the start of the book that questions the certainty and linearity of meaning, and rather offers a post-structuralist disorganisation showing struggles over meaning, uncertainties and multiple positionings which are tied in with complex power relations.

Figure 15.2 'Tree of Life' by
Suzanne deVeuve

Figure 15.3 'Tree of Life' by
Jan Paulus-Maly

Having deconstructed lifelong learning and articulated some of our perspectives of possible changes, we also want in this final chapter to return to the question of the recognition of nonformal and informal learning. Throughout the book we have thought about ways in which certain kinds of learning count, whilst others do not. We recognise that we have in the main focused on formal learning, a clear indication of the current state of play for lifelong learning. For example, in Chapter 13 on assessment practices we considered the ways in which formal accreditation processes make it almost impossible for the recognition of learning which takes place outside of formal educational institutions. We have also discussed the limitations of current AP[E]L frameworks which are bound up with the same sorts of practices and epistemological assumptions as other forms of accreditation.

Issues like these present challenges for reconceptualising lifelong learning and we use our stories to continue our own challenges, including those of constructions of learners and learning, as well as constructions of academic writing. In our vignettes we raise issues and scenarios that are challenging for lifelong learning and our perspectives of these, but we have resisted assuming any concrete conclusions from these stories which would cause us to slip back into hegemonic epistemological positions. Following each vignette we will offer multiple readings and images of the story from different perspectives, which will combine fictionalised interpretations with our own, and leave spaces for further interpretations.

Our first vignette is the story a mature white working-class man, Mark, who has committed himself to a full-time access course. Mark is somebody who has read widely and has a passionate political commitment to social justice. His working life was one of physical labour, which took its demands on his body. The possibility of more formal education suggested itself to him at the point of not being physically able to continue such work. However, he does not associate participation in further and higher education as about 'bettering himself'. Indeed, he worries that it poses a threat to his intellectual creativity. A formal access course might justify the time spent on reading and writing in ways that others around him would find acceptable, although he is wary of educational institutions as factories for the production of 'learning' rather than open and creative places. Despite his concerns, Mark found that there were times that he really enjoyed his access course, especially the social nature of study and the interaction with other students and his tutor. He contributed widely to critical discussions and was admired by his peers for his confident and intellectual insights. Mark is an independent thinker. For example, instead of the required written assignment he wrote an extended poem to articulate his thoughts on the interactions between his own experiences and the course materials. Mark became upset when he was told he had to resubmit his written work in the required format of an essay. However, Mark did well on his course, obtaining a good pass and receiving offers of places at the universities of his choice. After much soul searching, Mark came to the decision that he did not want to go on to study at university as he felt he risked being corrupted by the mindset of the academy, and he left the college.

There are multiple ways in which this story could be (re-)told. The stories below extend from some of the stories in Section II:

The **further education manager** thinks that this is a story about progression or lack of progression. He is concerned that the figures for this year's group show a decline in numbers progressing from access courses to university. This could reflect particularly badly on his faculty's annual review and impact on the funding he is allocated for the next year. He will see this story as yet another indication of the failure of his access team to ensure high progression rates to university. He is also concerned about the implications of this for future recruitment. He is likely to hold accountable the lecturing agency that is providing his staff to the course and is concerned about the quality of his team. His response to this story will be to hold a series of meetings aimed at communicating to his staff the importance of improving rates of progression. He will also be holding an immediate meeting with the course leader to identify the weaker teachers on the team, and to propose remedial action.

The **further education policy-maker** sees this as a story that reflects yet again the need to raise the aspirations of individuals from lower-income groups. She is frustrated that the work of AimHigher is focusing on raising aspirations of young people from disadvantaged groups but is not reaching out to individuals like Mark. She is aware that there is little she can do about national policy, although she will write a letter to voice her concerns to the widening participation team at HEFCE. In the context of her work in the college, she will introduce measures to support students in making a smooth progression into university from their access courses. She will put into place a policy that students will have a structured interview with a member of the career development team, as well as their tutor, in the final term of their access course. Those students who decide not to go on to university will have a special meeting arranged with the course leader to discuss their options.

The **learner** is one of Mark's peers in the class. He has always liked and admired Mark and even seen him as a role model for what working-class men can achieve.

He is shocked that Mark is not going to go on to university, especially as he has done so well on the course and has been offered places at all his university choices, including one that has a reputation for being really difficult to get into. He is disappointed because he had hoped that they might end up in the same university and feels angry at Mark for letting him down. He is also anxious that Mark will not be around any more to give him advice and support him in his studies. He thinks Mark is being arrogant and that he will regret the decision later on. He is still hoping though that he can change Mark's mind, and believes the truth is that Mark is scared to take up a university place.

The **access course teacher** recognises Mark as a student who is very talented; a critical, independent and free thinker. She feels proud that Mark has developed in the ways he has, and sees this as in part due to her own pedagogical practices and the critical texts she has introduced to Mark over the year. She empathises with Mark's decision, as she sees herself as a creative thinker who wants to challenge the assumption that the best thinkers are those in universities. However, she is concerned for Mark, not wanting to see him return to the hard labouring work that has damaged his health and may leave him with little time to pursue his intellectual interests. She recognises that, particularly as a working-class man, he is unlikely to have access to higher paid work without a degree. She is also aware that by supporting Mark's decision, she has left herself open to claims that she has a low progression rate in her class for which she will be held accountable.

Mark has had many sleepless nights over this decision and it has not been an easy one to make. He feels guilty about the financial support that his family has given him over the year although he suspects that they are relieved that he will be going back to work and bringing in some income again. None of his college friends understand and he misses the fun that they have enjoyed over the year, although his pre-college friends think he has seen sense at last in returning to his roots. He looks back over the year and remembers some critical moments that were valuable, especially in sociology, which sometimes stretched his thinking. There were lots of other times that he was really frustrated and he felt like he was back at school. This came to a head when he submitted his poem, which he thought was taking an original approach and making an important contribution to a reworking of Marxist ideas. Most disappointing of all was that he was asked to resubmit it, in essay form, by the one teacher who had encouraged his creativity and inspired him to take his own approaches. He can see that if he went on to university his thinking would be increasingly confined to dominant and class-bound ways of doing things.

Is Mark's act one of positive assertion of self as learner or is it a self-protection strategy to avoid the unfamiliar, shaped out of the politics of class and gender? In **our re-telling**, we suggest that Mark's story challenges the deficit constructions of working-class men that are implicit in widening participation policies. Mark's narrative brings into question some of the assumptions behind the notion of raising aspirations. Mark does not have low aspirations, nor does he have the kinds of aspirations linked to widening participation policies; i.e. to move from university into paid work, that we critiqued in Chapter 1. Learning for Mark is central to his political position, and this is linked in with his classed identity. He does not see this as a problem, or something he should want to leave behind, but it is a position which affirms who he is. Mark has a strong sense of what learning means to him and he does not see formal educational institutions as the only, or even the best, place for that learning to happen. He has a critical perspective of his experiences of formal learning but also a critical perspective of being a working-class man and what that means. As we showed in Chapter 8, constructions of our identities and subjectivities have a profound effect on our (lifelong) learning experiences. It appears that Mark does not take the hierarchies in society for granted and he does not assume that occupying a particular position means a higher level of knowledge. He also has many of the attributes associated with successful learning, and middle-class identities, such as 'being independent', 'being critical' and 'being intellectual'. He is a fluent reader and writer and has developed much of his understanding from engaging in these activities throughout his life outside of school and college.

There are of course other tellings and re-tellings of Mark's story/ies . . .

Here is a story about Matthew. Matthew decided to leave school in his final 'A' level year to travel abroad. He had been studying the new Advanced Vocational Art and Design course but found that it was not challenging him in the ways he had expected. He enjoyed making art, and he was already being commissioned for professional graphic design, but this was seen by his personal tutor as distracting him from his coursework and was strongly discouraged. School was frustrating for Matthew; although his parents and teachers kept telling him he needed the qualification, he did not feel he was learning anything new. His classes bored him and it was at home that he really enjoyed creating new work and developing new techniques through the internet, talking to his grandparents who were professional artists and playing around with the software he had available to him. But he also loved the more physical arts and his true love was Shaolin Kung Fu. It was when he was absorbed in mastering new techniques in Kung Fu that he felt happiest. When the opportunity to travel to China to study at the Shaolin Temple presented itself, he took it eagerly. In China he had to learn to live in new ways, giving up many of the luxuries he had enjoyed at home, but he loved this challenge. He met new people, formed new friendships, discovered and participated in the practices of the Shaolin monks and learned to speak in Mandarin. He began teaching as well as studying. He was happy but he was also aware that many people back home were critical of his decision and thought he should have finished his 'A' levels and gone on to university. He felt he could always study later, if and when it felt right. For now, he was living his dream and learning what he loved to do most and, despite the criticisms, he felt good about his decision.

Here are some of the stories about Matthew. Like the issues raised in Section III, identities and subjectivities, emotions and resistances appear in the telling of these stories. Also here are the impacts of hegemonic discourses of 'successful' learning, linked to both social class and gender.

Matthew's personal tutor sees this as a story of opportunity lost, and is very disappointed with the decision. Matthew was a very promising student and could have probably got into a prestigious art school if his attitude had been better. He had not prioritised his coursework but she had been willing to help him catch up, if he could have just been more positive about his studies. The fact that he had been awarded a commissioned piece was a huge distraction from his schoolwork and contributed to his arrogance that he could understand the subject without doing a proper course. She does not see a future for Matthew, which he has thrown away by dropping out of school. The commercial art world is increasingly competitive

Figure 15.4 Matthew in China

and Matthew does not have a chance of making it into that world without formal qualifications.

Matthew's mother sees this as a story of opportunity gained. She sympathises with her son and understands his frustration, and is proud that he has already produced work professionally. She believes in Matthew and, although she is frightened that he has traveled all the way to China alone, she knows he is happy. She is worried however that he might need more than this to get a well-paid job and have the kind of life she hopes for him. She thinks that maybe he will do a degree when he returns. She also listens out for indications that teaching martial arts might be a lucrative area of work in the future and is pleased when she hears announced on the radio that personal trainers will be one of the highest paid areas of work in the future. She wants to support her son in his aspirations but worries whether she is giving him the best advice as his mother.

Matthew's friend thinks that Matthew did not work hard enough, which annoys him because Matthew is such a talented artist. He talks to Matthew regularly on MSN Messenger and tells him that he needs to come back soon and finish his 'A' levels and do his degree. He is worried about his friend, but he is also intrigued with what he is doing. He is taking a gap year after finishing his 'A' levels although he is not sure what he wants to do. He is glad that his 'A' levels are over; they were hard work and he feels exhausted from studying. Matthew is trying to talk him into visiting China while he is on his gap year and he wishes he could. But his parents do not want him to do this, so where would he find the money? He is working three part-time jobs at the moment, trying to save for university. He is not quite sure what he wants to do in his life but he knows he must get a degree.

Matthew never enjoyed school and he is happy to be out of formal education and doing what he loves to do most. He knows his parents are worried but he is confident that he will be able to achieve his goals, earn a good living and do this without a qualification. However, he has not completely decided against formal education; he thinks he might do a degree in philosophy, perhaps with the Open University, when he returns home. He has found his core strength and understands this as being as much about his philosophical approach as his physical training. Matthew has also started teaching and has enjoyed explaining to his students certain key understandings behind the philosophy of martial arts – he knows this is what makes a good Kung Fu teacher. He feels frustrated with his friends who have been seduced into believing that just by doing a degree they will accomplish their dreams, especially as many of them do not know what they want to do with their lives. He is already living his dream, and he is learning more every day – more than he ever did at school.

From **our perspective**, Matthew's story raises a range of key challenges for (re)-conceptualising lifelong learning and particularly for notions of widening educational participation. Matthew's story raises questions about the dominant assumption that young people should study 'A' levels in preparation for a degree and then go on to university by the age of 18. Perhaps Matthew learns more of value through his travels than he would have in an educational institution in his home country. Furthermore, Matthew did not enjoy school, which he saw as simply an exercise in pleasing his parents and teachers in order to get a qualification that was meaningless to him. Formal learning in school was not inspiring Matthew and this suggests that policy-makers as well as teachers need to learn more about young people's different experiences and perspectives of formal learning. Matthew experienced formal learning as only instrumental and detached from his own aspirations and therefore de-motivating and unrelated to his life. Matthew's experiences led him to make new connections and to develop philosophical insights, and this attracted him to the possibility of studying philosophy. He likes the idea of self-study and learning independently.

Matthew's story suggests that for many young people the classroom is not always the best place to learn and that a range of forms of learning in different contexts should be available. His story highlights that nonformal and informal learning is as significant, and sometimes more significant, as formal learning but this raises questions about the recognition of different kinds of learning, issues which we raised in earlier chapters in this Section IV. How will Matthew's learning be counted and who will do the counting as well as the judging? Although we recognise his learning as valuable, as we showed in Chapter 14 it does present challenges for the recognition of learning outside of formal institutions. A way is needed for Matthew's learning to be formally recognised without moving back into the very structures that de-motivated him to begin with. Although Matthew might have the (right kind of) cultural capital to transform his learning into a recognizable learning experience, for example through AP[E]L, there are also issues of social class at play here and such opportunities will not be available for all young people. If all learning ultimately needs to be presented through the literacy practices of privileged groups in order to be socially validated, then the learning of those in marginalised positions with other kinds of literacy practices is less likely to be recognised, perpetuating the privileging of the already privileged. Matthew has the resources through his parents' (financial as well as emotional) support to pursue his dream and this kind of learning experience is not likely to be available to a young man from a poorer background. Additionally, young men may be more likely than young women to gain parental support for travelling alone . . .

Our final vignette is about Faith. Faith grew up in the 1960s, with expectations about her future centred on her becoming a wife and mother, which she did in her 20s, having left school at 16 with little in the way of formal qualifications. On becoming a mother Faith immediately gave up paid work to concentrate on her new role. She found learning to be a mother an intense, defining experience. She struggled with people's expectations of what it means to be a good mother, including her own expectations of self. She enjoyed learning with her children, finding her views and perspectives continually challenged through their questions, opinions and understandings. However, although she enjoyed her children and often felt fulfilled through motherhood, she also at times felt frustrated, isolated and even angry.

Faith entered formal education again through correspondence courses whilst at home with her children, and continued taking courses as her children were growing up. She returned to part-time paid work whilst they were at school, and later full-time. Although she had no career ambitions initially, Faith is now a middle manager in a large organisation. In that role she has learned much about herself, and has grown in self-confidence. Faith is surprised to recognise herself as ambitious, and she is keen to apply for promotion, although she is concerned about the development of her C.V., believing her organisation's definition of achievement is different from her own.

Although she has always considered herself working class, Faith now finds herself differently positioned by others, with her current salary and lifestyle indicating a middle-class lifestyle. Both her classed positioning and her changing identities as a (classed and racialised) Black woman have forced her to confront complex power relations, and she sees a key challenge of her job as learning how to use her management position to make changes that are sensitive to social relations and inequalities. She did undertake some management training, but found it individualist in nature and unhelpful in facilitating managers' understandings of how to develop sensitivities around power relations.

For **Faith**, formal, nonformal and informal learning are all interwoven so that the separation of these is unhelpful and fails to recognise the meaning that different experiences of learning develop. Experiences of formal learning can help give personal and political meaning to other lived experiences; and lived experiences, including the material and cultural, inform the ways in which we learn non/ in/formally. For example, motherhood has enabled Faith to learn from, with and

Figure 15.5 Amazing Grace by Nelson Young Jr.

through her children, although constructions of gender and (expectations of) motherhood have also limited formal and work-related learning opportunities. Hegemonic discourses of motherhood shape the intensity of experiences of and for women who mother, whilst also normalising motherhood as something to which all women should naturally aspire. This is linked to constructions of femininity and the normalisation of (hetero)sexuality, and is problematic both for women who are not mothers and women who are.

As discussed in Chapter 9, as a mother Faith will have had to give emotional labour to her children, and constructions of motherhood linked to femininity mean that she may also be emotionally supporting a partner. She is likely to be giving emotional labour to her colleagues, whom she is keen to support. Patriarchal capitalism demands that women give unconditionally of their labour, including emotional labour, in order that it may produce and reproduce itself. The demands of this labour will have also impacted upon Faith's learning opportunities. However, Faith is of course an active subject. In Chapter 10 we considered resistances: we know that Faith resented some of the demands of motherhood, and that she is resisting constructions made by others regarding her identity as a (Black) working-class woman. She is also attempting some resistance to neo-liberalism. Whilst in part she is buying into the system, she wants to do so in ways that enable her to facilitate the development of others. However, both resistance and facilitation are impacted by her gender, social class and race, which in turn impact upon her past and current opportunities, and future possibilities.

It is to possibilities that we now turn . . .

Refashioning lifelong learning

In this final section of the chapter, we interrogate the premise of the book – that critiquing the current field of lifelong learning helps to create transformation. How does a feminist post-structuralist critique help us to reconceptualise lifelong learning in ways that challenge deeply embedded social inequalities and misrepresentations? In our private discussions during the process of writing and rewriting this book, we have struggled with the concept 'lifelong learning' and have been attracted to the idea of throwing it out entirely and replacing it with something else. Our discomfort with 'lifelong learning' is that it carries certain meanings that we want to contest. We suspect that it is almost impossible to shift ways of thinking about lifelong learning if we have to use the same concept that has largely defined what it is. In our introduction to the book we struggled with concepts of 'life', of 'long' and of 'learning'. 'Lifelong learning' continues to speak to us of individualised lives, moving hierarchically and/or in a linear fashion through the processes of (formal) learning (hence the 'tree of life' image with which we opened this chapter). In connection with such concerns, we have attempted to think of other ways of articulating our reconceptualisation, for example *learning for life*, *critical learning* and/or *reflexive learning*.

However, all of these have their own serious limitations. *Learning for life* has the potential to move the emphasis away from the notion of continual (formal) learning for instrumental reasons to learning for *living*. This would highlight that learning is something that all human beings participate in as part of the human condition. *Learning for life* is about all aspects of social life, not only learning for paid work. However, we believe that this term could be easily appropriated by policy-makers, developing discourses of 'life' that are about economic citizenship. We also feel that this concept is limited in that it does not illuminate the collaborative, community-oriented and social aspects of learning and being a learner that we have wanted to foreground in our reconceptualisation; that is learning not as an individual but as a social and relational process.

The concept of *critical learning* emerges from our interest in critical pedagogies and the ideas in particular of Freire, which we discussed in Chapter 11. Freire talked of rewording the world, highlighting the discursive nature of learning and constructing knowledge. However, again, this has its limitations. Critical pedagogical approaches can be critiqued for their emphasis on structural theories of inequality, which pose the 'dominator' and 'dominated' in opposing and binary positions

(Ellsworth 1992). They are overly simplistic and do not account for the complexity of power and subjectivity.

Reflexive learning helps to consider the social aspects of the learner in relation to positionality and the different values and perspectives that learners bring to their experiences of learning. It helps to theorise the relational aspects of learning and to shed light on the ways that the personal is always the political. However, there have been important critiques of reflexivity (see, for example, Skeggs 2004), which bring into question to whom the tools of reflexivity are available, and in what ways they are helpful. Whereas white, middle-class subjects can utilise the tools of reflexivity to re/author-ise the self, racialised and working-classed subjects may be forced into reflexivity in ways that can misrepresent their subjectivities as the grotesque and despised Other. Reflexivity therefore is problematic, although we hold on to it as a useful concept in this book.

The way we have used reflexivity in this book is as a tool of deconstruction within the field of lifelong learning. Most importantly, reflexivity can enable those in the most privileged positions to understand that their identity is not individual but relational and intermeshed with wider power relations. This emphasises the need to interrogate the values, judgements and subjectivities they (we) bring to meaning-making as a result of their (our) social positioning. Although we argue that the responsibility of reflexivity should be placed on those in the most powerful positions in society (particularly as the policy of lifelong learning usually places most responsibility on the least privileged groups in relation to discourses of derision and deficit), learning reflexively is important to all groups, as all subjects have access to power and in this way should be reflexive about how they exercise that power in relation to others.

At the start of this chapter, we argued – as indeed we did in the introduction to the book – that change is important, no matter how small, as each act of resistance, subversion and refashioning in the discursive field of lifelong learning contributes to its transformation. In this Section of the book, we have focused our attention on the practices at play within that discursive field. We have deconstructed those practices and then considered where lifelong learning is now and where we would like it to be in the future. We have critiqued and reconsidered practices of pedagogy, curriculum, assessment and quality assurance and, as all are inter-dependent and connected, there have been key themes emerging from these four different chapters. These have included ways in which discourses, policies and practices of and for lifelong learning must be situated and contextualised within a socio/political framework. In particular, we have shown that there is the impera-tive to deconstruct the power relations that are embedded in societal, cultural, political and structural definitions of knowledge. New critical spaces must be created for learning communities to pool their fragmentary knowledges and expose the problematic assumptions behind their gendered, racialised, classed and sexualised experiences, identities and understandings.

We have proposed ways of reworking current practices in order to create possibilities for change. Related to this we have argued that formal, nonformal and informal learning are all interwoven so that the separation of these is unhelpful and does not recognise the competing meanings that different experiences of learning expose. However, we have demonstrated that the practices at play within formal learning institutions create a barrier to the recognition and valuing of learning that takes place outside of formal contexts. We have used the vignettes and images in this final chapter to highlight these points: that learning happens in a range of different social contexts; that learners contest hegemonic versions of who counts as a learner; that learners make the connections between their learning in different contexts and in ways that enrich and give power to their experiences of learning; that learning does not always happen in classrooms; that there are no linkages between learner and teacher to be taken for granted; and that learning happens in the everyday routines of life as well as in the structured pedagogical spaces created by formal institutions.

In the introduction to this book we stated that we engaged in this project because lifelong learning matters to us. However, whilst this book may have begun as a project to reconceptualise lifelong learning, it has ended with us wanting to go further. It may be that the term has become so appropriated, and is so embedded within neo-liberal discourses that do a major disservice to marginalised groups, that it no longer serves a useful purpose. Above all, we have argued that 'lifelong learning' supports individualised learning embedded in structural power relations and hegemonic meaning-making. It remains to be seen whether the discourses of lifelong learning can be refashioned into policies and practices that support critical and reflexive communal and social learning. We hope that this book has helped to deconstruct current practices of and for lifelong learning, including constructions of essayist practices and of academic work, but more than that we hope it has outlined some of the challenges and has opened possibilities for debate and change.

Bibliography

Aggleton, P. (1987) *Rebels Without A Cause: Middle Class Youth and the Transition from School to Work*, London: The Falmer Press.

AimHigher: Higher Education at UK Universities and Colleges of Further Education; available online at http://www.aimhigher.ac.uk/home/index.cfm (accessed 17 January 2005).

Ainley, P. (1994) *Degrees of Difference: Higher Education in the 1990s*, London: Lawrence and Wishart.

Alcoff, L. and Potter, E. (1993) *Feminist Epistemologies*, New York and London: Routledge.

Aldridge, F. and White, L. (eds) (2005) *Charting the Experiences and Achievements of Black Adult Learners*, Leicester: NIACE.

Anderson, P. (2001) 'Betwixt and Between: *Class*, ifying Identities in Higher Education', in P. Anderson and J. Williams (eds) *Identity and Difference in Higher Education: Outsiders Within*, Aldershot: Ashgate.

Anderson, P. and Williams, J. (2001) *Identity and Difference in Higher Education: 'Outsiders Within'*, Aldershot, Burlington, Singapore, Sydney: Ashgate.

Angelou, M. (1986) *The Heart of a Woman*, London: Virago.

Apple, M. (1982) *Education and Power*, London: Routledge and Kegan Paul.

Archer, L. (2003) 'Social Class and Higher Education', in L. Archer, M. Hutchings and A. Ross, *Higher Education and Social Class: Issues of Exclusion and Inclusion*, London and New York: Routledge Falmer.

Archer, L. (2006) 'Masculinities, Femininities and Resistance', in C. Leathwood and B. Francis (eds) *Gender and Lifelong Learning: Critical Feminist Engagements*, London: Routledge.

Archer, L. and Leathwood, C. (2003) 'Identities, Inequalities and Higher Education', in L. Archer, M. Hutchings and A. Ross, *Higher Education and Social Class: Issues of Exclusion and Inclusion*, Routledge Falmer.

Archer, L., Hutchings, M. and Ross, A. (2003) *Higher Education and Social Class: Issues of Exclusion and Inclusion*, London: Routledge Falmer.

Armitage, A., Bryant, R., Dunnill, R., Hayes, D., Hudson, A., Kent, J., Lawes, S. and Renwick, M. (2003) *Teaching and Training in Post-compulsory Education*, 2nd edn, Buckingham: Open University Press.

Baker, P. and Comfort, H. (eds) (2004) *Engaging Black Learners in Adult and Community Education*, Leicester, NIACE.

Ball, S. (1987) *The Micro-Politics of the School*, London: Methuen.

Ball, S. (1990) *Politics and Policy Making in Education*, London: Routledge.

Ball, S., Maguire, M. and Macrae, S. (2000) *Choice, Pathways and Transitions Post-16, New Youth, New Economies in the Global City*, London: Falmer.

Barkley, Elizabeth F., Cross, K. Patricia and Major, Claire Howell (2004) *Collaborative Learning Techniques: A Handbook for College Faculty*, New Jersey: Jossey-Bass.

Barr, J. (2002) 'Universities After Postmodernism', in *International Journal of Lifelong Education*, 21 (4): 321–33.

'Basic Skills for Offenders in the Community' (2004) Reports on efforts to improve the literacy and numeracy of offenders in the community, Coventry: Adult Learning Inspectorate; available online at http://docs.ali.gov.uk/publications/BasicSkillsOffenders Community.pdf (accessed 18 January 2007).

Behar, R. and Gordon, D. (eds) (1995) *Women Writing Culture*, Berkeley: University of California.

Benn, R., Elliott, J. and Whaley, P. (eds) (1998) *Educating Rita and Her Sisters: Women and Continuing Education*, Leicester: NIACE.

Bernstein, B. (1996) *Pedagogy, Symbolic Control and Identity*, London: Taylor and Francis.

Black Practitioners and Learners', Network, Leicester: NIACE; online at http://www. niace.org.uk/bpln/Default.htm (accessed 17 January 2005).

Bloomer, M. (2001) 'Young Lives, Learning and Transformation: Some Theoretical Considerations', in *Oxford Review of Education*, 27 (3): 429–49.

Bloomer, M., Davies, J. and Tedder, M. (2002) 'The Pink Collar Workers: Young Women, Vocational Identification and Learning', Paper presented at South-West Regional Learning & Skills Research Network Conference, Ilminster, 5 July 2002; available on-line at http://www.ex.ac.uk/education/tlc/docs/publications/EX_JMB_JD_MT_PUB_ 05.07.02.doc (accessed 18 January 2007).

Bourdieu, P. (1973) 'Cultural Reproduction and Social Reproduction', in R. Brown. (ed.) *Knowledge, Education and Cultural Change*, London: Tavistock.

Bourdieu, P. (1977) *Outline of a Theory of Practice*, Cambridge: Cambridge University Press.

Bourdieu, P. (1988) *Homo Academicus*, London: Polity Press in association with Basil Blackwell.

Bourdieu, P. (2001) *Masculine Domination*, Cambridge: Polity Press.

Bourdieu, P. and Passerson, J. (1977) *Reproduction in Education, Society and Culture*, London: Sage.

Bowl, M. (2003) *Non-traditional Entrants to Higher Education: 'They Talk about People Like Me'*, Stoke-on-Trent: Trentham Books.

Brah, A. (1996) *Cartographies of Diaspora: Contesting Identities*, London: Routledge.

Brah, A. and Phoenix, A. (2004) 'Ain't I A Woman? Revisiting Intersectionality', *Journal of International Women's Studies*, 5 (3): 75–88.

Brine, J. (in press 2006) 'Lifelong Learning and the Knowledge Economy: Those that Know and Those that Do Not – The Discourse of the European Union', in L. Blaxter, W. Brine, C. Hughes and S. Jackson (eds) *British Educational Research Journal*, Special Issue, *Gender, Class and 'Race', in Lifelong Learning: Policy and Practice in the UK and EU*.

Broadfoot, P. (1998) 'Records of Achievement and The Learning Society: A Tale of Two Discourses', *Assessment in Education: Principles, Policy & Practice*, 5 (3): 447–78

Burke, P. J. (2002) *Accessing Education: Effectively Widening Participation*, Stoke-on-Trent: Trentham Books.

Burke, P. J. (2006) 'Fair Access? Exploring Gender, Access and Participation Beyond Entry to Higher Education', in C. Leathwood and B. Francis (eds) *Gender and Lifelong Learning*, London: Routledge.

Burke, P. and Dunn, S. (2006) 'Communicating Science: Exploring Reflexive Pedagogical Approaches', *Teaching in Higher Education*, 11 (2): 219–32.

Burke, P. J. and Hermerschmidt, M. (2005) 'Deconstructing Academic Practices through Self-reflexive Pedagogies', *Literacies Across Educational Contexts: Mediating Learning and Teaching*, Philadelphia: Caslon Press.

Burke, P. J. and Kirton, A. (2006) 'The Insider Perspective: Teachers-as-Researchers', *Reflecting Education*, 2 (1): 1–4.

Burn, E. (2001) '"Good Girls Are Seen and Not Heard": A White Working-class Woman's Educational Story', BERA Annual conference, 13–15 September.

Butler, Judith (1997) *Excitable Speech: A Politics of the Performative*, New York: Routledge.

Butler, Judith (2005) *Giving an Account of Oneself*, New York: Fordham University Press.

Carlton, S. and Soulsby, J. (1999) *Learning to Grow Older and Bolder: A Policy Discussion Paper on Learning in Later Life*, Leicester: NIACE.

Chappell, C. (1999) 'Identity, Location and the Making of Adult Educators', SCUTREA, 5–7 July.

Citizenship Education Research Strategy Group (2005) *A Systematic Review of the Impact of Citizenship Education on Student Learning and Achievement*, London: Institute of Education.

Coare, P. and Johnston, R. (eds) (2003) *Adult Learning, Citizenship and Community Voices*, Leicester: NIACE.

Colley, H. (2002) 'A "Rough Guide" to the History of Mentoring from a Marxist Feminist Perspective', in *Journal of Education for Teaching: International Research and Pedagogy*, 28 (3): 257–73.

Colley, H. (2003) '"Children Can Wind You Up!": Learning to Labour in the Nursery', Paper presented at the Gender and Education Association Conference Revisiting Feminist Perspectives on Gender and Education University of Sheffield, 14–16 April 2003; available online at http://www.ex.ac.uk/sell/tlc/docs/publications/LE_HC_PUB_GENDERCONF_O4.03.htm (accessed 5 January 2007).

Colley, H. (2004) 'Learning to Labour with Feeling: Class, Gender and the Reform of Habitus in Vocational Education and Training', Paper presented at a seminar for the *Institute for Policy Studies in Education*, London Metropolitan University, 10 November 2004; available online at http://www.tlrp.org/dspace/retrieve/333/LE_HC_Institute+Policy+Seminar+Nov+04.doc (accessed 18 January 2007).

Colley, H. (2006) 'From Childcare Practitioner to FE Tutor: Biography, Identity and Lifelong Learning', in C. Leathwood and B. Francis (eds) *Gender and Lifelong Learning: Critical Feminist Engagements*, London: Routledge.

Colley, H., Hodkinson, P. and Malcolm, J. (2003) *Informality and Formality in Learning*, London: Learning and Skills Development Agency.

Colley, H., James, D., Tedder, M., and Diment, K. (2003) 'Learning as Becoming in Vocational Education and Training: Class, Gender and the Role of Vocational Habitus', *Journal of Vocational Education and Training*, 55 (4): 471–98.

Collins, P. H. (1990) *Black Feminist Thought: Knowledge, Consciousness, and the Politics of Empowerment*, Boston: Unwin Hyman.

Commission of European Communities (2005) Commission Staff Working Document, Towards a European Qualifications Framework for Lifelong Learning; available online at http://ec.europa.eu/education/policies/2010/doc/consultation_eqf_en.pdf (accessed 6 January 2007).

Community Learning Resource – Leadership and Management, online at http://www. aclearn.net/leadership (accessed 17 January 2005).

Connor, H., Tyers, C. *et al.* (2004) *Why the Difference? A Closer Look at Higher Education Minority Ethnic Students and Graduates*, Nottingham: Department for Education and Skills.

Côté, J. (1996) 'Sociological Perspectives on Identity Formation: The Culture-Identity Link and Identity Capital', in *Journal of Adolescence*, 19: 419–30.

Côté, J. and Levene, C. (2002) *Identity Formation, Agency and Culture*, New Jersey: Lawrence Erlbaum.

Cotterill, P., Jackson, S. and Letherby, G. (eds) (2007) *Challenges and Negotiations for Women in Higher Education*, Dordrecht: Springer Press.

Council of Europe (1998) 'Lifelong Learning for Equity and Social Cohesion: A New Challenge to Higher Education', Strasbourg, Council of Europe, DECS-HE 98/5 rev 2.

Coward, R. (1977) ' "Culture" and the Social Formation,', *Screen*, 18.

Creme, P. (2003) 'Why Can't We Allow Students to be More Creative', *Teaching in Higher Education*, 8 (2): 273–77.

Crick, B. (2000) *Essays on Citizenship*, London: Continuum.

Crowther, J., Hamilton, M. and Tett, L. (2001) *Powerful Literacies*, Leicester: NIACE.

Cultural Diversity – Responding to the Learning Needs of Older People from Black and Minority Ethnic Communities, Leicester: NIACE Briefing paper; available online at http://www.niace.org.uk/information/Briefing_sheets/35_Cultural_older.htm (accessed 17 January 2005).

Currie, J. (1998) 'Impact of Globalization on Australian Universities: Competition, Fragmentation, Demoralization', Paper presented at the International Sociology Association World Congress of Sociology, Montreal, 26 July to 2 August.

Currie, J., Thiele, B. and Harris, P. (2002) *Gendered Universities in Globalized Economies*, Lanham, Boulder, New York and Oxford: Lexington Books.

D'Andrea, V. (1999) 'Organising Teaching and Learning: Outcomes Based Planning', in H. Fry, S. Ketteridge and S. Marshall (eds) *A Handbook for Teaching and Learning in Higher Education*, London: Kogan Page.

Dadzie, S. (1993) *Older and Wiser: A Study of Educational Provision for Black and Ethnic Minority Elders*, Leicester: NIACE.

David, M. (2005) 'Personalised Learning in Higher Education: A Question of Feminist Pedagogy?', *Gender, Power and Difference*, Gender and Education Association 5th Annual Conference, Cardiff, 29–31 March.

Dearing, R. (1997) *Higher Education in the Learning Society*, (The Dearing Report) London: The National Committee of Inquiry into Higher Education.

Deem, R., Morley, L. and Tlili, A. (2005) *Negotiating Equity in Higher Education Institutions*, Final report to the Joint Funding Councils', EO Programme Steering Group.

Dehmel, A. (2006) 'Making a European Area of Lifelong Learning a Reality? Some Critical Reflections on the European Union's Lifelong Learning Policies', *Comparative Education*, 42 (1): 49–62.

Delors, J. (1996) *Learning: The Treasure Within*, Report to Unesco of the International Commission on Education for the Twenty-first Century, Paris: UNESCO.

Devos, A. (2002) 'Gender, Work and Workplace Learning', in F. Reeve, M. Cartwright and R. Edwards (eds) *Supporting Lifelong Learning: Organizing Learning*, London: Routledge Falmer.

Dewson, S., Aston, L., Bates, P., Ritchie, H., and Dyson, A. (2004) 'Post-16 Transitions: A Longitudinal Study of Young People with Special Education Needs, London: DfES, Research brief RB582; available online at http://www.dfes.gov.uk/research/data/uploadfiles/RB582.pdf (accessed 18 January 2007).

DfEE (1998) *The Learning Age: A Renaissance for a New Britain*, London: HMSO.

DfEE (1999) *Learning to Succeed – A New Framework for Post-16 Learning*, London: The Stationery Office Ltd.

DfEE (1998) February, booklet.

DfES (2003a) *Widening Participation in Higher Education*, Norwich: The Stationery Office Ltd.

DfES (2003b) *21st Century Skills: Realising our Potential*, London: HMSO.

DfES (2003c) *Pathways in Adult Learning Survey*, London: HMSO.

DfES (2003d) *The Future of Higher Education*, London: HMSO.

DfES (2004a) *Further Education and Work-based Learning for Young People – Learner Outcomes in England: 2002/2003*, London: DfES, ILR/SFR04; available online at http://www.dfes.gov.uk/rsgateway/DB/SFR/s000478/index.shtml (accessed 18 January 2007).

DfES (2004b) *Further Education and Work-based Learning for Young People and Adult and Community Learning – Learner Numbers in England 2003/4*, London: DfES, ILR/SFR045.

DfES (2004c) *Five Year Strategy for Children and Learners*, London: HMSO.

DfES (2005) *14–19 Education and Skills White Paper*, London: HMSO.

DfES (2006) *Further Education: Raising Skills, Improving Life Chances*, London: HMSO.

Dill, D. (2001) 'The Regulation of Public Research Universities: Changes in Academic Competition and Implications for University Autonomy and Accountability', *Higher Education Policy*, 14 (1): 21–35.

Duke, C. (1992) *The Learning University: Towards a New Paradigm?*, Milton Keynes: Open University Press.

Education and Training Statistics for the United Kingdom 2004 Edition (2004) London: DfES; available online at http://www.dfes.gov.uk/rsgateway/DB/VOL/v000538/ed_train_final.pdf (accessed 18 January 2007).

Ellsworth, E. (1992) 'Why Doesn't This Feel Empowering? Working Through the Repressive Myths of Critical Pedagogy', in C. Luke and J. Gore (eds) *Feminisms and Critical Pedagogy*, London and New York: Routledge.

Epstein, D. (1997) 'Love's Labours – Playing it Straight on the Oprah Winfrey Show', in D. Steinburg, D. Epstein and R. Johnson (eds) *Border Patrols: Policing the Boundaries of Heterosexuality*, London: Cassel.

Epstein, D., O'Flynn, S. and Telford, D. (2003) *Silenced Sexualities in Schools and Universities*, Stoke-on-Trent: Trentham Books.

Epstein, D., Elwood, J. *et al.* (1998) *Failing Boys? Issues in Gender and Achievement*, Buckingham: Open University Press.

European Council (2000) 'Lisbon European Council 23 and 24 March 2000: Presidency

Conclusions'; available online at http://www.europarl.europa.eu/summits/lis1_en.htm (accessed 5 January 2007).

Evans, K. (2001) 'Learning to be Citizens in Adult Life', in *Journal of Adult and Continuing Education*, 4: 57–71.

Evans, M. (2004) *Killing Thinking: The Death of the Universities*, London: Continuum.

Ewen, D. and Watters, K. (2002) *Using Quality Schemes in Adult and Community Learning: A Guide for Managers*, London: Learning and Skills Development Agency; available online at http://www.lsda.org.uk/files/pdf/1326A.pdf.

Field, J. (2000) *Lifelong Learning and the New Educational Order*, Stoke on Trent: Trentham Press.

Field, J. (2001) 'Adult Education and Active Citizenship: Recent Developments in the UK', in *Journal of Adult and Continuing Education*, 4: 17–28.

Field, J. (2005) *Social Capital and Lifelong Learning*, Bristol: Policy Press.

Field, J. and Leicester, M. (eds) (2000) *Lifelong Learning: Education Across the Lifespan*, London: Routledge Falmer.

Finger, M. and Asún, J. M. (2001) *Adult Education at the Crossroads: Learning our Way Out*, Leicester: NIACE.

Foley, G. (ed.) (2004) *Dimenstions of Adult Learning: Adult Education and Training in a Global Era*, Maidenhead: Open University Press.

Foster, A. (2005) *Review of the Future Role of FE Colleges*, London: DfES.

Foucault, M. (1972) *The Archeology of Knowledge*, London: Tavistock.

Foucault, M. (1973) *The Order of Things: An Archeology of the Human Sciences*, New York: Vintage Books.

Foucault, M. (1974) *The Archaeology of Knowledge*, London: Tavistock.

Foucault, M. (1977) *Discipline and Punish: The Birth of the Prison*, trans. A. Sheridan, New York: Pantheon Books.

Foucault, M. (1980) 'Two Lectures', in C. Gordon (ed.) *Michel Foucault: Power/Knowledge*, London: Harvester Wheatsheaf.

Foucault, M. (1984) *The History of Sexuality: Volume 1: The Will to Knowledge*, London: Allen Lane.

Foucault, M. (1988) *The History of Sexuality: Volume 2: Use of Pleasure*, London: Penguin Books.

Francis, B. (2002) 'Is the Future Really Female? The Impact and Implications of Gender for 14–16 year olds', Career Choices', *Journal of Education and Work*, 15 (1): 75–88.

Francis, B. and Skelton, C. (eds) (2001) *Investigating Gender: Contemporary Perspectives in Education*, Buckingham: Open University Press.

Freidson, E. (2001) *Professionalism: The Third Logic*, Chicago: University of Chicago Press.

Freire, P. (1972) *Pedagogy of the Oppressed*, New York: Herder and Herder.

Freire, P. (2004) *Pedagogy of Indignation*, Boulder: Paradigm.

Fry, H., Ketteridge, S. and Marshall, S. (eds) (1999) *A Handbook for Teaching and Learning in Higher Education*, London: Kogan Page.

Further Education Funding Council (2000) *Citizenship for 16–19 year olds in Education and Training*, Report of the Advisory Group, Coventry: FEFC.

Further Education National Training Organisation (2005) 'Roles and Characteristics of the Part-time Lecturing Staff; available online at http://www.fento.org/res_and_dev/reports/pt_lect_report_roles.htm (accessed 17 January 2005).

Fuwa, K. (2001) 'Relationship Between Adult Education and Citizenship', in *Journal of Adult and Continuing Education*, 4: 1–4.

Gee, J. P. (1990) *Social Linguistics and Literacies: Ideologies in Discourses*, London: Falmer Press; 2nd edn, Basingstoke: Falmer Press, 1996.

Gender Research Forum (2002) London: Women and Equality Unit.

Gerwirtz, S. (2001) 'Cloning the Blairs: New Labour's Programme for the Re-socialization of Working-class Parents', *Journal of Educational Policy*, 16(4): 365–78.

Gillborn, D. and Youdell, D. (2000) *Rationing Education: Policy, Practice, Reform and Equity*, Buckingham: Open University Press.

Giroux, H. (1992) *Border Crossings: Cultural Workers and the Politics of Education*, New York: Routledge.

Gore, J. (1993) *The Struggle for Pedagogies: Critical and Feminist Discourses as Regimes of Truth*, New York: Routledge.

Green, A. (2002) 'The Many Faces of Lifelong Learning: Recent Education Policy Trends in Europe', *Journal of Education Policy*, 17 (6): 611–26.

Hall, S. (1990) 'Cultural Identity and Diaspora', in Rutherford, J. (ed.) *Identity: Community, Culture, Difference*, London: Lawrence & Wishart.

Hall, S. (1992) 'Introduction: Identity in Question', in S. Hall, D. Held and T. McGrew, *Modernity and Its Futures*, Cambridge: Polity Press.

Hall, S. (2000) 'Who Needs "Identity"?', in P. du Gay, J. Evans and P. Redman (eds) *Identity: A Reader*, London: Sage.

Hammond, C. (2002) *Learning to be Healthy*, The Wider Benefits of Learning Papers No. 3, London: Institute of Education.

Haraway, D. (1988) 'Situated Knowledges: The Science Question in Feminism and the Privilege of Partial Perspective', *Feminist Studies*, 14 (3): 575–99.

Harding, S. (1987) *Feminism and Methodology*, Milton Keynes: Open University Press.

Harding, S. (1993) *The 'Racial', Economy of Science: Toward a Democratic Future*, Bloomington and Indianapolis: Indiana University Press.

Harris, R., Hall, J. and Muirhead, A. (2004) 'Impact of E-learning on Learner Participation, Attainment, Retention and Progression: A Scooping Study', London: DfES; available online at http://www.dfes.gov.uk/research/data/uploadfiles/RW15.pdf (accessed 18 January 2007).

Harrison, R. (2003) 'Languaging Learners: Constructions of Identity Through Discourses of Lifelong Learning', SCUTREA 33rd Annual Conference, 1–3 July 2003, Bangor, Wales.

Hawkes, G. (2005) *Edge Learner Forum*, London: Edge.

HEFCE (Higher Education Funding Council for England) (2005) *Young Participation in Higher Education*, Bristol: HEFCE.

Henkel, M. (1998) 'Evaluation in Higher Education: Conceptual and Epistemological Foundations', *European Journal of Education*, 33 (3): 285–97.

Hernàndez, A. (1997) *Pedagogy, Democracy and Feminism: Rethinking the Public Sphere*, New York: State University of New York Press.

Hey, V. (2004) 'Perverse Pleasures – Identity Work and the Paradoxes of Greedy Institutions', *Journal of International Women's Studies*, Special Issue: *Feminist Challenges: Crossing Boundaries*, 5 (3): 33–43.

Hillier, Y. (2002) *Reflective Teaching in Further and Adult Education*, London: Continuum.

Hillier, Y. and Thompson, A. (eds) (2005) *Readings in Post-compulsory Education: Research in the Learning and Skills Sector*, London: Continuum.

Hochschild, A. R. (1983) *The Managed Heart: The Commercialization of Human Feeling*, Berkeley: University of California Press.

hooks, bell (1991) *Yearning – Race, Gender and Cultural Politics*, London: Turnaround Publishers.

hooks, b. (1994) *Teaching to Transgress*, London: Routledge.

Hughes, C. (2002) *Key Concepts in Feminist Theory and Research*, London: Sage.

Hughes, C. (2006) 'A Methodologically Contested Present? Contemporary Dilemmas for Gender and Lifelong Learning Research', Methodologies in Lifelong Learning: ESRC seminar series on Gender and Lifelong Learning, University of Warwick, 26 May.

Hughes, C. and Tight, M. (1998) 'The Myth of the Learning Society', in S. Ranson (ed.) *Inside the Learning Society*, London: Cassell.

Hussey, T. B. and Smith, P. (2003) 'The Uses of Learning Outcomes', *Teaching in Higher Education*, 8 (3): 357–68.

Illich, I. (1976) *Deschooling Society*, Harmondsworth: Penguin.

Institute for Employment Research (2003) 'National Employers Skills Survey: Key Findings', Coventry: Learning and Skills Council; available online at http://www.lsc. gov.uk/NR/rdonlyres/ekts4w3fnotnxdfacwiaq6myaaadkxxdb4a3j7xbfnczytk6virmwdh umha3snqwp7spzyk4y5rnfd/NESS2004.pdf.

International Labour Office (2000) *World Labour Report 2000: Income Security and Social Protection in a Changing World*, Geneva: International Labour Office.

Ivanic, R. (1998) *Writing and Identity: The Discoursal Construction of Identity in Academic Writing.*, Amsterdam and Philadelphia, PA: John Benjamins Publishing Company and John Benjamins North America.

Jackson, C. (2003) *Working with Young Adults*, Leicester: NIACE.

Jackson, S. (1998) 'In a Class of Their Own: Women's Studies and Working-class Students', *The European Journal of Women's Studies*, 5: 195–215.

Jackson, S. (1997) 'Crossing Borders and Changing Pedagogies: From Giroux and Freire to Feminist Theories of Education', *Gender and Education*, 9 (4): 457–67.

Jackson, S. (1999) 'Learning and Teaching in Higher Education: The Use of Personal Experience in Theoretical and Analytical Approaches', *Journal of Further and Higher Education*, 23 (3): 351–58.

Jackson, S. (2002) 'Citizens of the Classroom: Appropriating Bernstein for Women in Higher Education', *Education and Society*, 20 (1): 63–77.

Jackson, S. (2003) 'Lifelong Earning: Lifelong Learning and Working-class Women', *Gender and Education*, 15 (4): 365–76.

Jackson, S. (2004a) *Differently Academic? Developing Lifelong Learning for Women in Higher Education*, Dordrecht: Kluwer Academic Press.

Jackson, S. (2004b) 'Widening Participation for Women in Lifelong Learning and Citizenship', *Journal of Widening Participation and Lifelong Learning*, 4 (1): 5–13.

Jackson, S. (2005a) 'When Learning Comes of Age? Continuing Education into Later Life', *Journal of Adult and Continuing Education*, 11 (2): 188–99.

Jackson, S. (2005b) *Learning Citizenship – The National Federation of Women's Institutes*, unpublished research report.

Jackson, S. (2006) 'Jam, Jerusalem and Calendar Girls: Lifelong Learning and the WI', *Studies in the Education of Adults*, 38 (1): 74–90.

Jackson, S. and Clarke, R. (2003) 'Rural Proofing Lifelong Learning?', *FCE Occasional Paper*, London: Birkbeck, University of London.

Jamieson, A. and Adshead, L. (2001) 'Education and the Adult Years: A Study of Students of the Faculty of Continuing Education', *FCE Occasional Paper*, London: Birkbeck, University of London.

Johnson, R. (2000) 'The Authority of the Student Evaluation Questionnaire', *Teaching in Higher Education*, 5 (4): 419–34.

Journal of International Women's Studies (2004) Special Issue, *Feminist Challenges: Crossing Boundaries*, 5 (3): 75–86.

Keep, E. and Rainbird, H. (2002) 'Towards the Learning Organisation?', in M. Cartwright and R. Edwards (eds) *Supporting Lifelong Learning: Organizing Learning*, London: Routledge Falmer.

Knowledge Transfer Partnerships Online, Department of Trade and Industry, http://www.ktponline.org.uk (accessed August 2006).

Lave, J., and Wenger, E. (1991) *Situated Learning: Legitimate Periperal Participation*, Cambridge: Cambridge University Press.

Lea, M. R. and Street, B. (1997) 'Student Writing and Staff Feedback in Higher Education: an Academic Literacies Approach', Swindon: Economic and Social Research Council.

Lea, M. R. and Street, B. (2000) 'Student Writing and Staff Feedback in Higher Education: An Academic Literacies Approach', in M. Lea and B. Stierer, *Student Writing in Higher Education: New Contexts*, Buckingham: The Society for Research into Higher Education and Open University Press.

Learning through voluntary work; available online at http://www.direct.gov.uk/Topics/Learning/AdultLearners/FinancialSupport/FinancialSupportArticle/fs/en?CONTENT_ID=4016520&chk=Jf%2BwzK (accessed 17 January 2005).

Letherby, G. (2003) *Feminist Research in Theory and Practice*, Buckinham: Open University Press.

Light, G. and Cox, R. (2001) *Learning and Teaching in Higher Education: The Reflective Practitioner*, London: Paul Chapman.

Lillis, T. (2001) *Student Writing: Access, Regulation, Desire*, London: Routledge.

Lillis, T. M. and Ramsey, M. (1997) 'Student Status and the Question of Choice in Academic Writing', *Research and Practice in Adult Learning Bulletin*, Spring: 15–22.

Lister, R. (1997) *Citizenship: Feminist Perspectives*, London: MacMillan.

Lorde, A. (1984) *Sister Outsider*, California: Crossing Press.

LSC (2005) *Agenda for Change*, publication no. 304, Coventry: Learning and Skills Council.

McGivney, V. (1999a) *Informal Learning in the Community: A Trigger for Change and Development*, Leicester: NIACE.

McGivney, V. (1999b) *Excluded Men: Men who are Missing from Education and Training*, Leicester, NIACE.

McGivney, V. (2002) *A Question of Value: Achievement and Progression in Adult Learning*, Leicester: NIACE.

McNay, L. (1999) 'Gender, Habitus and the Field: Bourdieu and the Limits of Reflexivity', *Theory, Culture and Society*, 16 (1): 95–117.

McWilliam, E. and Hatcher, C. (2004) 'Emotional Literacy as a Pedagogical Product', in *Journal of Media and Cultural Studies*, 18 (2): 179–89.

'Making an Impact on Individuals and Communities: The Effect of Adult and Community

Learning Provision Today' (2004) Coventry: Adult Learning Inspectorate; available online at http://docs.ali.gov.uk/publications/MakingAnImpact041109133603.pdf.

Manley, I. (2003) 'The UK/U3A approach to Life Long Learning', Paper presented to the Third Age Trust; available online at http://www.u3a.org.uk/natoffice/general_info/lifelong_learning.htm (accessed August 2006).

Marks, A. (2003) 'Welcome to the New Ambivalence: Reflections on the Historical and Current Cultural Antagonism Between the Working Class Male and Higher Education', *British Journal of Sociology of Education*, 24 (1): 83–93.

Martino, W. (1996) 'Boys and Literacy: Addressing the Links Between Masculinity and Learning', Paper presented at the Gender Networking Conference for the Department of School Education, Sydney, 28–29 May [forthcoming in B. Comber and A. Simpson (eds) *Negotiating Critical Literacies in Local Sites*, London: TheFalmer Press].

Martino, W. (1997) '"Dick Heads", "Pooftas", "Try Hards" and "Losers": Addressing Masculinities and Homophobia in the Literacy Classroom', Paper presented at the Gender & Literacy Forum, Primary English Teachers'Association (PETA), Sydney, 27 September.

Martino, W. (1999) '"Cool Boys", "Party Animals", "Squids" and "Poofters": Interrogating the Dynamics and Politics of Adolescent Masculinities in School', *British Journal of Sociology of Education*, 20 (2): 239–63.

Maynard, M. and Purvis, J. (eds) (1994) *Researching Women's Lives from a Feminist Perspective*, London: Taylor and Francis.

Mayo, M. and Thompson, J. (1995) *Adult Learning, Critical Intelligence and Social Change*, Leicester: National Institute of Adult Continuing Education.

'Meeting the Needs of Older Learners – A Briefing for LSCs', Leicester: NIACE; available online at http://www.niace.org.uk/information/Briefing_sheets/Meeting_needs_older_learners.htm (accessed 17 January 2005).

Miller, J. (1995) 'Trick or Treat? The Autobiography of the Question', *English Quarterly*, 27 (3): 22–6.

Mirza, H. (2006) 'The In/visible Journey', in C. Leathwood and B. Francis (eds) *Gender and Lifelong Learning: Critical Feminist Engagements*, London: Routledge.

Mirza, H. S. (2003) '"All the Women Are White, All the Blacks Are Men – But Some of Us Are Brave": Mapping the Consequences of Invisibility for Black and Minority Ethnic Women in Britain', in D. Mason (ed.) *Explaining Ethnic Differences: Changing Patterns of Disadvantage in Britain*, Bristol: Policy Press.

Mohanty, Chandra Talpade (2002) *Under Western Eyes: Feminist Scholarship and Colonial Discourses*, Stanford: Stanford University Press.

Mojab, S. (2006) 'War and Diaspora as Lifelong Learning Contexts for Immigrant Women', in C. Leathwood and B. Francis (eds) *Gender and Lifelong Learning: Critical Feminist Engagements*, London: Routledge.

Morley, L. (1997) 'Change and Equity in Higher Education', *British Journal of Sociology of Education*, 18 (2): 231–42.

Morley, L. (1999) *Organising Feminisms: The Micropolitics of the Academy*, Hampshire: Macmillan Press.

Morley, L. (2001) 'Subjected to Review: Engendering Quality and Power in Higher Education', *Journal of Education Policy*, 16 (5): 465–78.

Morley, L. (2003) *Quality and Power in Higher Education*, Berkshire, England and Philadelphia: Society for Research in Higher Education and Open University Press.

Morrell, J., Chowdhury, R. and Savage,s B. (2004) 'Progression from Adult and

Community Learning', London: DfES, NOP Social and Political, Research report RR546; available online at http://www.dfes.gov.uk/research/data/uploadfiles/RR546.pdf (accessed 18 January 2007).

Morris, J. and Feldman, D. (1996) 'The Dimensions, Antecedents, and Consequences of Emotional Labor', in *Academy of Management Review*, 21 (4): 986–1010.

National Association of Teachers in Further and Higher Education, *Part-Time Work: Department of Trade and Industry Public Consultation: NATFHE response to DTO consultation*; available online at http://www.natfhe.org.uk/help/helppt01.html (accessed 17 January 2005).

Newby, H. (2004) 'Doing Widening Participation: Social Inequality and Access to Higher Education', *Jim Bell Memorial Lecture*, University of Bradford.

Nicoll, K. and Edwards, R. (2004) 'Lifelong Learning and the Sultans of Spin: Policy as Persuasion?', *Journal of Education Policy*, 19 (1): 43–55.

Nowotny, H. (1981) 'Women in Public Life in Austria', in Cynthia Fuchs Epstein and Rose Laub Coser (eds) *Access to Power: Cross-National Studies of Women and Elites*, London: George Allen & Unwin.

Nutt, Kathleen (2006) 'Teacher "MOT" Plan to Raise Standards', in *The Sunday Times*, 23 July 2006.

OECD (2001) *Economics and Finance of Lifelong Learning*, Paris: OECD.

Older People and Learning – Some Key Statistics, Leicester: Niace; available online at http://www.niace.org.uk/information/Briefing_sheets/Older_Learners_Stats.htm (accessed 17 January 2005).

Orr, S. and Blythman, M. (2005) 'Transparent Opacity: Assessment in the Inclusive Academy', in C. Rust (ed.) *Improving Student Learning*, Oxford: Oxford Brookes University Press.

Osborne, M. (2003) 'Increasing or Widening Participation in Higher Education? – A European Overview', *European Journal of Education*, 38 (1): 5–24.

Overcoming Social Exclusion Through On-line Learning: Project: NIACE/Open University; available online at http://www.niace.org.uk/online/index.htm (accessed 17 January 2005).

Owston, Ronald (1997) 'The World Wide Web: A Technology to Enhance Teaching and Learning?', *Educational Researcher*, 26 (2): 27–33.

Parker, P. (2002) 'Negotiating Identity in Raced and Gendered Workplace Interactions: The Use of Strategic Communication by African American Women Senior Executives Within Dominant Culture Organisations', *Communication Quarterly*, 50: June.

Participation Rates in Higher Education: By Social Class: Social Trends 34; available online at http://www.statistics.gov.uk (accessed 17 January 2005).

Pratt, J. (1997) *The Polytechnic Experiment, 1965–1992*, Milton Keynes: Society for Research into Higher Education and Open University Press.

Prince, C. and Beaver, G. (2001) 'The Rise and Rise of the Corporate University: The Emerging Corporate Learning Agenda', *International Journal of Management Education*, 1 (2); available online at http://www.business.ltsn.ac.uk/publications/journal/vol1no2/paper3/beaver.pdf (accessed 18 January 2007).

Purvis, J. (1987) 'Social Class, Education and Ideals of Femininity', in M. Arnot and G. Weiner (eds) *Gender and the Politics of Schooling*, London: Unwin Hyman in association with the Open University Press.

Putman, R. (2000) *Bowling Alone: The Collapse and Revival of American Community*, New York: Simon & Schuster.

QAA (Quality Assurance Agency) (2003) 'Access to Higher Education Key Statistics'; available online at http://www.qaa.ac.uk/crntwork/access/statistics/key_stats_2003.htm: 1–8.

Quinn, J. (2003) *Powerful Subjects: Are Women Really Taking over the University?*, Stoke-on-Trent: Trentham.

Radford, M. (2002) 'Educating the Emotions: Interior and Exterior Realities', in *Pastoral Care in Education*, 20 (2): 24–9.

Ramazanoglu, C. and Holland, J. (2002) *Feminist Methodology: Challenges and Choices*, London: Sage.

Readings, B. (1996) *The University in Ruins*, Cambridge MA: Harvard University Press.

Reay, D. (1998) 'Surviving in Dangerous Places: Working Class Women, Women's Studies and Higher Education', in *Women's Studies International Forum*, 21 (1): 11–19.

Reay, D. (2001) 'Finding or Losing Yourself?: Working-class Relationships to Education', *Journal of Education Policy*, 16: 333–46.

Reay, D. (2002) 'Gendering Bourdieu's Concept of Capitals?: Emotional Capital, Women and Social Class', Paper presented at the Feminists Evaluate Bourdieu Conference Manchester University 11 October 2002; available online at http://www.socialsciences.manchester.ac.uk/sociology/Seminar/documents/dianereaybourdieu.doc (accessed 18 January 2007).

Reay, D. (2003) 'A Risky Business? Mature Working-class Women Students and Access to Higher Education', *Gender and Education*, 15: 301–17.

Reay, D. (no date) 'Working Your Heart Out: Gender, Class and Emotional Labour in the Academy', available online at http://www.shef.ac.uk/education/events/monday.pdf (accessed April 2006).

Reay, D., David, M. and Ball, S. (2005) *Degrees of Choice: Social Class, Race and Gender in Higher Education*, Stoke-on-Trent: Trentham Books.

Reay, D., Davies, J., David, M. and Ball, S. (2001) 'Choices of Degree or Degrees of Choice? Class, "Race" and the Higher Education Choice Process', *Sociology*, 35: 855–74.

Retention and Achievement Data from Work-based Learning Inspections (2003) Coventry: Adult Learning Inspectorate; available online at http://docs.ali.gov.uk/publications/Retentionachievementrates03030912150804.pdf (accessed 18 January 2007).

Reuters (2005) 'GCSE Results Out Amid Criticism', in *Daily Mirror, Online*, http://www.mirror.co.uk, 25 August 2005.

Richie, J. and Lewis, J. (2003) *Qualitative Research Practice*, London: Sage.

Ritzer, G. (1995) *The McDonaldization of Society*, New York: Sage.

Roberts, S. (ed.) (2003) *A Ministry of Enthusiasm: Centenary Essays on the Workers Educational Association*, London: Pluto Press.

Robinson, E. (1968) *The New Polytechnics*, Harmondsworth: Penguin.

Roseneil, S. and Seymour, J. (eds) (1999) *Practising Identities: Power and Resistance*, Basingstoke: Macmillan.

Rossatto, C. A. (2005) *Engaging Paulo Freire's Pedagogy of Possibility: From Blind to Transformative Optimism*, Lanham: Rowan and Littlefield.

Rowland, S. (2002) 'Overcoming Fragmentation in Professional Life: The Challenge for Academic Development', *Higher Education Quarterly*, 56 (1): 52–64.

Sand, B. (1998) 'Lifelong Learning: Vision, Policy and Practice', *Journal of Access and Credit Studies*, Winter 1998: 17–39.

Sargent, N. with Field, J., Francis, H., Schuller, T. and Tuckett, A. (1997) *The Learning Divide: A Study of Participation in Adult Learning, in the United Kingdom*, Leicester: NIACE.

Scheutze, H. G. and Slowey, M. (2000) *Higher Education and Lifelong Learners; International Perspectives on Change*, London: Routledge-Falmer.

Schuller, T. (2001) 'Tracing Links Between Adult Education and Civic Participation', *Journal of Adult and Continuing Education*, 4: 5–16.

Schuller, T. (2002) 'Age, Equality and Education', *IPPR Seminar Series on Age and Equality*, London.

Schuller, T. (2004) 'Visual Imagery, Lifecourse Structure and Lifelong Learning', in *Studies in the Education of Adults*, 36 (1): 72–85.

Schuller, T., Baron, S. R. and Field, J. (eds) (2000) *Social Capital: Critical Perspectives*, Oxford: Oxford University Press.

Schuller, T., Preston, J., Hammond, C., Brassett-Grundy, A., and Bynner, J. (2004) *The Benefits of Learning: The Impact of Education on Health, Family Life and Social Capital*, London: Routledge Falmer.

Selwyn, N., Gorard, S. *et al.* (2004) 'Adults', Use of ICTs for Learning: Reducing or Increasing Educational Inequalities?', *Journal of Vocational Education and Training*, 56 (2): 269–90.

Senge, P. (1990) *The Fifth Discipline: the Art and Practice of the Learning Organization*, New York: Doubleday.

Shay, S. (2005) 'The Assessment of Complex Tasks: A Double Reading', *Studies in Higher Education*, 30 (6): 663–79.

Shepherd, J. (2006) 'Staff are Silenced by Fear of Reprisals', in *Times Higher Education Supplement*, 4 August: 1.

Skeggs, B. (1997) *Formations of Class and Gender: Becoming Respectable*, London: Sage.

Skeggs, B. (2002) 'Techniques for Telling the Reflexive Self', in T. May (ed.) *Qualitative Research in Action*, London: Thousand Oaks, New Delhi: Sage Publications.

Skeggs, B. (2003) *Class, Self, Culture*, London: Routledge.

Skeggs, B. (2004) *Class, Self, Culture*, London and New York: Routledge.

Skelton, C. (2001) *Schooling the Boys: Masculinities and Primary Education*, Buckingham and Philadelphia: Open University Press.

Smith, J. and Spurling, A. (2001) *Understanding Motivation for Lifelong Learning*, Leicester: NIACE.

Snape, D., Bell, A. and Jones, A. (2003) *Pathways in Adult Learning Survey*, London: DfES; available online at http://www.dfes.gov.uk/research/data/uploadfiles/RR559.pdf (accessed 18 January 2007).

Sommer, J. (1995) *The Academy in Crisis: The Political Economy of Higher Education*, New Jersey: Transaction Publishers

Sources of Funding for Older Learners, England and Wales, Leicester: NIACE; available online at http://www.niace.org.uk/information/Briefing_sheets/FundingOlder.htm (accessed 17 January 2005).

Stanley, L. and Wise, S. (1993) *Breaking Out Again: Feminist Ontology and Epistemology*, London: Routledge.

Stuart, M. (2000) 'Beyond Rhetoric: Reclaiming a Radical Agenda for Active Participation in Higher Education', in J. Thompson, *Stretching the Academy: The Politics and Practice of Widening Participation in Higher Education*, Leicester: NIACE.

Stuart, M. and Thomson, A. (eds) (1995) *Engaging with Difference: The 'Other', in Adult Education*, Leicester: NIACE.

Student and Community Voice: 4 (2002) London: Collaborative Widening Participation Project.

Tapper, T. and Brian, S. (2003) 'Interpreting the Process of Change in Higher Education: The Case of the Research Assessment Exercises', *Higher Education Quarterly*, 57 (1): 4–23.

The Future of Corporate Learning (2000) London: Department of Trade and Industry.

Thompson, J. (2000) 'Introduction', in J. Thompson, *Stretching the Academy: The Politics and Practice of Widening Participation in Higher Education*, Leicester: NIACE.

Trends in Higher Education in Further Education Colleges; available online at http://www.hefce.ac.uk/learning/FEFund/trends/FEtrends.doc (accessed 17 January 2005).

Tuckett, A. and McCauley, A. (2005) *Demography and Older Learners: Approaches to a New Policy Challenge*, Leicester, NIACE.

UNESCO (1998a) 'The Mumbai Statement on Lifelong Learning, Active Citizenship and the Reform of Higher Education', The 5th International Conference on Adult Education, Hamburg, UNESCO.

UNESCO (1998b) 'Higher Education in the Twenty-First Century: Vision and Action', World Conference on Higher Education, Paris.

UUK/SCOP (2005) *Higher Education Sector Improving Access for Disadvantaged Students*, available online at http://www.universitiesuk.ac.uk/mediareleases/show.asp? MR=444 (accessed 6 January 2007).

Vygotsky, L. S. (1978) *Mind in Society*, Cambridge, MA: Harvard University Press.

Walkerdine, V. (1992) 'Progressive Pedagogy and Political Struggle', in C. Luke and J. Gore (eds) *Feminisms and Critical Pedagogy*, London: Routledge.

Walkerdine, V. (1998) *Democracy in the Kitchen: Regulating Mothers and Socialising Daughters*, London: Virago.

Ware, L. (2001) 'Writing, Identity and the Other', *Journal of Teacher Education*, 52 (2): 107–23.

Webb, S., Brine, J. and Jackson S. (2007 forthcoming) 'Gender, Foundation Degrees and the Knowledge-driven Economy', in *Journal of Vocational Education and Training*.

Weiler, K. (ed.) (2001) *Feminist Engagments: Reading, Resisting and Revisioning Male Theorists in Education and Cultural Studies*, New York: Routledge.

Weinstein, K. (1999) *Action Learning: A Practical Guide*, Aldershot: Gower.

Welch, P. (1994) 'Is a Feminist Pedagogy Possible?', in S. Davies, C. Lubelska and Quinn, J. (eds) *Changing the Subject: Women in Higher Education*, London: Taylor & Francis.

Wenger, E. (1999) *Communities of Practice: Learning, Meaning and Identity*, New York: Cambridge University Press.

Whetherly, J. (1995) 'What is Action Learning?', *Action Learning News*, 14 (3): 5–7.

Whetherly, J. (1996) 'Action Learning: Developing the Person and the Organization', *Personnel Training and Education*, 3 (2); available online at http://www.junewhetherly.co.uk/person_amd_organisation.htm (accessed 6 January 2007).

White, L. (2002) *Engaging Black Learners in Adult and Community Education*, Leicester: NAICE.

Williams, J. (1997) 'The Discourse of Access: The Legitimisation of Selectivity', in J. Williams (ed.) *Negotiating Access to Higher Education: The Discourse of Selectivity and Equity*, Buckingham: Society for Research into Higher Education & Open University Press.

Willis, P. (1977) *Learning to Labour*, Farnborough, Saxon House.

Withnall, A. and Percy, K. (1994) *Good Practice in the Education and Training of Older Adults*, Aldershot: Ashgate.

'Working Together: A Strategy for the Voluntary and Community Sector and the Learning and Skills Council' (2004) Learning and Skills Council; available online at http://www. niace.org.uk/bpln/downloadable_documents/Working-Together-Final.pdf (accessed 18 January 2007).

Yeaxlee, B. (1929) *Lifelong Education*, London: Cassell.

Youdell, D. (2006) *Impossible Bodies, Impossible Selves: Exclusions and Student Subjectivities*, Netherlands: Springer.

Young, M. (1998) *The Curriculum of the Future: From the 'New Sociology', of Education*, London: Routledge Falmer.

Index